THIRD WAVE
AGENDA

THIRD WAVE AGENDA

BEING FEMINIST, DOING FEMINISM

Leslie Heywood &
Jennifer Drake, editors

University of Minnesota Press
Minneapolis
London

Third printing, 2002

Published by the University of Minnesota Press
111 Third Avenue South, Suite 290
Minneapolis, MN 55401-2520
http://www.upress.umn.edu

Library of Congress Cataloging-in-Publication Data

Third wave agenda : being feminist, doing feminism / Leslie Heywood and
    Jennifer Drake, editors.
        p.   cm.
    Includes index.
    ISBN 0-8166-3004-6 (hardcover : alk paper). — ISBN 0-8166-3005-4
(pbk. : alk. paper)
    1. Feminism—United States.   2. Women—United States—Social conditions.
3. Feminist theory—United States.   I. Heywood, Leslie.   II. Drake, Jennifer.
HQ1421.T455   1997
305.42—dc21   97-20301
                                                                          CIP

Printed in the United States of America on acid-free paper

The University of Minnesota is an equal-opportunity educator and employer.

To all those who have, past, present, and future,
called themselves *feminist, womanist*;
to those persons "committed to the radical notion
that women are people."

Contents

Acknowledgments

This book was put together to offer witness to the complications of contemporary culture and the difficulties of thinking between and among them. Our debts are no less complicated. I (Leslie) thank my feminist teachers and colleagues, in and outside academia, in friendship and in the classroom, who, through giving me understanding, have sometimes literally saved my sense of dignity and my life: Susan Bordo, Susan Strehle, Liz Rosenberg, Jerry Hogle, Susan Aiken, Lynda Zwinger, Beth Darnell, Barbara Spackman, Racquel Goldsmith, Simi Aziz, Nancy Henry, and Sidonie Smith. I especially thank my collaborator, Jennifer Drake, the sanest, strongest woman I know, for patience, tolerance, and wisdom, for a relationship that is creative and sustaining in ways the importance of which it is difficult to articulate fully, and for helping me stand when I am falling down. I also thank the contributors to this book, whose commitments and passionate voices have given me hope. And I thank Lisa Freeman, director of the University of Minnesota Press, who believed in this book when others didn't, and who gave it the chance to do the cultural work that it does.

I (Jennifer) acknowledge the women with and through whom I came to feminism: Ro Bagatell, Lynn Bell, Rebecca Busansky, Anita Kostecki, Sarah Lammert, Emily Lucero, Jenn Lynch, Linda Ramsdell, Janet Shaffer, Rachel Sheinkin, Cecilie Surasky, Marilyn Weigner, Julia Whitney, Claudia Yellin. Here's to all our versions of feminism and activism, to talking the hell out of stuff and laughing a lot, to communal cooking and living, to good sex and cool clothes (whatever that means to each of us), to the women we wanted to be and are becoming. Thanks also to my teachers Mei-Mei Berssenbrugge, Flora Keshgegian, Constance Coiner, Sidonie Smith; my mother, Audrey Drake; and the many women writers and artists to whose work I turn again and again. Finally, thanks to Leslie Heywood, for talk that could riff from hair to chick rock to the academy to feminist activism to poetry to competitive individualism to collaboration to body politics to relationships to athletics and back around, so that we could flesh out the connections and contradictions, so that we could think harder and write better together.

Introduction

Leslie Heywood and Jennifer Drake

Recently much media attention has been given to writings about third wave feminism, often labeled "postfeminism." In the perpetual battle of representation and definitional clout, the slippage from "third wave feminism" to "postfeminist" is important, because many of us working in the "third wave" by no means define our feminism as a groovier alternative to an over-and-done feminist movement. Let us be clear: "postfeminist" characterizes a group of young, conservative feminists who explicitly define themselves against and criticize feminists of the second wave.

Not surprisingly, it is these conservative feminists who are regularly called upon as spokespersons for the "next generation." Writers such as Katie Roiphe, Rene Denfield, and Naomi Wolf argue against feminist critiques of rape, sexual harassment, and abortion. They publish books, appear on op-ed pages, and write for popular young women's magazines such as *Glamour* and *YM*. Conservative postfeminism is in every way more visible than is the diverse activist work that terms itself "third wave." The one anthology that explicitly refers to a "third wave" of feminism, *The Third Wave: Feminist Perspectives on Racism*, cited in a *Genders* article in 1994, reflects on how the "third wave" is defined by the challenge that women-of-color feminists posed to white second wave feminism. This book, unlike the work of conservative white feminists, has seen a difficult road to publication. Perhaps because this book challenges easily assimilated feminist stereotypes and because it is being published by a small, independent house, the book's production has seen problems that rarely occur in the large, mainstream publishing houses to which conservative feminism has easier access.[1]

Two third wave feminist anthologies that have gained some prominence and are written in a less conservative vein, Barbara Findlen's *Listen Up: Voices from the Next Feminist Generation* and Rebecca Walker's *To Be Real: Telling the Truth and Changing the Face of Feminism*, present the reading public with a version of third wave feminism that relies, for the most part, on personal anecdote for their definitional and argumentative strategies.[2] These writings tend to be autobiographical and experiential, giving the insiders' "view from the heart," a glimpse of the social preoccupations and problems facing this "next generation" of feminists. Yet as important as these two books have been in addressing the experiences of this next generation, the writing rarely provides consistent analysis of the larger culture that has helped shape and produce those experiences.

Third Wave Agenda picks up where these other collections left off, joining the efforts of Nan Bauer Maglin and Donna Perry, editors of the 1996 anthology *"Bad Girls"/"Good Girls,"* to present a group of writers who work as cultural critics, activists, and teachers, whose life stories are informed by an intense engagement with the most vital cultural theory available today.[3] These are personal voices mediated by their grounding in research, theory, and social practice, an engaged scholarship that combines new interdisciplinary methodologies with an autobiographical style. Fusing the confessional mode of earlier popular feminisms with the more analytic mode that has predominated in the academy since the 1980s, both *Third Wave Agenda* and *"Bad Girls"/"Good Girls"* comprise essays that give an emotional life and a personal stake sometimes missing from academic writing, while maintaining an analytic focus. But, unlike *"Bad Girls"/"Good Girls," Third Wave Agenda* presents a generational perspective, gathering the voices of young activists struggling to come to terms with the historical specificity of our feminisms and with the times in which we came of age (the late 1970s through the late 1980s).

Because our lives have been shaped by struggles between various feminisms as well as by cultural backlash against feminism and activism, we argue that contradiction—or what looks like contradiction, if one doesn't shift one's point of view—marks the desires and strategies of third wave feminists. Whereas conservative postfeminist thinking relies on an opposition between "victim feminism" (second wave) and "power feminism" (third wave), and suggests that "power feminism" serves as a corrective to a hopelessly outmoded "victim feminism," to us the second and third waves of feminism are neither incompatible nor opposed. Rather, we define feminism's third wave as a movement that contains elements of second wave critique of beauty culture, sexual abuse, and power structures while it also acknowledges and makes use of the pleasure, danger, and defining power of those structures. Conservative postfeminist Christina Hoff Sommers splits feminism into two camps only: equity feminists (power feminists) and gender feminists (victim feminists).[4] She defines equity feminists as those who "stay within the bounds of traditional scholarship and join in its enterprise." She defines gender feminists as those who "seek to transform scholarship to make it 'women-centered'" (55). For Sommers, and for postfeminists in general, anyone who speaks of "oppression" or is "woman-centered" is in the "victim" camp.

One group of feminists not accounted for by this polarity—ourselves among them—is young feminists who grew up with equity feminism, got gender feminism in college, along with poststructuralism, and are now hard at work on a feminism that strategically combines elements of these feminisms, along with black feminism, women-of-color feminism, working-class feminism, pro-sex feminism, and so on. A third wave goal that comes directly out of learning from these histories and working among these traditions is the development of modes of thinking that can come to terms with the multiple, constantly shifting bases of oppression in relation to the multiple, interpenetrating axes of identity, and the creation of a coalition politics based on these understandings—understandings that acknowledge the existence of oppression, even though it is not fashionable to say so. We know that what oppresses me may not oppress you, that what oppresses you may be something I participate in, and that what oppresses me may be something you participate in. Even as different strains of feminism and activism sometimes directly contradict each other, they are all part of our third wave lives, our thinking, and our praxes: we are products of all the contradictory definitions of and differences within feminism, beasts of such a hybrid kind that perhaps we need a different name altogether.

In the important second wave collection *The Feminist Papers*, Alice Rossi contests the position that feminism "died" after the suffrage movement and came to life again in the late 1960s. Instead, she argues, there is a continuity between feminist generations that doesn't seem like continuity:

> [T]he public heroines of one generation are the private heroines
> of the next. . . . [B]etween 1920 and 1960 . . . [women] private[ly]
> consolidated . . . gains made by their mothers. . . . [S]trong-
> minded descendants of the suffragists were pouring much of their
> energy into education and employment, and if they were married,
> they did double duty at work and at home; such a profile leaves
> little time and energy for political involvement.[5]

Facing classrooms of young women and men who are trained by the
media caricature of "feminazis," who see feminism as an enemy or say
"feminist" things prefaced by "I'm not a feminist, but . . . ," finding
little time in our own overextended, economically insecure lives for
traditional public activism, we may be experiencing a repetition of the
historical pattern Rossi documents.

In the current historical moment, then, third wave feminists often
take cultural production and sexual politics as key sites of struggle,
seeking to use desire and pleasure as well as anger to fuel struggles for
justice. These forms of third wave activism don't always look "activist" enough to second wave feminists. But, as Rossi argues, exploring different activist practices doesn't mean we're not feminists: "[T]he
[less publicly activist] generation, unnoted by historians, may consoli-
date gains and provide the foundation on which the [next] generation
takes off again into public and historical notice" (619). Within the
"generation" addressed in *Third Wave Agenda*, whose birth dates fall
between 1963 and 1974, we can see this historical dialectic in opera-
tion. Those of us on the older end of this spectrum have tended to
spend more time establishing our careers, whereas those of us on the
younger end have had more experience with public activism. But, as
Third Wave Agenda attempts to establish, we are all third wave feminists, bringing the specificity of our historical situation to our widely
variable definitions of that term.

One public figure who demonstrates some of the contradictions
that third wave feminism brings together is Courtney Love, the punk
rock musician who bridges the opposition between "power feminism"
and "victim feminism." She combines the individualism, combative-
ness, and star power that are the legacy of second wave gains in opportunities for women (which arrived in conjunction with cultural backlash against such gains), with second wave critiques of the cult of
beauty and male dominance. Love is a prototype of female ambition
and a sharp cultural critic of both the institutions that sustain that am-

bition and those that argue against it. Glamorous and grunge, girl and boy, mothering and selfish, put together and taken apart, beautiful and ugly, strong and weak, responsible and rebellious, Love bridges the irreconcilability of individuality and femininity within dominant culture, combining the cultural critique of an earlier generation of feminists with the backlash against it by the next generation of women, legacies of Reagan Republicanism who are busy reclaiming the province of beauty for female power in ways that can only fail because they have been critiqued too thoroughly.

Love's most famous song, "Doll Parts," contradictorily combines the second wave critique of "I am / doll eyes / doll mouth / doll legs" with the third wave postmodern individualism facilitated by the second wave—"I want to be the girl with the most cake / I fake it so real I am beyond fake"—but returns to the lived cost of female ambition: "[S]omeday, you will ache like I ache."[6] Love's media persona combines the reality of female competitiveness with a feminist sensibility and a vocal support of other women: in conversation, Love often cites Susan Faludi's *Backlash* and raves about some women's performances at the same time that she defines herself competitively against others. Even in her mass media incarnation as Althea Flynt in Miloš Forman's *The People vs. Larry Flynt* and her January 1997 layout in *Vogue*, Love is still throwing an unfashionable feminism in the face of fashion, tongue in cheek. Love was "bossily laying into me," the *Vogue* reporter writes, "about anorexic models, the power of fashion magazines to determine national standards of body mass." "I can't stand it, that whole thing," Love says, "sitting around with your girlfriend and kvetching about weight. It takes all your confidence. . . . [T]hat's my big feminist lecture for today."[7] Love is aware of the social context that now makes a "big feminist lecture" unhip, thus harming chances for individual success, yet does it anyway.

Love's star quality and personal ambition may be a legacy of the Reagan 1980s and a quality discouraged by the collective movement ethos of second wave feminism, but it was the second wave that made ambition a realizable possibility for women. Equity feminist, postmodern feminist, and victim feminist all at once, Love combines the contradictory aspects of these discourses in a way that recognizes and makes use of complications that young women working within dominant culture face today. For better and for worse, she may be our Gloria Steinem, in that she is a highly visible lightning rod for third wave issues. Stylistically, however, Love emerges more from the playful, parodic tradition of the late 1960s WITCH (Women's International Conspiracy from Hell) and women's liberation guerrilla theater movements.[8]

African American hip-hop artist Me'Shell NdegéOcello is another public figure who exemplifies third wave feminist hybridity, contradiction, and activism. With her deep voice, barely there hair, and sexily androgynous clothing, NdegéOcello plays the edges of boy and girl, masculine and feminine, while her music voices a bisexual feminist sensibility strongly grounded in African American culture and hip-hop's hybrid logic.[9] Many of the songs on *Plantation Lullabies* (1993) call for love between black men and women, "a love that is essential to the loving of one's self," whereas on *Peace beyond Passion* (1996) NdegéOcello attacks homophobia in "Leviticus: Faggot" and speaks to a woman lover in "Who Is He and What Is He to You."[10] In songs such as "Two Lonely Hearts (on the Subway)," gendered desire becomes less important than raced desire and connection. The lyrics addressed an unspecified "you" whose "lovely black face" the speaker wants to get to know, perhaps by reading Ntozake Shange or the *Village Voice* together. Collaborative escape into love and language, the speaker suggests, might provide an antidote to "singin' the blues on the subway." NdegéOcello's songs enact the pleasures of desiring and desirable blacknesses, and show how love's necessary and healing power mingles with the outrage of "livin' in the midst of genocide." Loving Black men *and* Black women in such a world, and saying this out loud, is one way for NdegéOcello to live her whole, complex self.

The movement between love and outrage also characterizes NdegéOcello's take on religion, particularly evident in *Peace beyond Passion*. Taking Old Testament books as song titles, and collaging verses and images that recall Moses and Diaspora, human divinity, Mary Magdalene's prostitute-beauty, racial uplift, and some Christians' biblical justification for condemning homosexuality, NdegéOcello seeks healing through a redefinition of Christian faith and tradition. Revising, hybridizing, and reclaiming a spirituality that can do what she needs it to, NdegéOcello also turns to other religions, naming one song "God Shiva" and dedicating another to Kahlil Gibran. As *Rolling Stone* writer Ann Powers observes, in this activist work NdegéOcello "joins the chorus of contemporary women—Tori Amos, Joan Osborne,

Polly Jean Harvey, Jewel—re-imagining the mystical through the vehicle of pop, using music's power to challenge conceptions and build some myths of their own."[11] NdegéOcello's engagements with spirituality also participate in a key aspect of black feminist praxis. Taken together, the various facets of her performances work the edges of contradiction in a powerfully feminist way.

In the introduction of *To Be Real*, Rebecca Walker lists contradiction as a generative force for her collection but sets third wave hybridity in opposition to what she describes as a rigidly ideological second wave feminism:

> Constantly measuring up to some cohesive fully down-for-the-feminist-cause identity without contradictions and messiness and lusts for power and luxury items is not a fun or easy task. . . . For many of us it seems that to be a feminist in the way that we have seen or understood feminism is to conform to an identity and way of living that doesn't allow for individuality, complexity, or less than perfect personal histories.[12]

Third Wave Agenda makes things "messier" by *embracing* second wave critique as a central definitional thread while emphasizing ways that desires and pleasures subject to critique can be used to rethink and enliven activist work. We see the emphasis on contradiction as continuous with aspects of the second wave, whereas many writers in *To Be Real* seem eager to distance themselves from the second wave by forgetting or dismissing its legacies. The politics, however, that their essays advocate is very much indebted to the work of women of color who are generationally second wave—Walker's mother among them.

Perhaps ironically, this politics is perhaps best expressed today in the inclusive feminist activist collective Third Wave, which Rebecca Walker founded. Third Wave is a good example of a coalition-politics activism that defines itself, and its politics, through the multiple subject positions and diverse community affiliations of its members. Third Wave's mission statement reads as follows:

> Third Wave is a member-driven multiracial, multicultural, multi-sexuality national non-profit organization devoted to feminist and youth activism for change. Our goal is to harness the energy of young women and men by creating a community in which members can network, strategize, and ultimately, take action. By using our experiences as a starting point, we can create a diverse community and cultivate a meaningful response.

Third Wave makes the inclusion of persons of various genders, sexualities, nationalities, and classes a top priority and combines elements of equity feminism and gender feminism in a grassroots feminism that still fights for equal access and equal pay for equal work but also seeks to transform the structures within which young people work.

The lived messiness characteristic of the third wave is what defines it: girls who want to be boys, boys who want to be girls, boys and girls who insist they are both, whites who want to be black, blacks who want to or refuse to be white, people who *are* white *and* black, gay *and* straight, masculine *and* feminine, or who are finding ways to be and name none of the above; successful individuals longing for community and coalition, communities and coalitions longing for success; tensions between striving for individual success and subordinating the individual to the cause; identities formed within a relentlessly consumer-oriented culture but informed by a politics that has problems with consumption. Although many third wave writings make provocative use of these contradictions, they often posit a cleaner break between the second and the third wave than *Third Wave Agenda*'s contributors are willing to advocate, and those writings often do not mention where these contradictions have previously been most powerfully voiced.

From the Third World to the Third Wave: Our Debts

Characterizing the "third wave" as a movement defined by contradiction is not new. In fact, the definitional moment of third wave feminism has been theorized as proceeding from critiques of the white women's movement that were initiated by women of color, as well as from the many instances of coalition work undertaken by U.S. third world feminists. As Kayann Short notes in an article in *Genders*, "[S]ome feminists of color use the term 'the third wave' to identify a new feminism that is led by and has grown out of the challenge to white feminism posited by women of color."[13] As early as 1981, which saw the publication of the landmark anthology *This Bridge Called My Back: Writings by Radical Women of Color*, and 1983, the year of the publication of Barbara Smith's *Home Girls: A Black Feminist Anthology*, contradiction was claimed as a fundamental definitional strategy, a necessary, lived, embodied strategy.[14] Why, then, has there been in mainstream media representation no "third wave" until the 1990s?

What is the relationship between the self-named U.S. third world feminism of *This Bridge Called My Back* and the third wave feminism of the "next generation"?

As we finished compiling this manuscript and reading through individual contributions, we were struck by the fact that most of them, our own included, cited the work of bell hooks and her emphasis on coalition politics as a model for third wave activist theory and praxis. Contributors to this volume have looked to hooks in particular as a model for hope, for some sense of what to do next, but hooks's work itself is situated within the hybrid and intersecting discourses of black feminism and U.S. third world feminism. Chela Sandoval's important 1982 essay on U.S. third world feminism and white feminist racism, "Feminism and Racism: A Report on the 1981 National Women's Studies Association Conference," argues for a feminist movement defined by difference: "What U.S. third world feminists are calling for is a new subjectivity, a political revision that denies any one perspective as the only answer, but instead posits a shifting tactical and strategic subjectivity . . . no simple, easy sisterhood for U.S. third world feminists."[15] And what third wave feminists seek and find in the writing of hooks, Hazel Carby, Audre Lorde, Gloria Anzaldúa, Maxine Hong Kingston, Ntozake Shange, Patricia Hill Collins, Bharati Mukherjee, Patricia Williams, Ana Castillo, Coco Fusco, Toni Morrison, and so many others, is languages and images that account for multiplicity and difference, that negotiate contradiction in affirmative ways, and that give voice to a politics of hybridity and coalition. *Third Wave Agenda* acknowledges how fully third wave feminism comes out of this groundbreaking work, and how U.S. third world feminism changed the second wave of the women's movement for good.

In acknowledging the profound influence of U.S. third world feminism on the third wave, it is imperative to recognize the dangers of appropriation, as well as the ways that, as Hazel Carby argues, "feminist theory has frequently used and abused [the writing of black women] to produce an essential black female subject for its own consumption."[16] For example, as important as hooks's work has been for U.S third world feminism and third wave feminism, she is often read and taught as *representing* black feminist thought. And, as Patricia Hill Collins notes, "While black women's particular location provides a distinctive angle of vision on oppression, this perspective comprises neither a privileged nor a complete standpoint."[17] A definitive aspect of third wave feminist movement, then, is negotiating multicultural and antiracist standpoints amid the ongoing tensions between borrowing and appropriating. As Vron Ware points out in *Beyond the Pale: White Women, Racism, and History*, "[T]he extent to which this borrowing, or appropriating, is acknowledged obviously varies a great deal, but I think it can potentially provide an important link between different types of struggles . . . [leading] to forming alliances."[18] White U.S. feminism has a long history of borrowing from, allying with, and betraying African American liberation movements, and a consciously multicultural third wave feminism must continuously work with and through these tensions. Perhaps this is where the concept of "feminist generations" is most useful: as an articulation of feminist *movement*, ongoing change, and struggle.[19]

If "whiteness" has been assumed by white women to mean privilege, visibility, belonging, and sisterhood, many of the writers in *Third Wave Agenda* have spent their lives feeling the often inchoate failures of whiteness, white femininity, and competitive individualism. As James Baldwin argued so eloquently, there *is* no white community: "America became white—the people who, as they claim, 'settled' the country became white—because of the necessity of denying the Black presence, and justifying the Black subjugation. No community can be based on such a principle—or in other words, no community can be established on so genocidal a lie."[20] And, as historian David Roediger writes, "Whiteness describes, from Little Big Horn to Simi Valley, not a culture but precisely the absence of culture. It is the empty and therefore terrifying attempt to build an identity based on what one isn't and on whom one can hold back."[21] In a world whose population is expected to double in the next ten years, where social criticism and angst are treated by Prozac, and where Republicans and Democrats alike trumpet the vision of "family values" and nuclear, single-career families precisely when so many of us make alternative families and seek dual careers by choice *and* because we must—in this world, the old motivator of individual distinction, required and perpetuated by the lies of whiteness and assimilation and equal opportunity, often feels like the dustiest myth. In this historical moment we are motivated by "despair, uncertainty, and loss of a sense of grounding" to do something other than adopt "the ideology of individualism that assumes a competitive view of the individual."[22]

Yet that oh-so-American ideology has been ingrained into our deepest senses of ourselves, an ironic legacy of the second wave feminist and civil rights struggles that fought for equal access to the opportunities of white men. Despite our knowing better, despite our knowing its emptiness, the ideology of individualism is still a major motivating force in many third wave lives. Further, our struggles to negotiate individualism's powerful seductions and betrayals provide the third wave with an odd form of common ground, linking us across our many differences. So many of us are panicked about our futures and places, or lack thereof, in the world. With hundreds or sometimes thousands of applications for every "good job"—that is, a job with benefits that is not temporary or part-time—it is hard to think in terms of joining together with others rather than competing against them. The specter of anonymity, linked as it is with the threat of un- and underemployment for all workers, is one of our generation's biggest fears. As David Wild writes in an article on MTV's *The Real World* for *Rolling Stone*,

> One senses *The Real World* speaks to an entire generation of viewers that can hardly wait to get a camera crew on its ass. An application in *The Real Real World* book led to 10,000 new young bodies anxious to sign on for house duty. One imagines packs of pushy twentysomethings lying in wait for a quick way out of the ghetto of obscurity.[23]

In a time of radically diminished economic opportunity, the reality of this "ghetto of obscurity" generates an almost panicked impulse to escape, a panic that makes pushiness and ruthless competition easy. It is a panic that makes other bodies look, on certain mornings, like so many bowling pins to bump out of the way. It is a panic that fuels the current backlash against affirmative action programs, the tightening of border security and anti-immigration laws, and the legislation ending welfare as we know it. The powerful motivating force of this fear often bumps up against a more reasoned knowledge that this adversarial attitude only contributes to the sense of placelessness. Competition can appear to be the most readily available survival strategy even as we know it ensures our extinction. This is a contradiction that feminism's third wave has to face: an often conscious knowledge of the ways in which we are compelled and constructed by the very things that undermine us.

This isn't just "Generation X" whining but, rather, a form of spiritual sickness that most compels generationally third wave men and women to activism and that most works as a galvanizing force for social change. Bell hooks writes in "Postmodern Blackness":

> The overall impact of postmodernism is that many other groups now share with black folks a sense of deep alienation, despair, uncertainty, loss of a sense of grounding even if it is not informed by shared circumstance. Radical postmodernism calls attention to those shared sensibilities which cross the boundaries of class, gender, race, etc., that could be fertile ground for the construction of empathy—ties that would promote recognition of common commitments, and serve as a basis for solidarity and coalition.[24]

Although hooks points out that a longing for community is specific to middle-class white women who have been allowed to join the competitive fray of the dominant culture, it may be this longing that helps fuel white participation in third wave activism. Hooks writes that white feminism "did not question whether masses of women shared the same need for community. . . . [T]he focus on feminism as a way to develop shared identity and community has little appeal to women who experience community, who seek ways to end exploitation and oppression in the context of their lives."[25] But it may be that the longing for community that is characteristic of some white feminists will serve as a motivation to form coalitions that seek to "end exploitation and oppression" affecting lives other than just their own. In addition, the concept of "equal rights," which obscures the complex ways that exploitation and oppression work and are normalized, is also a concept that, *because* most young Americans internalize it naively, can lead to coalition. While growing up, we take "equal rights" seriously, assuming that they apply to all Americans, and we are often horrified when we realize, sooner or later, that in practice, "equal rights" apply only to a few.

Shaped by hegemonic privileges, white women's paths to a coalition-based feminist consciousness have often been based in ignorance, contradiction, and confusion. In some fundamental ways many of us still don't "get it." Striving for the success and equality with white men that second wave feminism made possible, white women in particular often became so focused on individual achievement and success that we became wholehearted supporters of the very structures we most wanted to contest. Third wave women and men of color who have gained access to these kinds of "opportunities" also get caught in this bind. In short, many of us have been clueless, swallowing status quo gambits whole, not choking until we find they have eaten us up from the inside—our hearts, livers, stomachs, lungs—until we can't feel or eat or breathe. We once *could* eat and breathe, and because we could, others couldn't. Third wavers know in theory that, as hooks wrote in 1984, "[B]roader perspectives can only emerge as we examine both the personal that is political, the politics of society as a whole, and global revolutionary politics."[26] But we don't always know how to accomplish this.

Perhaps these are some of the reasons that, for most women who are generationally third wave, the feminist-separatist, pro-woman "gynocriticism" and "goddess worship" of some feminisms, although they sometimes sounded nice, seemed all too wishful and frilly and arcane to make any sense of our lives. Although we also owe an enormous debt to the critique of sexism and the struggles for gender equity that were white feminism's strongest provinces, it was U.S. third world feminism that modeled a language and a politics of hybridity that can account for our lives at the century's turn. These are lives marked by the realities of multicultural exchange, fusion, and conflict, lives that combine blackness, whiteness, brownness, gayness, bisexuality, straightness. These are lives that combine male-identification and female-identification, middle-class status and staggering debt, lives that are hopeful and stressed and depressed, empowered and exhausted and scared. As Gloria Anzaldúa writes in her foreword to the second edition of *This Bridge Called My Back*, "[W]e have come to realize that we are not alone in our struggles nor separate nor autonomous but that we—white black straight queer female male—are connected and interdependent."[27] We hope that in these pages we have begun—provisionally, slowly, making some dumb mistakes—to pay our debts to those women whose work has sometimes literally saved our lives.

Keeping a Faith

Essays in *Third Wave Agenda* try to answer the question, What is the third wave? in a variety of ways. Coming out of a turn in the academy that tended to privilege a feminist theory that often seemed like a disembodied language game, three years ago in a bookstore in Ithaca, New York, we—both of us academic activists with creative writing backgrounds—sat down in frustration in the feminist theory section.

We wanted, needed, more than anything to see a kind of writing that addressed our historical perspective, a writing that was intellectually rigorous and heartfelt and unpretentious at once. Without knowing it, we were looking for the kind of writing that reflected a faith, a writing that Cherríe Moraga characterizes as "believing that we have the power to actually transform our experience, change our lives, save our lives. . . . It is the faith of activists I am talking about."[28] We wanted the kind of writing that Moraga and Anzaldúa name "theory in the flesh" and that bell hooks calls "lived theory," one that could articulate the historically situated experiences of our "generation."[29] Not finding examples of this kind of writing by third wave writers yet hoping it was out there somewhere, we sent out a nationwide call for papers to both nonacademic and academic venues, and we received contributions from academics, activists, and artists. The hybridity of language we were looking for—the hybridity characteristic of our identities, our lives—proved more difficult to find than we had imagined. We wanted good storytelling *and* critical analysis without jargon, lived personal experience that was tied to the larger social scene. But readers as well as contributors often were uncomfortable with language that wasn't clearly one or the other. We have struggled to keep both forms of discourse in play, to keep the faith that writing itself can be transformative.

The essays in *Third Wave Agenda* are organized into four sections: (1) What Is the Third Wave? Third Wave Cultural Contexts; (2) The Third Wave and Representation; (3) Third Wave Negotiations; and (4) Third Wave Activism and Youth Music Culture. "What Is the Third Wave?" articulates some of the questions most pressing for third wave feminism, examining possibilities for activism in the context of the economy, multiple identity positionality, and a cultural climate hostile to feminism. The section includes Michelle Sidler's "Living in McJobdom: Third Wave Feminism and Class Inequity," which argues that the choice for which second wave feminists fought—equal access to the workforce—is no longer a choice, because the U.S. workforce is now part of a global economy based on turnover and lower wages for all workers. Sidler calls for "a new feminist political agenda [that] work[s] to relieve the economic disparity facing twentysomethings," and argues that it is now under- and unemployment that are the most pressing problem for feminism, not "patriarchy." Our "We Learn America like a Script: Activism in the Third Wave; or, Enough Phantoms of Nothing" explores the emptiness of some of the traditional forms of empowerment, as well as some possible sources of the hunger for community and coalition that fuels contemporary activism. Deborah Siegel's "Reading between the Waves: Feminist Historiography in a 'Postfeminist' Moment" looks at some of the complications of theorizing feminism in the 1990s, including a backlash culture and "postfeminism." She concludes that "we must recognize that there can be no single representative subject of feminism, while, at the same time, we must continue to speak in a collective voice that articulates political demands on behalf of a group called 'women.'" The section concludes with "*HUES* Magazine: The Making of a Movement," an essay by three women who themselves are examples of third wave feminist practice, *HUES* magazine editors Tali Edut, Dyann Logwood, and Ophira Edut. They discuss the importance of biracial coalition and activism in the third wave and the story behind their brand of activism, which took the form of a nationally distributed fashion magazine that is a multicultural, feminist alternative to mainstream women's magazines such as *Glamour* and *Mademoiselle*. In a different way, each piece in this section articulates the importance of the contradictory and fragmentary identities in the third wave, making connections between racial, sexual, and gender identities, categories that make no sense if considered in isolation.

Section 2, "The Third Wave and Representation," explores multiple ways that fan culture and engagement with media figures have been empowering, if problematic, to third wave feminism, and how media promotion of conservative feminists has led to the highly distorted public perceptions of both second and third wave feminisms that conservative feminists love to attack. Leigh Shoemaker's exposé of and identification with singer Henry Rollins in "Part Animal, Part Machine: Self-Definition, Rollins Style" explores the relationship between contemporary configurations of masculinity and feminist male identification, which she argues is the result of the mixed messages of the backlash: "second wave feminism had taught me that, as a girl, I could do anything I wanted to do, but the backlash let me know that this was possible only as long as I wasn't a *girl*—as long as I wasn't soft and feminine and weak." She theorizes Rollins as the practitioner of our culture's latent fascist tendencies that problematically appeal to the malaise and the sense of disenfranchisement of third wavers. Jennifer Reed's "Roseanne: A 'Killer Bitch' for Generation X" explores the possibilities of "bitchiness" and identification with media figures for personal and political empowerment, offering Roseanne as the creator of "a new subjective space for women" that "both parodies and embraces glamour, . . . a construction committed to working with the contradictions and the irreconcilability" that characterize such a space. Carolyn Sorisio's "A Tale of Two Feminisms: Power and Victimization in Contemporary Feminist Debate" critically engages the Camille Paglia–Katie Roiphe–Naomi Wolf representation of third wave feminism. She argues for the value of feminist history and the need to make that history a more vital, present part of contemporary culture. Because Paglia-Roiphe-Wolf's popular work ignores much academic feminism and feminist history, particularly the work of feminists of color, and returns to a universalized concept of woman, this elision further indicates that "academic feminists must intensify efforts to speak to the overall feminist community. Otherwise, we will constantly remain in the same place, reinvent the same wheel, and learn nothing from the past." Together, the pieces in this section examine the role of representation in creating feminist identities and feminist histories (or lack thereof), arguing for the centrality of popular culture and an audience that goes beyond the academy to activist strategies in the third wave.

Section 3, "Third Wave Negotiations," presents some key sites of contradiction that characterize third wave experience. Carol Guess writes a meditation on the relationship between gay identity, academia, queer feminism, and feminist practice in "Deconstructing Me: On Being (Out) in the Academy," addressing the difficulties of negotiating lesbian identity and Butlerian poststructuralism. Lidia Yukman's "Feminism and a Discontent" performs in its language the hybridity that we argue is most characteristic of third wave activist strategy, pointing to the difficulties of negotiating creative and critical language and cross-gender/racial/sexual/class affiliations in the classroom, and arguing that ideas and words and writing are forms of activism that can save a person's life. And in "Masculinity without Men: Women Reconciling Feminism and Male-Identification," Ana Marie Cox and others negotiate between feminism and male identification. Writing in dialogue form, they discuss how, instead of being opposed to feminism, they have found male identification an enabling, embodied form of third wave feminist praxis.

The final section of the book, "Third Wave Activism and Youth Music Culture," highlights what many have found to be the most productive site for activism in the third wave. Because contemporary rap, rock, and alternative music is produced and consumed primarily by persons in the third wave, music has emerged as a site for activist coalition and community building like no other and has led to activist projects that link gender activism with other interventions. Riot Grrrl activists in Washington, D.C., for instance, first came together to produce girl-oriented music and fanzines, and then diversified their activist work to include literacy projects, self-defense projects, and empowerment initiatives in the wider community. Melissa Klein's "Duality and Redefinition: Young Feminism and the Alternative Music Community" is a firsthand account of that activism, providing a history of Riot Grrrl and the way the movement has branched out. "I have had to step outside the punk scene," Klein writes, and "into social service work to confront race, aging, and poverty issues, because the punk scene remains predominantly young, white, and middle class." Fellow activist Jen Smith discusses the evolution of musical production into diverse forms of "punk feminist cultural productions" in "Doin' It for the Ladies—Youth Feminism: Cultural Productions/Cultural Activism." And Jeff Niesel, a freelance music critic for the *Orange County Register* and the *San Diego Union-Tribune*, analyzes, in "Hip-Hop Matters: Rewriting the Sexual Politics of Rap Music," the politics and possibilites of rap music for race activism and its complicated relationship to feminism, emphasizing an alternative tradition in hip-hop that embodies and encourages coalition. This hip-hop alternative argues that only an examination of race and gender as related forces can make for meaningful cultural (ex)change. Together, the pieces in "Third Wave Activism and Youth Music Culture" argue persuasively for cultural production as a powerful activist site, perhaps the site where the third wave has made its strongest interventions.

Communities today have to be imagined on different bases than that of the separatism of identity politics, bases such as what bell hooks calls a "commonality of feeling."[30] Unlike Naomi Wolf, who is most often called upon as a spokesperson for third wave feminism, the writers in *Third Wave Agenda* believe that living in a world that preserves the status quo of free market competition and upward mobility is not enough to maintain our sanity and human dignity, if it is even possible. Always personal and engaged while maintaining a scholarly focus, these essays perform a kind of hybrid thinking and writing that marks part of a critical agenda for the third wave, a place of discussion and disagreement that is also a place of community. Writers in *Third Wave Agenda*, although their positions are by no means comprehensive of the diversity of the third wave, engage the possibility of rethinking and reshaping. Following the lead provided by the work of bell hooks, Susan Bordo, and others that has reshaped the critical paradigms of our time, we try to confront the complications of contradiction in ways that begin to expand comfortable cultural polarities and situate youth culture squarely within lived experience and cultural practices. We also begin to chart a series of directions for third wave feminism at a cultural moment when mainstream hostility to such projects has reached new peaks. We are able to do so only with the help of all the feminisms that have come before us and of the ways in which feminist work, more than anything else in contemporary culture, has made it possible for us still to have hope, to think, to keep the faith, to survive.

Notes

1. *The Third Wave: Feminist Perspectives on Racism*, edited by Lisa Albrecht et al., is being published by Kitchen Table: Women of Color Press and has been rescheduled for publication in spring 1997. Small presses often run into funding problems and get by with volunteer staffs.

2. See Barbara Findlen, ed., *Listen Up: Voices from the Next Feminist Generation* (Seattle: Seal, 1995); and Rebecca Walker, ed., *To Be Real: Telling the Truth and Changing the Face of Feminism* (New York: Doubleday, 1995).

3. See Nan Bauer Maglin and Donna Perry, eds., *"Bad Girls"/"Good Girls": Women, Sex, and Power in the Nineties* (New Brunswick, N.J.: Rutgers University Press, 1996).

4. See Christina Hoff Sommers, *Who Stole Feminism? How Women Have Betrayed Women* (New York: Simon and Schuster, 1994).

5. Alice Rossi, *The Feminist Papers* (Boston: Northeastern University Press, 1973), 616–17. Our thanks to Susan Bordo for suggesting this source.

6. Hole, "Doll Parts," *Live through This* (Geffen, 1994).

7. Vicki Woods, "Labor of Love," *Vogue*, January 1997, 135.

8. Our thanks go to Susan Bordo for her insights on this point.

9. Cultural critic Greg Tate signifies on hip-hop complexity in the liner notes for NdegéOcello's *Plantation Lullabies*:

> There's no such thing as alternative hiphop because the only known alternative to hiphop is dead silence. . . . Hiphop is the inverse of capitalism. Hiphop is the reverse of colonialism. Hiphop is the world the slaveholder made, sent into niggafide future shock. Hiphop is the black aesthetic by-product of the American dream machine. . . . Hiphop is the first black musical movement in history that black people pimped before the white boys got to it. Hiphop converted raw soul into fetishized commodity. Hiphop has

no morals, no conscience, and no ecological concern for the scavenged earth or the scavenged American minds wrecked in the pursuit of new markets. Unlike Sigourney Weaver's nemesis Alien, hiphop is not the other man's rape fantasy of the black sex machine gone berserk. Hiphop is James Brown's pelvis digitally grinded [*sic*] into technomorphine. Hiphop is DOPE-KNOWLOGY, THE ONLY KNOWN ANTIDOTE FOR PRIME TIME SENSORY DEPRIVATION.

10. Me'Shell NdegéOcello, *Plantation Lullabies* (Maverick Recording, 1993) and *Peace beyond Passion* (Maverick Recording, 1996).

11. Ann Powers, "Black and Blue," *Rolling Stone*, September 5, 1996, 34.

12. Walker, *To Be Real*, xxxi.

13. Kayann Short, "Coming to the Table: The Differential Politics of *This Bridge Called My Back*," *Genders* 20 (1994): 3–44.

14. Gloria Anzaldúa and Cherríe Moraga, eds., *This Bridge Called My Back: Writing by Radical Women of Color* (Latham, N.J.: Kitchen Table: Women of Color Press, 1981); Barbara Smith, ed., *Home Girls: A Black Feminist Anthology* (New York: Kitchen Table: Women of Color Press, 1983).

15. Chela Sandoval, "Feminism and Racism: A Report on the 1981 National Women's Studies Association Conference," in *Making Face/Making Soul: Haciendo Caras*, ed. Gloria Anzaldúa (San Francisco: Aunt Lute Books, 1990), 67.

16. Hazel Carby, "The Multicultural Wars," in *Black Popular Culture*, ed. Michele Wallace and Gina Dent (Seattle: Bay, 1992), 192.

17. Patricia Hill Collins, "What's in a Name? Womanism, Black Feminism, and Beyond," *Black Scholar* (winter/spring 1996) 26:1, 16.

18. Vron Ware, *Beyond the Pale: White Women, Racism, and History* (London and New York: Verso, 1992), 240. See also Sara Evans, *Personal Politics: The Roots of Women's Liberation in the Civil Rights Movement and the New Left* (New York: Random House, 1979).

19. On the concept of feminist generations, see Nancy Whittier, *Feminist Generations: The Persistence of the Radical Women's Movement* (Philadelphia: Temple University Press, 1995). Whittier's book is problematic because of its lack of substantive discussion on the impact of women-of-color feminism. "Feminist Generations" was also the name of a conference devoted to the generational theme, held at Bowling Green State University in February 1996, and an anthology is planned based on the papers given there.

20. James Baldwin, "On Being White and Other Lies," *Essence*, April 1984, 92.

21. David Roediger, *Towards the Abolition of Whiteness* (London and New York: Verso, 1994), 13.

22. Zillah Eisenstein, introduction to *The Radical Future of Liberal Feminism*, quoted in bell hooks, *Feminist Theory: From Margin to Center* (Boston: South End, 1984), 8.

23. David Wild, "Television Reality Bites Back," *Rolling Stone*, September 5, 1996, 71.

24. Bell hooks, "Postmodern Blackness," in *Yearning: Race, Gender, and Cultural Politics* (Boston: South End, 1990), 27.

25. Hooks, *Feminist Theory*, 28.

26. Ibid., 25.

27. Gloria Anzaldúa, foreword to the second edition of *This Bridge Called My Back: Writings by Radical Women of Color*, 2d ed., ed. Gloria Anzaldúa and Cherríe Moraga (Latham, N.Y.: Kitchen Table: Women of Color, 1983).

28. Cherríe Moraga, preface to Anzaldúa and Moraga, *This Bridge*, xviii.

29. "Theory in the Flesh" is a subtitle of one section of Anzaldúa and Moraga, *This Bridge*. See also hooks's discussion of "lived theory" in her "Theory as Liberatory Practice," in *Teaching to Transgress: Education as the Practice of Freedom* (New York: Routledge, 1994), 59–75.

30. See bell hooks, *Outlaw Culture* (New York: Routledge, 1994). The way hooks engages the widest possible audience by letting her work appear in an amazing diversity of publications, from her many books to popular magazines to the feminist self-defense music compilation *Free to Fight! An Interactive Self-Defense Project* (Candy-Ass Records, 1996), is a crucial political strategy for progressive third wavers. Susan Bordo's work has been similarly influential, opening areas such as medicine, philosophy, and sociology to the possibility of cultural critique. The discussion of eating disorders in *Unbearable Weight* (Berkeley: University of California Press, 1993), for instance, has had an impact on medical paradigms for treatment. These kinds of analysis—ones that do actual cultural work—are the third wave's best hope as well as its point of departure.

WHAT IS THE THIRD WAVE? THIRD WAVE CULTURAL CONTEXTS

Copyright 1993 by Barry Baldridge   *Courtesy of HUES Collective*

Courtesy of HUES Collective

WHAT IS THE THIRD WAVE? THIRD WAVE CULTURAL CONTEXTS

It is necessary to look at how cultural context shapes feminist strategies and concerns. Early, "first wave" feminists, for example, worked for abolition, voting rights, and temperance causes. Second wave feminists concentrated on the ERA and wage equity, developed "gender" and "sexism" as key categories of analysis, critiqued beauty culture, and often worked in black, gay, and New Left movements. Although third wave feminists draw upon these histories and continue these struggles, our worlds and our issues have changed.

Essays in this section begin to articulate how third wave feminisms are shaped by intersections of contemporary sociopolitical forces. An increasingly unstable economy and insecure job market for all workers becomes a primary feminist concern. Gender activists might consider how to use technologies as part of a new politics, but such a project would also have to demand broad-based access to technical education and forms of knowledge. Third wave feminisms must remain aware of the complex ways that power, oppression, and resistance work in a media-saturated global economy so that what at first glance looks like progress might not be the change we most need, and what looks like regression might actually be progressive.

Our praxis is shaped by the questions that are our legacy. How to forge a movement, or even rethink what a movement might look like, in a generation that has learned to ask Which personal? and Whose politics? How to think "sisterhood" in terms of difference and hybridity? How to avoid dismissing the feminists who came before us in an attempt to articulate our own identities, and how to repay our debts to their work? How to build coalitions? How to negotiate both our sense of entitlement and cultural backlash? How to make room for our younger sisters and daughters, our younger brothers and sons? How to keep feminist movement strong?

CHAPTER ONE

Living in McJobdom: Third Wave Feminism and Class Inequity

Michelle Sidler

I recently read *Changing Subjects: The Making of Feminist Literary Criticism* (Greene and Kahn 1993), a collection of essays by women who were leaders in second wave feminism—literary scholars and teachers who came of age in the 1960s and 1970s. Many of the essays were personal and reflective, recounting the difficulties of working in departments as the first and only woman professor. These feminists defied blatant sexism and existing cultural norms against working women to fulfill their potential as intelligent, independent people. I was moved by the dedication to literary studies that initially led so many of the women to attend graduate school, where they often faced an unreceptive academia dominated by male scholars.

It occurred to me that when I entered graduate school in 1991, I did not anticipate gender barriers, partially because of my own naïveté, but also because of an undergraduate experience within an English department almost exclusively made up of women. It was at this moment that I realized to the fullest my indebtedness to second wave feminism—all of the female instructors of undergraduates whose brilliance and support fostered my eventual career in English studies were part of the second wave feminist movement. If not for the vital social and political work of these women, I might not have been in a position to consider even the possibility of obtaining a doctoral degree.

But looking closer at my reason for entering graduate school directly after receiving my bachelor's degree, I must confess that my decision had less to do with an overwhelming desire to study Milton or Joyce or even Welty than with my fear of facing a bleak job market holding, as I did, few technical skills and a liberal arts degree. Too many friends before me had fallen into McJobs,[1] working in part-time or temporary positions with no benefits and no hope of advancement. If I can just make it through graduate school, I thought, I will have it all—job security, benefits, great working hours, and an academic position that will allow me to engage in two of my favorite activities, teaching and writing. In a time when temporary employment agencies such as Manpower are among the most prosperous American companies, such economic concerns loom large.[2] My choices were discouragingly simple: either survive graduate school and work in academia, or risk being swallowed up into the black hole of McJobdom and losing the security and prospects of my middle-class upbringing. Indeed, going to graduate school seemed the only foreseeable alternative to what Jeff Giles in *Newsweek* magazine called, "for newly minted grads, arguably the worst job market since World War II" (1994, 65).

Many second wave feminists were faced with an either/or dilemma also: either get (or stay) married and sacrifice their own professional ambitions, or follow their desires as self-sustaining, intelligent women. Rachel Blau DuPlessis writes of the mixed messages she received at college in the 1960s: "A major contradiction lay between the culture's incessant (and our internalized) demand for instantly ratifying engagement and marriage, and any sense of independence, self-definition, autonomy, social commitment" (1993, 98). She, like other second wave feminists, found herself torn between two conflicting messages: raise a family or be economically self-sufficient. Second wave feminists, driven by a sense of independence and a need for equality, struggled to break down that either/or dilemma.

For many young women now, the choice whether or not to work is no longer an either/or proposition. Most twentysomething women do not question the possibility of work, and not necessarily because we feel particularly empowered or independent. With stagnant wages in many fields, women often must work just to stay afloat, even if they are married to working husbands. Generally, women no longer feel trapped into housekeeping and motherhood; on average, we are waiting later and later to have children. Since women's liberation, more women than ever are entering the professional workplace. According to Robert Reich in *Rolling Stone*, "In 1973, 57 percent of women in their 20's were in the workforce. Twenty years later, the figure had climbed to 73 percent" (1994, 119). However, many young women do not view this new presence in the workforce as an opportunity. Many, like myself, feel trapped by lower wages for all workers and know that even for married couples, two incomes are quickly becoming a necessity.

Second wave feminism helped bring about professional self-sufficiency for women, and their work paved the way for new feminisms, such as that being constructed by young women of the post–baby boom generation. But postmodernism and the new global economy have brought on concerns about the homogeneity of the so-called bourgeois white feminism of the second wave. Who has reaped the benefits of the women's movement of the 1960s and 1970s? To what extent did second wave feminism help the rise of women in *all* classes, including those outside privileged classes, and to what extent must feminism revamp itself in the wake of the new global economy? What can we learn from second wave feminism as we face an economy driven by profits, with workers edged out by technology and global competition?

The rise of women in the workplace sounds like bright news, but it begins to take on a new face when I consider again my own shaky job dilemma. Like many other twentysomethings, I feel job security slipping out from under me. Economic restructuring has destabilized employment for both men and women. Women can no longer depend on the security of a husband's income (or their own, for that matter). Nor can they assume that jobs are available; often women just have not had access to them. Even young working men are finding more McJobs and lower salaries. Third wave feminism will have to face these harsh economic conditions.

Academia itself poses an excellent example of this new destabilization. Women (and men) in academia have less encouraging economic prospects than did second wave feminists. Since my entrance into graduate school, I have found that most of the academic perks I once looked forward to are not guaranteed. Due to budget crunching and an overabundance of out-of-work academics, many universities have turned to hiring professors part-time or temporarily, thus eliminating higher salaries, benefits, and the security of tenure. In the new restructuring of faculty, many professors are paid by each course hour they teach, prompting them to teach heavy loads and leaving little time for professional development. The shortage of positions was a minor problem when most second wave feminists looked for their first academic appointments. As second waver Elizabeth Ermath writes, "When I began looking for a tenure-track job in 1969–70 the job market was just beginning to get pinched" (1993, 227). After twenty-five years, that pinch has become a painful squeeze. Doctoral students feel the economic pressure even before they graduate. While they pursue degrees, most endure their own versions of McJobs—teaching assistantships with salaries so low (and often few benefits) that many are forced to take out even more student loans, thus increasing their post-doctoral debt.

I am not alone in my pessimism about the economy. Many young Americans, so-called Generation Xers, have continued to list the economy as a concern; from *Time* magazine's groundbreaking feature on twentysomethings by David Gross and Sophfronia Scott in 1990 to *Newsweek*'s 1994 cover story by Giles, the economy continues to haunt postboomers. These two articles frame what has become a confusing and controversial discussion about exactly what Generation X is. Many of the initial media characterizations of twentysomethings have been proven inaccurate, such as the claims that they are "slackers" or "whiners." Some polls, in fact, show that Generation Xers work as hard as, and moan less than, members of older generations (Giles 1994, 65; Aley 1994). However, young workers are having an increasingly difficult time grappling with their economic conditions.

For the most part, twentysomethings have resisted the media characterizations, like one man who remarked, "Generation X is . . . a media fabrication" (qtd. in Giles 1994, 65). In many ways the generational category is just a convenient label. But even Giles, who attempted to debunk what he called "myths" about Generation X, could not dispute one overarching concern for twentysomethings—the economy. He concluded that "even leaving aside the $4 trillion debt, Xers have had a lot to contend with," including skyrocketing student loan debt and comparatively lower incomes with which to pay it off (1994, 65). These factors, along with the economic uncertainties such global trade agreements as NAFTA and GATT are likely to bring about, have left young workers with more than their share of financial worries. Further, Giles cites economist Gary Shilling, who "thinks that global wage competition will prevent the Xers from doing as well as the previous small cohort of the '50's" (67). The new global economy will certainly lessen, and may eradicate, any worker shortage as the large boomer generation retires. This new development complicates many analysts' claims that postboomers will eventually fare as well as, if not better than, their boomer predecessors because they will have a greater job pool in the near future.[3]

And we still have to address the current employment crisis for young workers. Among the countries represented at the March 1994 G7 conference (excepting only Germany), the jobless rate for people under twenty-five was worse than that for older workers.[4] In America, youth joblessness is not as bad as it is in most countries, but the employment available for twentysomethings in the United States is "often ill-paid or temporary or both" (Generation 1994, 27). This trend will only continue in the future, as new technologies and overseas job competition remain threats for working people. And we cannot rely on technological fields to create new jobs, because the number of jobs created by these fields is a fraction of what is needed to relieve U.S. and global unemployment (Rifkin 1995, xvii). Jeremy Rifkin notes that the future of many U.S. workers may be dire because of technology: "more than 90 million jobs in a labor force of 124 million are potentially vulnerable to replacement by machines" (1995, 5). In the specialized world of technologies, there are simply not enough jobs for all of these workers, and educated young Americans are already feeling the effects. According to the Bureau of Statistics, "Approximately 25% of under-35 college graduates have jobs that do not require college degrees" (Lane 1995, 106). Many of these twentysomethings work in temporary, part-time, and low-wage jobs. Temporary jobs alone employ 8.1 million Americans (Thurow 1996, 165).

These statistics have been proved in my personal life: I have seen many of my college friends (most of whom have four-year degrees) bounce from one McJob to another. And the financial situation continues to look as grim for women as it did in the past. According to Giles's statistics, women between twenty-five and thirty-four are still making an average salary only 82 percent that of their male counterparts. In *Working Woman*, Pamela Krueger notes that for college-educated women, future finances are even more complicated by the desire to have a family (1994, 62). The best-educated and most-skilled young women are demanding flexibility in the workplace. This goal will be difficult, if not impossible, to achieve, even for professionally prepared women, in the current economic instability.

Further, the situation is particularly drastic for young Americans with little education or professional skills. Reich notes that women and men ages twenty-five to thirty-four without a high school diploma make less than half the income of their counterparts with a college education—"the largest gulf between high earners and low earners in our nation's history" (1994, 119). This statistic is no surprise to those who observed the shrinkage of the middle class throughout the 1980s. The *Economist* agrees: "In an economy where earnings are tied ever more tightly to skills, and where employers use education as a proxy for such skills when hiring young workers, the 75% of Americans who do not graduate from college face a grim future of stagnant or falling real wages" (Generation 1994, 27–28). With fewer jobs to go around, most Americans without enough skills or education will find themselves in an economic crisis, creating a new class of the impoverished. Due to technology and global competition, downsizing and reduction of jobs remain the trend. Even for those with skills, competition for jobs will continue to tighten.

Annette Fuentes and Barbara Ehrenreich recognize the motivating force behind the worldwide employment crisis—multinational corporations guided by the "profit motive" (1983, 57). They argue that we must create a global network among working women for support and recognition. Although such a goal is an essential first step, much more needs to be done, and soon. Women, men, and feminism must redirect the profit motive, confront the widening gap between the wealthy and the underclasses, and produce options beyond the present corporate model. To prepare for such a challenge, women of all classes must familiarize themselves with economics as an integral part of feminism and of their daily lives. This need has never been greater or clearer than it is now in my generation. We can expect little improvement in these economic conditions as long as corporations value profit more than workers.

Marxist feminists argue that the union of capitalism and patriarchy leads to the domestic oppression of women.[5] These feminists have exposed the oppression of women, through domestic labor, as the reproducers of the capital workforce. However, the image of women as domestic servants to patriarchy first and capitalism second is quickly becoming outdated. Many families cannot afford the traditional family structure of the domestic mother when one-third of all men from twenty-five to thirty-four years of age earn less than what is needed to keep a family of four out of poverty (Thurow 1996, 31). Men do not have the luxury of an unemployed wife. Most women of my generation must work, whether we have families or not, to survive economically. Feminism can use the experience of resisting the oppressive yet ingrained patriarchal system to fight capitalism, but we must begin to move away from viewing patriarchy as the immediate cause of oppression and try to combat the even larger threat of American and worldwide economic hardship.

Without a new economic theory and political mission, feminism risks alienating this new generation of women, many of whom experience economic instability and, in some cases, a drop in class status. With the added insecurity of McJobs comes the decline of raw salary figures: between 1973 and 1992, real wages dropped for people at all levels of income except those in the top 20 percent (Rifkin 1995, 23). If this trend continues (and it most certainly will with the rising of corporate downsizing and global job competition), only women in the top 20 percent will have a choice about working. Material feminists must change their priorities from fighting the patriarchy first and capitalism second. Women's oppression must be seen as, first, a function of wage earning and, second, a result of domestic servitude, because soon there will be few homes without working mothers. Second wave feminists did not enter an economic forecast so grim; they had no way of knowing that my generation would need their help to counter the raw face of global profit-driven capitalism.

So how can a new feminist political agenda work to relieve the economic disparity facing twentysomethings? First, we must recognize that gender equality in the workforce does not automatically bring economic progress. Feminism in the 1960s and 1970s worked toward giving women the same economic opportunities as men. Now, however, there will be fewer economic opportunities for either gender, so we have to broaden our concerns to include issues previously viewed as gender neutral. In "The Long Goodbye," Linda Kauffman calls for a renewed sense of a feminist project that will readdress the current state of affairs, with its list of injustices that goes beyond those tackled by second wave feminism. She proposes a women's movement that addresses "injustices that might not normally be regarded as specifically feminist concerns because it is precisely the interconnection of feminist issues with other injustices that urgently needs our attention in the '90's" (1993, 141). This interconnection involves not just recognizing the plight of others but also learning how all injustices are an integral part of feminism itself.

Feminism can begin interconnecting by addressing at least three areas: academics, the media, and technology. These structures function broadly on economic, social, and cultural levels, and they have all been important in the progression of feminism. They also work on a personal level for me, as a teacher of using computers for writing. In my experience, academics, the media, and technology usually exist as contradictory forces. Feminists have been actively trying to usurp these structures as places of empowerment and change for women. But these areas have proved detrimental to twentysomethings, women, and workers. In many ways academics, the media, and technology are complicit in the workings of corporate oppression and the profit motive.

A new agenda must include mobility between the academic politics of second wave feminism and young workers both in and out of the academy. The academy is, after all, no less susceptible to economic adversity than is any other profession or institution. New doctoral graduates, especially those in the liberal arts, are facing a horrible job market as colleges and universities give in to the pressure of a technologically based economy, hiring full-time tenured faculty mostly in only those fields that will give students skills for professionalization. Higher education's need to compete in the corporate marketplace has taken priority before less economically tangible areas of study, such as the liberal arts. The academy presents a representative case of the current economic crisis and can act as a starting point, like the informant of a joint movement, one that recognizes mutual oppression where binaries such as academic/popular and man/woman still take prevalence.

At the scholarly level, we can begin by looking for theorists' discussions of the current economy that have immediate implications for twentysomething workers. Jacques Derrida recognizes injustices created by the current economy in his *Specters of Marx*. He lists ten "plagues of the new world order," the social, political, and economic structures created by multinational markets and the "New International Law" (1994, 81–84). Changing conditions in late capitalism are leading to global abuse of human rights, and the first of these on Derrida's list is unemployment:

> The function of social inactivity, of non-work or of underemployment[,] is entering into a new era. It calls for another politics.
> And another concept. The "new underemployment" no more resembles unemployment, in the very forms of its experience and its calculation, than what in France is called the "new poverty" resembles poverty. (1994, 81)

Through the creation of a global pool of workers, capitalism has constructed joblessness on a grand scale. No longer can we consider unemployment a fluctuating curve in the economy; we have entered an era of chronic work shortage and poverty. Neither women nor men can assume that jobs are out there to be had and that economic stability is a function of gender equality. We must overhaul feminism to operate within this "new world order," recognizing not just the absence of work equality for women, but the absence of work for *everyone*. We need, as Derrida states, a new concept of sustained unemployment. Academics like me who face job shortages have a vested interest in addressing the theoretical issues behind our employment crisis and in translating those issues into a new feminist agenda.

The economic adversity of young workers can also be transformed on political and social levels, particularly through the media. The women's movement of second wave feminism learned hard lessons that can aid in this struggle. One way is to stop the cycle of blame on twentysomethings. As Susan Faludi spells out so effectively in *Backlash* (1991), feminism was reflected back onto the women's movement when much popular press in the 1980s claimed that feminism was its own worst enemy. A similar backlash has begun in response to reports of the economic plight of twentysomethings. Exploiting the false stereotypes about my generation, some members of the popular press blame young workers for their financial problems. David Martin, for example, labels twentysomethings "the Whiny Generation" and argues, "Instead of blaming everyone for this state of [economic] affairs, the Whiners should acquire more skills, education and specialized knowledge for the careers of the 21st century" (1993). Of course, Martin is mistaken about the possibilities for careers of the next century; with fewer jobs even for the educated, many skilled workers will be underemployed. In addition, as technology speeds up the progression of the market, many skills acquired now by young people will be obsolete soon.

Further, Martin's statement presents a problem facing twentysomethings that feminism also faces. Martin blames young workers themselves for their dissatisfaction, asserting that they were spoiled by privileged childhoods with high standards of living and economic prosperity. Ignoring for the moment Martin's obvious overgeneralizations about the standards of living for all postboomer youth, his blame tactics echo those chronicled in Faludi's book. Such reports targeted the "triumph of women's equality" as the cause of reports of increased stress and unhappiness among women (Faludi 1991, xiii). Feminism learned valuable lessons from this type of conservative media reaction, lessons that could now be used to counter backlash in the popular press concerning economic inequality for young men and women. Such lesson sharing is a realization of the interconnectedness between feminism and other movements that Kauffman identifies.

Moving again to the theoretical level, a surprising connection can be drawn between Martin's comments and Donna Haraway's calls for a new feminism (Haraway 1990, 211). Haraway advocates using the power of technology in the postmodern era to promote a new feminist agency. Although her theory concerns the economic disadvantage of women specifically, it applies equally well to twentysomething workers—both men and women—who are in positions of economic disadvantage. She argues that "we are living through a movement from an organic, industrial society to a polymorphous, information system" that posits great power in the knowledge of technology (203). Haraway asserts that unemployment itself stems from the new technologies but that women can learn to use technology to create new, empowering social realities. Haraway believes that the forces of capitalism can be fought through the tools of technology: "An adequate socialist-feminist politics should address women in the privileged occupational categories and particularly in the production of science and technology that constructs scientific-technical discourse, processes, and objects" (211). Haraway argues that a new feminist agenda should support and encourage women who are in positions of technological power. Her feminist agenda assumes that we can use the tools of technology to fight oppression, but this approach seems simplistic. Haraway's theory sounds much like Martin's advice to young workers—just get the right kind of technical and communicative skills, and you will get the right kind of economic power.

The current economic plight of twentysomethings complicates Martin's and Haraway's insistence on the power of technology. Haraway and Martin simplify the privilege of class as a basis for acquiring knowledge of technology, particularly for young workers. As the importance of technology rises, so does the pay gap between those with and those without the economic means to attend college. The 1980s brought on a shrinking middle class and an increased necessity for a college education, but that education has gotten more and more expensive, even for those left in the middle class. As John Heilemann notes in the *Washington Monthly*, the rise in tuition for higher education is outrageous: "Between 1980 and 1990 the cost of attending the average college soared by an astonishing 126 percent—way ahead of inflation and, more importantly, way ahead of the median family income" (1993, 43). Acquiring the necessary skills and knowledge costs more now than ever, making it more difficult for those in lower classes to obtain gainful employment, and sustaining higher education as an institution predominantly for the privileged classes. With the shrinkage in the 1980s of federal grant funds for higher education, students without the means from their families and/or scholarships find themselves taking out large student loans to finance their education (Heilemann 1993, 43). Martin and Haraway address the advantages of technology from different perspectives, but both sustain its position as powerful for those with privilege.

This brings the discussion back to the personal level, to my stake in this economic inequity as a member of the twentysomething workforce. I am looking for a new feminism that tackles the issue of affording an education that will lead to economic prosperity, a struggle that parallels the employment equality sought by second wave feminists. I am personally invested in this problem not only as a student in higher education but also as a teacher in higher education. As a student, I have had to contend with the rising cost of my studies, at both the undergraduate and the graduate levels. I have already superseded the average $35,000 debt incurred by students seeking graduate degrees (Heilemann 1993, 42). And I am not alone—as of the 1991–92 school year, student loans overtook grants as the largest source of federal educational funds that college and graduate students receive (Financial 1993). This is no surprise as I consider my college classmates, some of whom graduated from our private, four-year university with debts totaling $5,000, $20,000, even $40,000. And with direct student loan dispersal (through increased technology, students can receive their checks as soon as seventy-two hours after applying), this trend will no doubt continue to rise (Wilkinson 1994).

Whereas many women in second wave feminism faced difficult decisions between family or school, or family or work, twentysomethings have little choice in these matters. First, higher education is quickly becoming a necessity; we are told there is no longer a job for us on the factory floor, so we must incur heavy debt to obtain a degree.

Second, we must put off decisions such as having children for five, ten, maybe even twenty years because of the financial burden left by our education. This too is a feminist concern. Young women may not feel as much pressure to have children as did the previous generation of women, but their decision has become even more complicated by debt.

As an instructor in academia, I bring these concerns to my classroom and discuss them with my students. Teaching technical writing to seniors, I empathize with them as they surf the Internet desperately for the job that will take them out of this debt cycle. Some succeed; many do not. And my students are the ones on "the right path," obtaining the technical degrees touted as the promise of the twenty-first century. What of those students, like me, who did not choose "the right path," who obtained liberal arts degrees not for the money expected after graduation but for the desire to learn, to teach, and, in my case, to write? As I watch my students, I often wonder, if I had the chance to go back, would I choose a different direction, perhaps one with a more promising economic outlook?

And so I return again to those undergraduate English professors who supplied me with strong female role models in academic positions of power, juggling families and careers so skillfully. Their stories echo those told in *Changing Subjects* (Greene and Kahn 1993), as many of those women also came to grips with their own sexuality, independence, and social power through second wave feminism. But even with the professional and personal barriers they overcame, there were lessons that my professors did not know to teach me, struggles they had not faced as women pursuing careers. Mass job shortage was not a hardship they had needed to overcome; neither was oppressive, lingering debt. These conditions must be concerns of a third wave feminism. Yet we can learn from the struggles fought by second wavers against oppression, transforming the aggressor from patriarchy to capitalism.

Many boomer feminists found that patriarchy could be fought not on a mass level (the bitter defeat of the Equal Rights Amendment attests to that), but in smaller, more localized ways over a long period of time. Whereas their activism took the shape of hard work in positions that pushed on the glass ceiling, a third wave activism might take the form of denying or resisting corporate America by starting worker-friendly businesses or by helping employees unite to buy out their companies, thus returning the wealth and capital of the company to those who fostered it. Whereas second wave feminists strove for equality with men, third wave feminists cannot reasonably expect equality from capitalism. But we can fight to preserve basic rights and decent working conditions for people.

Another concern—another connection and contradiction—will be the importance placed on technology. Who will benefit from a feminism that finds its economic (as well as social and political) answers in the power of or power over technology? Personal computers and instant information did not influence the economy for second wave feminists as it does now. Whereas my undergraduate professors completed their dissertations on typewriters, I am learning the Internet in graduate school and submitting papers through E-mail. Although a new feminist agenda must keep up with the changes in technology, we must not lose sight of the economic privilege required and sustained by these machines. Technologies are, after all, the master's tools, created by men for the advancement of capitalism. Haraway argues that we must usurp those tools and use them for our benefit, but I am more skeptical about our chances. The Internet, for example, should be a place for open, global discussion and organization, much along the lines that Fuentes and Ehrenreich describe (1983). However, it is quickly becoming a place of commodification, a quick and easy instrument for corporations. We cannot turn our backs on this powerful medium, but we must understand its contradictions and limitations as well.

The McJobdom inhabited by so many twentysomethings is but a local manifestation of a growing economic condition. The condition is so subtle and pervasive that women and men of my generation do not know how to fight it. We have to recognize that global capitalism is overtaking many of the social structures under which second wave feminists operated. Academia is no longer a place of support for critically conscious scholars, media representations of the underprivileged and marginalized are often suspect, and technology is as much a hindrance to women and workers as it is an empowering tool. Leaving domestic roles to pursue a career is no longer a political statement either; it is a necessity that does not constitute activism for twentysomething women. A new, third wave feminism must combine our forces in the areas of academia, the media, and technology, constructing alliances against the profit motive and looking for the interconnection Kauffman describes. Such connections now supersede the traditional academic/popular, male/female binaries, providing the opportunity to explore injustice and inequity in new ways. But we also have to understand the contradictions inherent in many of the areas available for connection. We have to create an agenda with skepticism, looking closely and critically at the avenues we choose. Second wave feminism's identity politics gave twentysomething women the opportunity to enter the workforce and empowered us to create our own agenda, but with the rise of class instability we face a new playing field complicated by factors such as unemployment, debt, and technology. In short, third wave feminism needs a new economy.

Notes

1. Douglas Coupland describes "McJobs" as "Low pay, low prestige, low benefits, low future" (1991, 5).

2. Jeremy Rifkin describes the magnitude of Manpower: "Manpower, the nation's largest temp agency, is now the country's single largest employer, with 560,000 workers" (1995, 190).

3. Maggie Mahar's column about women and employment possibilities (1994) is an example of this argument.

4. The G7 conference is an annual summit of labor and finance leaders from the "Group of Seven," seven countries with some of the largest economies in the world, Italy, France, Canada, Britain, Japan, Germany, and the United States. The conference is primarily a chance to exchange information and discuss possible economic strategies. It is also known for producing a lot of talk but little action. For more information about the 1995 G7 conference, see "The G7 Summit: A Modest Proposal" (1995).

5. Barbara Hartmann provides an excellent discussion of the theoretical bases for the primacy of patriarchy (1981).

Works Cited

Aley, James. 1994. "Slacker Myths." *Fortune*, 21 February, 24.

Coupland, Douglas. 1991. *Generation X: Tales for an Accelerated Culture*. New York: St. Martin's.

Derrida, Jacques. 1994. *Specters of Marx*. Translated by Peggy Kamuf. New York: Routledge.

DuPlessis, Rachel Blau. 1993. "Reader, I Married Me: A Polygynous Memoir." In *Changing Subjects: The Making of Feminist Literary Criticism*, edited by Gayle Greene and Coppelia Kahn, 97–111. London: Routledge.

Ermath, Elizabeth. 1993. "On Having a Personal Voice." In *Changing Subjects: The Making of Feminist Literary Criticism*, edited by Gayle Greene and Coppelia Kahn, 226–39. London: Routledge.

Faludi, Susan. 1991. *Backlash*. New York: Crown.

"Financial Need and Loans Soar." 1993. *USA Today*, April, 10.

Fuentes, Annette, and Barbara Ehrenreich. 1983. *Women in the Global Factory*. Boston: South End.

"The G7 Summit: A Modest Proposal." 1995. *Economist*, 10 June,19–21.

Generation X-onomics. 1994. *Economist*, 19 March, 27–28.

Giles, Jeff. 1994. "Generalizations X." *Newsweek*, 6 June, 62–72.

Greene, Gayle, and Coppelia Kahn, eds. 1993. *Changing Subjects: The Making of Feminist Literary Criticism*. London: Routledge.

Gross, David M., and Sophfronia Scott. 1990. "Proceeding with Caution." *Time*, 16 July, 56–62.

Haraway, Donna. 1990. "A Manifesto for Cyborgs." In *Feminism/Postmodernism*, edited by Linda J. Nicholson, 190-231. London: Routledge.

Hartmann, Barbara. 1981. "The Unhappy Marriage of Marxism and Feminism." In *Women and Revolution: A Discussion of the Unhappy Marriage of Marxism and Feminism*, edited by Lydia Sargent, 1–41. Boston: South End.

Heilemann, John. 1993. "Debt 101." *Washington Monthly*, March, 42–44.

Kauffman, Linda S. 1993. "The Long Goodbye: Against the Personal Testimony or, An Infant Grows Up." In *Changing Subjects: The Making of Feminist Literary Criticism*, edited by Gayle Greene and Coppelia Kahn, 129–46. London: Routledge.

Krueger, Pamela. 1994. "Superwoman's Daughters." *Working Woman*, May.

Lane, Randall. 1995. "Computers Are Our Friends." *Forbes*, 8 May, 102–8.

Mahar, Maggie. 1994. "Why Baby Boomers Aren't Going Bust." *Working Woman*, April, 22.

Martin, David. 1993. "The Whiny Generation." *Newsweek*, 1 November, 10.

Reich, Robert. 1994. "Hire Education." *Rolling Stone*, 20 October, 119–25.

Rifkin, Jeremy. 1995. *The End of Work: The Decline of the Global Labor Force and the Dawn of the Post-Market Era*. New York: Tarcher/Putnam.

Thurow, Lester C. 1996. *The Future of Capitalism: How Today's Economic Forces Shape Tomorrow's World*. New York: Morrow.

Wilkinson, Francis. 1994. "Clinton's Credit: The 72-Hour Student Loan." *Rolling Stone*, 25 August, 53.

CHAPTER TWO

We Learn America like a Script: Activism in the Third Wave; or, Enough Phantoms of Nothing

Leslie Heywood and Jennifer Drake

Embarrassed, heels in track gravel, wearing a borrowed suit, I heard myself named homecoming queen. Applause. A look of hate from my ex–best friend in the bleachers. People had joked that she and I must be lovers, we spent so much time together, and it was like a breakup when after five years I pulled away from her and her obsessions with guys, hair, makeup. At the time I had no language to talk about the intensity of that relationship or about how I had publicly become the beauty-queen image I had rejected in rejecting her. I had no way to speak about how shaming it was to be crowned, playing a role I hated yet felt compelled toward and couldn't quite get the fuck out of, not yet, not without feminism.

Actually, this guy named Danny Byrnes won the title of queen, but the principal wouldn't let him have it because a guy as queen wouldn't reflect well on the school. Huh. Homophobe. Well, gender-bending-phobe. I wonder what Danny is doing now? Straight and married? He wore a purple dress to the dance, and I gave him the crown. It was a rhinestone tiara. Really. When people find out this bit of auto-biographical information (not to mention the part about cheerleading), they wonder how I turned out so well, by which they mean my politics or my current wardrobe, or they confess their own sordid little "success" stories, or we discuss how obsolete and annoying homecoming queens are and always were, the bitches.

The image "homecoming queen" is a lie. Like other appearances of American success and normalcy, it carries with it the shadow of its otherness, my shadow side and that of all the people who could never "win," because they were already marked, masked, in other ways: The woman everyone said whored around to make money for her crazy mother. The "brainy" woman who went to a school dance with another woman. The woman no one really knew because she spent her nonschool time downtown hanging out with other African Americans, escaping suburban whitewash. I like to think, from this distance, that my discomfort with representing success as homecoming queen came from my discomfort with what the image designated as privileged in my upstate New York school: whiteness, straightness, nice clothes, popularity, and being smart but not overtly brainy. (Be careful of how you speak, what you say. Don't tell anyone how much you read, what you think, what you know, what you fantasize and desire. Don't tell your family's secrets, or other people's family secrets. Don't threaten the social order. Rebel only temporarily, through what you wear or the music you buy. Don't learn anything from these excursions into alternative cultural styles. Go to a good college and get a good career and get married and have a couple of nice kids. Repeat.) This was the early 1980s.

At the same time, I was, and still am, though in different ways, invested in my construction as smart, attractive, "together," and deserving of "success." Playing my updated version of the role can sometimes get me through a shitty day in the social minefields. But this is the danger: *needing* to live the lie of the image. If I need this affirmation, if I am rewarded for living the mask, even if it is a more "progressive" version of one, then the privilege I am given, and might come to think I deserve, comes at great cost, because that privilege is based on the socially sanctioned negation of what and who I seem *not* to be: the women, for example, who could not be homecoming queens because they didn't look or act the part. Becoming invested in the images of individual success that are applauded by the dominant culture keeps political action from happening. Living up to images of success requires keeping secrets. Interpreting these particular bodies and lives as successful requires collusion with approved scripts. Keeping the peace, as in "Can't everybody just get along?" requires silencing dissent. A lot of our "individual" and communal selves is invested in the work of keeping silent, shoring up images and narratives that we *think* help us survive but that are actually killing (the other in) us. These silences locate violences, every day. But I have to ask: how can breaking silence about pain and grief and desire and anger and violence and joy work so as to not participate in the banal self-help cultural conversation, or in tell-all talk show exhibitionism, or in language-use-as-cover-up? How can I talk about the ways that privilege is constructed to look like it is *not* oppressive, when in fact these images of success perpetuate logics and practices of domination? How can I not end up sounding Gen-X whiny, as in "I'm oppressed too"?

When I was in high school I didn't study. I read books on my own, and I ran. And ran and ran and ran and ran. Both present and future was promised by the times I clocked, the track and cross-country meets I won, the media attention I attracted. There was nothing else beyond the next workout, next mile, the next piece of cake I wouldn't eat. I was going to win the state meet in my senior year. Vague shadows of scholarships and college, but for now my life was the state meet. So, through injuries and sickness and forced time off to heal, I lived for one date: May 19.

In April 1993 at the University of California at Irvine, Barbara Ehrenreich gave a talk entitled "Third Wave Feminism and the New Anger," a kind of "passing the torch" discussion. She formulated where feminist theory had been and speculated about where it might be headed as a generation of women who grew up feminist, the products of the second wave women's movement, begin their careers. One feature that characterizes us as a generation of feminists, Ehrenreich argued, is our anger. Whereas the generation before us was often characterized by exhilaration and fatigue, we are distinguished by anger. But why?

People speak of the fierceness of athletes, their single-minded dedication to their goals. That single-mindedness is praised, the self-sacrifice it involves held up on an altar of American performance, a directedness and purpose so complete that no one notices what is lost along the trajectory from one performance to the next, one foot in front of the other. Heroic performance. It was 1982.

Call us "third wave" feminists, or, perhaps more pointedly, white middle-class feminists on the cusp of a generational divide. Feminist thinking was always a vital presence for those of us who are now entering the professional world. Many our age aren't; given these privileges, why should we be angry? Having reaped the benefits of our mothers' struggles and our race and class positions, having grown up with a sense of entitlement so strong that as girls in high school we virulently denied that any form of sexism existed, what do we have to be angry about? Shouldn't we be strong, self-assured, happy, whole, and able to carry the torch in a way that our mothers, fatally disabled by sexism, never could? We were raised to think we could do anything that (white) men could do, that we have the same opportunities, can compete with men equally, man to man. Indeed, many of us *have* competed with men, literally, proving our mettle in a concrete, physical way. Often we were publicly included in the realm of male entitlement, competition, and struggle. And often it was our race that included us. When we said "women," we usually thought of ourselves as the prototype. But was this an error of feminism, of sisterhood? According to Susan Douglas,

> The notion that all women were "sisters," bound together across ethnic, class, generational, and regional lines by their common experiences as an oppressed group, was the most powerful, utopian, and, therefore, threatening concept feminists advanced in the 1970's. . . . [N]othing was more dangerous to the status quo than the concept of sisterhood. Hence, the absolute importance of the catfight to demonstrate as simply and vividly as possible that sisterhood was, in fact, a crock of shit. . . . We had been raised to compete over men and to scrutinize ourselves and other women to see who was thinner, younger, sexier, nicer, prettier. And we had grown up with a notion of a female hierarchy in which some women—the Waspy, wealthy, young, and beautiful— were at the top of the pyramid and other women—the poor, the dark-skinned, the ugly, the old, the fat—were at the bottom. Multimillion-dollar industries were built on this foundation of female competition, and it was a notion wired into our sense of self. The competitive spirit was what animated individualism, and it is hard to think of an American value more enduring than rugged individualism. . . . [E]ach of us was encouraged to imagine herself as apart from the herd. . . . [S]o many women greeted the sisterhood concept with ambivalence.[1]

Maybe it was the media's pervasive antifeminism, as well as the emphasis on all "the things that kept women divided and apart."[2] Maybe it was the racism of white-dominant culture that some factions of feminism tried to challenge, that ensured that post–baby boom women like me would think that white experience could stand for all experience. Maybe it wasn't just feminism. Maybe if I had had feminism, sisterhood, I could have seen other women, black or white, Chicana or Asian American, as something other than obstacles it was my job to overcome.

    "Apart from the herd," without "sisterhood," I slammed the path

of the "rugged individual" with a fierceness I often couldn't understand: *Four miles at five. Sit-ups at six. Classes at eight. Training at
two: sprints and distance, distance and sprints. Weight training at five.
Another three miles at seven. Asleep by eight. Again and again:*

> Being one of the guys doesn't seem to bother Leslie. "They (the
> boys on the team) help me out a lot," she said. "They always
> push me." And she pushes the guys, too, says girls coach Tom
> Birch. "There's a lot of mutual benefit. If she beats one of the JV
> runners, then we can rib them and they'll work a little harder."
> The only place either of the coaches sees a problem is in what
> Birch calls the team concept. He says that without Heywood
> working with the girls team, the other girls don't think they can
> compete with her. "I would like all of the girls to believe that they
> can compete with Leslie for at least the first mile or so. . . ."[3]

It was an age of opportunity, fulfillment, equality. There I was, in the
paper; still, I could beat only JV runners, not varsity. These runners
were ashamed that I, as "just a girl," could beat them, and therefore
they strove harder (actually, some of them quit) to reclaim their manli-
ness and valor—defined as superiority to women. Any girl who can
beat any guy is "better than" the women's team. Only the exceptional
woman, capable of "real" achievement, is given the label of cultural
value—"one of the guys." I remember how proud I was to claim that
label then, how vindicated I felt to have it written in black and white
for all to see. I had arrived, I thought, had dragged myself out of the
shadows.

The fish that got away. And yet. Simon Reynolds and Joy Press
on Chrissie Hynde: "the tough chick tomboy . . . gets to hang out with
the rough guys.";[4] "the tough chick facade . . . cracks . . . to reveal the
precariousness of the she-rebel lifestyle. . . . [I]ndependence seem[s]
like insecurity. She imagines being a figure of gossip, watching the outlaw status she once craved become unheroic and pathetic as she gets
older" (240).

*The morning after the state meet, I woke up and looked around.
The room was unbearably quiet. I sat up, quite still. For a long time I
thought, what is wrong? The bed held its position along the wall. The
windows remained in place. The stereo, bureau, all intact. So why did I
feel like I was floating, uncertain where to place my feet? I didn't know
what to do. There I was in the morning paper. A tired smile, blond hair
in place against black ink. What now? Maybe a short run. What now?*

My throat got tight, my skin a little chilly. I've done everything I was supposed to. What now?

Like our counterparts in the general workforce, as women in academia we are offered access to positions previously held mostly by (white) men. Departments across the nation stress hiring women; white male students joke that they are "dead" and bitterly complain that they won't get jobs, and some of the hiring statistics seem to support this.⁵ We are allowed—*we are allowed*—to teach courses such as "Feminist Cultural Criticism" or "Postmodern Women Writers" instead of "Keats and Shelley" or "Milton," and feminist theory is considered one of the "major" theoretical approaches. Our books, often dealing with issues specific to or primarily focused on women, create great interest. So what's wrong with this picture?

Peggy Orenstein, who conducted a two-year case study on contemporary adolescent girls, reports that

> [My] results confirmed something that many women already
> knew too well. For a girl, the passage into adolescence is not just
> marked by menarche or a few new curves. It is marked by a loss
> of confidence in herself and her abilities, especially in math and
> science. It is marked by a scathingly critical attitude toward her
> body and a blossoming sense of personal inadequacy.⁶

A few years into college, mornings like that morning after the state meet became part of a daily battle to move. The listlessness of spirit crept from a terrified emptiness of mind, and the body that sustained it started to quit. First there were the chronic-use injuries: bursitis in a shoulder, hip, stress fractures in the feet. Then the core meltdown: random attacks of high fevers and chills, joints so swollen I couldn't hold a toothbrush in my hand. It took them seven months to decode it: my immune system was attacking my own tissues, joints. As if my own body were a threat.

Peggy Orenstein:

> By sixth grade, it is clear that both girls and boys have learned
> to equate maleness with opportunity and femininity with
> constraint. . . . [T]he girls I spoke with were from vastly different
> family structures and economic classes, and they had achieved
> varying degrees of academic success. Yet all of them, even those
> enjoying every conceivable advantage, saw their gender as a
> liability. (xiv–xv)

How did the promise bequeathed to us by an earlier generation of feminist critics, role models, and mothers fail? If that promise was equal access and—as white women, we had it, each of us intact in her individual achievements—where does this depression creeping up in the dull, flat hours of early morning, a paralysis we confess to each other in secret, come from? Voices—my friends', my students', mine: *"I can't move." "I've got straight A's and a boyfriend—I don't know what's wrong. . ." "I make movies about self-mutilation. I'll show you the one where I'm slitting my wrists."* Armed with trophies, college letters, certificates of achievement, and degrees, why do we feel so empty? As if those confessions—the stumbling, tentative reaching out—are the only warmth thawing the rigidity of our individual profiles: *"They've changed the dose of my Prozac again, and they're trying it along with something else . . ." "I threw up again last night. I'm out of control, I just can't stop . . ." "I've got the esophagitis and the irritable bowel syndrome again. Most times, he won't even touch me."* As if our aberrations are the only connections we have. And while struggling to speak to each other, to find some way of getting at what feels so wrong with our lives in the face of the rhetoric and appearance of opportunity, equality, and fullness everywhere, we find that thinking only about ourselves and those around us is part of the emptiness we feel.

Now, today, June 1996, I have spent roughly 16,040 hours of my life in the gym, another 8,552 running down roads and trails, conquering monstrous hills. Twenty-three percent of my waking hours, almost one-fourth of my life since adolescence, has been spent working out. Susan Douglas:

> The women's fitness movement was a site of resistance, as women sought to break into sports previously restricted to men and other women simply sought to get strong. But one of capitalism's great strengths—perhaps its greatest—is its ability to co-opt and domesticate opposition, to transubstantiate criticism into a host of new, marketable products. And so it was with fitness.
>
> Instead of group action, we got escapist solitude. Instead of solidarity, we got female competition over men. . . . [N]arcissism as liberation is liberation repackaged, deferred, and denied. . . . [O]f all the disfigurements of feminism, this, perhaps, has been the most effective.[7]

I have worked out for 24,592 hours and counting. Those hours have been my sanity, my identity, my life. The weight plates, coiling the hours to nowhere, the runs down the sidewalk for interminable miles, my eyes straight ahead, focused on nothing. If Douglas is right about her generation, "baby boomers [had the] sense of being part of something bigger" (160). I've spent my whole life trying to distinguish myself from that "something bigger" all around, to keep it from wiping me out cold. Distinguishing myself is all I know. The idea of belonging, of being "part of something," feels like the friend who moved away before I met her.

Many of us are critical of dominant and homogenizing cultural constructions of "Generation X." According to the most widely publicized construction of the third wave, "we" hate our bodies, ourselves, our boring little lives, yet we focus incessantly on ourselves, our bodies, and our boring little lives. "We" hate our parents for their divorces or their dysfunctions or their boring little lives. "We" hate Bill and Hillary and George Bush and Jesse Helms alike, if we think about politics at all. "We" appropriate the images of Angela Davis, Malcolm X, Leonard Peltier, and Cesar Chavez, putting them on T-shirts and stripping them of their activist histories. "We" believe that the glamorization of nihilism is hip and think that any hope for change is naive and embarrassing. "We" as a generation can be represented by the figure, or consumer profile, of a disenfranchised, (semi-)college-educated, (ex-)middle-class, straight, white boy-cum-musician with or without a McJob. Think Ethan Hawke or Leonardo DeCaprio.

The Gen-X writers and artists who get the most attention, such as Douglas Coupland and Elizabeth Wurtzel, do little to contest this bleak portrait. Taking their cues from postmodern white male writing and brat-pack 1980s writing, texts marketed as "Gen-X" express anxiety about the death of the author and the family and the nation and language and narrative and faith in anything. Yet, somehow, anxious postmod men get to be avant-garde. First the brat-packers and then the Gen-Xers get to represent cultural cool and cultural disintegration at the same time, and the whole discourse resonates in pretty eerie ways with the nostalgic language of the radical Right, who get to run the country. Whether the call for a "return" to "better days" happens through avant-garde textual cool or the rhetoric of family values or Gen-X pop-culture nostalgia or anti-immigration legislation or the fashion industry's mid-1990s glamorization of 1950s housewives and debutantes, it still spells the erasure of the violences that those "better days"

worked so hard to justify and conceal. So often, these systemic violences play out in the targeting of bodies marked "other," and popular
"Gen-X" texts are marketed as alternatives to the dominant social order
without providing models of cultural critique or social change at all.

The Gen-X portrait of the artist as a bored young man shores up
the discourse of and about "angry white males" by placing the lives
and concerns of this particular constituency front and center, again.
Just the clothes change. In this America, girlfriend seems like she might
be interesting if you judge by her clothes, but she's hanging out in the
background, overshadowed by this guy. Everyone around is white. The
downwardly mobile twentysomethings have college degrees and parents who drive really nice cars. No one can talk to each other. Privileg-
ing this white middle-class dude version of Generation X means that
public discussions of twentysomething culture, anger, and disenfranchisement in postindustrial America rarely make key connections
among youth cultures, so they rarely offer complex readings of third
wave cultural practices and points of view. But what would happen if
Generation X were publicly defined by the creative, critical, and political relationships among African American, Chicano, Latino, pan-Asian,
Anglo, feminist, working-class, middle-class, and queer youth cultures? What complex narratives might be forged in the cultural connections among, and differences between, rappers and Riot Grrrls and
metalheads and young PWAs and sorority chicks and cholos and athletes and cyberpunks and academic achievers and baby dykes and farm
kids and recent immigrants and Kurt Cobain wanna-bes and activists
of all kinds?

As "Gen-Xers," we have no utopias. We live, as Gloria Steinem puts it,
in "a generation of translation and backlash."[8] That translation and
backlash frames the rightfully conceived charge of what Gina Dent
calls "the familiar error of Western feminism, of extending the category of woman across time and space with little regard for cultural or
historical specificity."[9] That translation also means that we never experienced a time when we claimed a community based on "women."
That error, the argument goes, divided the second wave feminist community based on a false unity: the idea that the experience of the white,
middle-class woman was the same as that of other women of differing
races, ethnicities, sexual orientations, and historical periods. Translation and backlash mean that this false unity is the interpretation of

"sisterhood" by our generation, whereas some second wave feminists, many of them feminists of color, made transracial coalition central to their political agendas of improving conditions for all working women, lobbying for affordable child care, and ensuring reproductive rights of all types. "There are times," writes Steinem in her foreword to Rebecca Walker's third wave feminist anthology *To Be Real*, "when I—and perhaps other readers over thirty-five—feel like a sitting dog being told to sit."[10]

Translation and backlash mean that we as third wavers have bought into the media demonization of "sisterhood." We are letting ourselves, to use Susan Douglas's word, "catfight," both with second wavers and across racial divides. The arguments that women scholars of color introduced into the dominant feminist paradigms in the 1980s have become the most powerful forms of feminist discourse in the 1990s. The arguments are true, compelling, make sense. But there is some confusion between these arguments and the translation and backlash we seem to have swallowed whole. There is a consequence of the way divisions currently play out for white "Generation X cusp feminists," those on the bridge between the second and the not fully conceived third waves who have never experienced the second wave feminist sense of belonging to something, but instead live the isolation and emptiness that are the legacy of male-identification. The chance to form communities is now even more difficult. Factionalization is our world.

In the context of fitting into the dominant cultural community that bell hooks calls "white supremacist capitalist patriarchy," white middle-class Generation X feminists are the right race but the wrong gender.[11] In terms of fitting into the alternative cultural community formed by progressive feminists of color, we are the right gender but sometimes the wrong race. So, without a community, we have a hunger to bridge, to "border-cross," but we are conscious that this desire can be read as a desire to appropriate some greater "life," sense of soul, or warmth that women of color are stereotypically said to offer—a little fire to melt the ice queens, bring our deadness back to life. Stuck in Siberia looking for a way out, sometimes we have the sense that, as Jean Rhys writes, "the door will always be shut."[12]

And what we haven't talked about enough is what "power feminism," with its ready accusations of "victim feminism," would force us to remain silent about: what it's like to be an ice queen, seeing everything else in the world as something to compete with, to overcome. "Stop whining and join the old girl network," power feminism would say. "There's nothing bad about competition and achievement. Women have got to stop crying and get on with it." Power feminist tracts often eerily echo my old male coaches, who reacted to expressions of physical pain with "Don't be a wuss; suck it up!" But after twenty years of "sucking it up," a lot of us know the empty frozenness such a philosophy brings, and we know that "power feminism" is the voice of the father in his latest disguise. "Third wave feminism," feminism in Generation X, is not "power feminism." It's not about trying to be men or women either. It's about trying to think through what "coalition" might mean and on what basis a "community" might really come into being.

As "feminists" such as Camille Paglia begin to evoke the myth of the femme fatale and push sexual power as a means to achievement and to controlling men, and as Katie Roiphe shrugs off second wave feminist concerns such as sexual harassment and date rape, and as the media at large hails the "sexy" feminist and the "return" of femininity, young women have more and more chimeras to fight, and the hard lessons of feminist history are forgotten and lived again. The legacy of Generation X, of those of us who formed identities and "grew up" in a time of "cultural fascism" beginning with the Reagan years, may be a powerful form of the kind of "yearning" bell hooks so directly names:

> At dinner last night when I looked around me across differences, I wondered "What is uniting us?" All of us across our different experiences were expressing this longing, this deep and profound yearning, to just have this domination *end*. And what I feel unites you and me is: we can locate in one another a similar yearning to be in a more *just* world. So I tried to evoke the idea that if we could come together in that site of desire and longing, it might be a potential place of community-building. Rather than thinking we would come together as "women" in an identity-based bonding we might be drawn together rather by a *commonality of feeling*. I think that's a real challenge for us now: to think about constructing community on different *bases*.[13]

If, as "third wave feminists," we no longer think unproblematically of "natural" bonds between "women," to come out of isolation and thaw out, we need bases for connection like those hooks evokes. I can think of no clearer basis than a "commonality of feeling," a "deep and

profound yearning . . . to just have this domination *end.*" But where do
I find it?

Many young cultural workers from a wide variety of communities *are*
making these connections, building coalitions, and positioning themselves as participants in the ongoing history of radical thought and action. Refusing to panic about the complexity of public life and public
dialogue in the contemporary United States, these third wave activists
approach American culture *as* multiculture; hybrid, creole, made and
remade in dialogue and conflict. But, as if to distract attention from
the radical potential in recognizing the *mutual* constitution of African
American culture and "white" culture, or hetero culture and queer culture, "multiculture" has also come to signify both "political correctness" and apolitical fashion grooviness. Third wave activists might buy
into hip multiculti style, but we also critically explore the possibilities
produced by liberation struggles of the 1930s and 1960s that cracked
the facade of national consent and opened up the discussion of U.S.
multiculture in the first place. Granted, we weren't there. We've
learned about these traditions from parents, teachers, books, media
images, cultural apocrypha. But these images and stories—representations of the "real"—*are* as "real" as it gets, because they make and
are made by the social scripts that we live. We learned this as we began
to learn about all the American histories and knowledges we had never
before learned. Remember hearing about the Japanese internment
camps for the first time? the Chinese exclusion act? the use of rape
throughout world history as a genocidal tool? the treatment of Mexi-
can migrant workers in the United States? Remember bringing this shit
home? How could you begin to renarrate those ineffable events rack-
ing your town, your family, and your body? Remember beginning to
see how bodies are marked and judged, how bodies are targeted for
violence because of what they signify?

Continuing the struggle to unlearn American scripts and to expose America's betrayals of the democratic project, third wave activists
are well aware of the power of representations to promote or contest
domination. Since we understand the "real" as an effect of representation and understand that representational effects play out in material
spaces and in material ways, we take critical engagement with popular
culture as a key to political struggle. Besides, we're pop-culture babies;
we want some pleasure with our critical analysis. So we inhabit that

contradictory space between critiquing what various movies, videos, songs, ads, and fashions say and do to uphold structures of domination, even as we're into these same hip cultural productions, *knowingly* (yet as if we did *not* know) spending money on them, consuming them, and making them. It is this edge, where critique and participation meet, that third wave activists most (must?) work to further contentious public dialogue in and about the multicultural United States.

Our hybrid engagement with culture and/as politics sometimes looks problematic to second wave activists, who might accuse us of exchanging engagement with institutional and economic inequities for a self-referential politics that overestimates the power of critiquing, reworking, and producing pop- and subcultural images and narratives. But, as third wave activists, we contest a politics of purity that would separate political activism from cultural production. We acknowledge the tension between criticism and the pleasures of consumption, and we work the border between a critical, even cynical, questioning of things-as-they-are and a motivation to do something anyway, without the "support" of a utopian vision. We draw upon the languages, images, knowledges, and practices of many U.S. liberation struggles, and we know there will be no onetime or single-issue revolution. Rather, a socially conscious pragmatism—"The work will not end anytime soon"—fuels our cultural work. The third wave activists I am thinking of are *not* doom-and-gloom slackers or conservative Republicans or style-without-substance Gen-Xers or pseudopolitical I-wear-organic-cotton-and-I-rocked-the-vote-ers. Working to forge activist struggle in and for the postboomer, post-1960s, post-Vietnam, post-Reagan, now-we're-stuck-with-Newt generation, we take popular culture as just one pedagogical site that materializes our struggles with some of the ways power works.

Our lives are often acts of desperation. We start talking about this here in an attempt to figure out why. To figure out concrete ways to change. So the paralysis won't shut us down. So that when Republicans become governors and cut funds for education more radically than they have ever been cut in American history, along with welfare and education opportunity programs and tuition assistance programs, the funds that create possibility for and give visibility to all those students who aren't rich and white; when *Vogue* magazine runs high-fashion layouts selling stiletto heels as a form of female power while posing the models in wheelchairs or in handicapped braces; when so many women have breast implants and plastic surgery and call it "personal choice"; when the J. Crew catalog starts to sell its shirts based on stereotypes of African Americans and "soul"; when the top female bodybuilders start to pose in soft-porn centerfolds and call that power; when feminist or racialist criticisms of such representations are called "politically correct" or "extreme"—so that then we will have something to counter these forces with. We are enough. It's time to start acting on it, to stop living out lives that disintegrate into pain. There is little comfort in "passing" for white men, or in exclusively striving for individual achievement, staying within a world all fixed and divided and neat, us and them. We want out.

Like other cultural critics, we've taken our training as academics and felt a bottomless hunger to apply it to our lives, to challenge the assumption that, as hooks puts it, "to be truly intellectual we must be cut off from our emotions."[14] Like hooks, like many second wave feminists and the first wave feminists before them, we don't accept the old idea based on the separation of mind from body, work from life, reason from emotion, that the work we are doing isn't "real" work because it's about us and our lives. We're fighting for our lives, with some knowledge that being able to fight for intellectual, spiritual, and emotional expression is a position that most people, fighting for enough money for food and school tuition, won't ever hold, especially in this political climate. We're trying not to stay insulated in an academic world, to move our work into the larger public, to be part of the cultural work going on all around us, from literacy project volunteers to the self-defense workshops taking place before some of the Riot Grrrl concerts. We're trying to bring critical thinking and "book learning" together with our daily struggles to make meaning in a culture that is sometimes hostile to anything but the most restricted forms of meaning.

But if we are the "third wave," we can't fall into the trap of rejecting the second wave and all it has to offer in order to make ourselves stand out, fully differentiated from what we see as the "foolishness" of our mothers. In 1962, *Harper's* reported that "American women 'were repelled by the slogans of old-fashioned feminism,'" thus pitting one generation against the next;[15] today, article after article reports the same, and we buy it. Remember the snottiness in graduate-school circles that upheld "feminist theory" over anything second wave and dismissed that wave as "not theoretical enough"? Or students or friends who react to the word "feminist" like you just said "cancer"? We should not be so repelled. We've hated our mothers (and ourselves) long enough. Their struggles are still our struggles, if in different forms. Bridging generations as much as races, as much as classes, as much as all our other bisecting lines, and being humble enough to realize that our ideas are not so new, is one fine way to fight paralysis, to move, to shake, to rock the world one more time.

Notes

1. Susan Douglas, *Where the Girls Are: Growing up Female in the Mass Media* (New York: Random, 1995), 224.

2. Ibid.

3. John Truitt, "Amphi's Heywood 'One of the Guys,'" *Arizona Daily Star*, October 15, 1980.

4. Simon Reynolds and Joy Press, *The Sex Revolts: Gender, Rebellion, and Rock 'n' Roll* (Cambridge: Harvard University Press, 1995), 238.

5. "Jobtracks" in the March/April 1994 issue of *Lingua Franca* contains a list of hirings for tenure-track positions in 1994; nearly two-thirds of those hired were women.

6. Peggy Orenstein, *School Girls: Young Women, Self-Esteem, and the Confidence Gap* (New York: Doubleday, 1994), xvi.

7. Douglas, *Where the Girls Are*, 260, 268.

8. Gloria Steinem, foreword to *To Be Real: Telling the Truth and Changing the Face of Feminism*, ed. Rebecca Walker (New York: Doubleday, 1995), xx.

9. Gina Dent, "Black Pleasure, Black Joy: An Introduction," in *Black Popular Culture* (Seattle: Bay, 1992), 4.

10. Steinem, foreword, xxii.

11. Bell hooks's phrase, from *Black Looks* (Boston: South End, 1992) and *Outlaw Culture: Resisting Representations* (New York: Routledge, 1994), despite the flak she mentions getting for it (*Outlaw Culture*, 197–98), seems to us exactly right.

12. Jean Rhys, *Good Morning, Midnight* (New York: Norton, 1986), 31.

13. Hooks, *Outlaw Culture*, 217.

14. Hooks, *Teaching to Transgress* (New York: Routledge, 1994), 155.

15. Quoted in Douglas, *Where the Girls Are*, 123.

CHAPTER THREE

Reading between the Waves: Feminist Historiography in a "Postfeminist" Moment

Deborah L. Siegel

> *For it will not be time to speak of postfeminism until we can*
> *legitimately speak of post-patriarchy.*   —Nancy Fraser

In the spring of 1995, Gloria Steinem came to my town. When I announced the lecture in my first-year composition class, my students looked at me blankly. "Gloria who?" asked a woman in the front row. At twenty-six, I was baffled to find that my assumption that Steinem mattered was not necessarily shared by a new generation of women. Waiting in line with the other ticket holders on the night of the event, I stared in disbelief as a number of protesters—grown men in baseball caps and plaid shirts—passed out flyers that read, "Take Back the Penis!" Fed up with the tired tactics of the penis gang, on the one hand, and dissatisfied with the number of polls that showed young women supporting feminist issues but rejecting the label, on the other, I took matters into my own hands.

On the morning after Steinem's visit, I headed for the stalls of the women's restroom in the undergraduate library. I scrawled the following question on the bathroom door: "*Is* feminism dead?" My survey was met with indignation. "Is the pope dead?" wrote the first respondent; "Hell no!" added a second; "It'll only die if we let it," scrawled a third. In the lively debate that followed, anonymous scribbling women struggled with definitions of feminism, challenging assumptions about who can be one: "Can a woman who works at Hooters really be a feminist, as she claims she is?" "If I'm pro-life, can I be pro-feminist?" "What *is* a feminist, anyway?" For an exhilarating week during daily trips to the second stall, I watched as women of the third wave embraced the topic of feminism with the revolutionary fervor of public restroom philosophers. By Friday the bathroom door was covered with query and contradiction, qualification and commitment—a living testimony of feminism's future that would, I think, make Steinem proud. "Feminism," wrote one woman toward the end of the week, "the ability of a woman to transcend barriers of racism, classism, and sexism in order to intellectualize and experience life to the fullest." While this particular forum vanished with a swipe of the janitor's rag, I hope that the third wave will continue to find such unabashedly personal political spaces where we may intellectualize and experience our lives. To me, this is feminism's best legacy. We are not the first generation to contend with penis gangs and disbelievers. Nor will we be the last.

Preface: On the Politics of Prefixes

In a 1979 essay entitled "Words and Change," Gloria Steinem poses the following question to her primarily white, middle-class, heterosexual baby boomer readership: "Think for a minute. Who were you before this wave of feminism began?"[1] As a young witness of Steinem's autobiographical disclosures, I frequently find myself quite moved by her revolutionary words. Yet, as a third wave reader inclined always to ask, Which personal? and Whose politics? I find that in reading Steinem I bear witness not merely to the politicized personal revelations of a feminist foremother but also to the epistemological assumptions of an earlier generation of feminist writing.

A chronologically informed positivist epistemology, that is, an understanding of eras and consciousnesses that can be labeled "pre" and "post," underlies much of Steinem's writing.[2] A faith in the feminist historian's ability to get at the Real of history informs such statements as the following: "In this wave, words and consciousness have forged ahead, so reality can follow."[3] In her early writing, Steinem draws upon allegorical tropes of discovery, revelation, and rescue, as is evident in the following excerpt from a 1972 essay entitled "Sisterhood": "If it weren't for the women's movement, I might still be dissembling away. But the ideas of this great sea-change in women's view of ourselves are contagious and irresistible. They hit women like a revelation, as if we had left a dark room and walked into the sun."[4] According to such an epistemology, when the ideas of the women's movement "hit," the recipient of the blow is miraculously rescued from her prior solitary and oppressive existence. The Sun of Feminist Consciousness illuminates Truth and redeems Her witnesses from the pre-feminist conditions of Dissembling and Falsehood. In this universe one is either a rescuer, safely anchored on the Bank of Post-Consciousness, or a victim, dissembling away in the Pre-Consciousness River. "We've spent the first decade or so of the second wave of feminism on the riverbank, rescuing each other from drowning," Steinem maintains in a 1978 retrospective entitled "Far from the Opposite Shore." "Now, some of us must go to the head of the river and keep the victims from falling in."[5]

If Steinem speaks with confidence about the possibility of rescu-ing victims from the dark room or wild river of pre-feminist existence, a survey of current popular writings by young feminist authors and ac-tivists reveals the extent to which third wave feminists agree not on the location of the river, nor on the conditions of the spaces we inhabit (What are the contours of that dark room and who gets to walk in the sun? Is the riverbank muddy or solid? How deep is that river?), nor, and perhaps most significant, on the status and function of three of second wave feminism's foundational words: *we, feminist,* and *victim.*[6] In a more recent essay entitled "Doing Sixty," Steinem reminds today's readers that the "essential idea" of the early consciousness-raising groups was to provide a space in which the isolated "I" could, by means of instantaneous and unqualified identification, collapse into a collective, rescuing, rebellious "we": "Tell your personal truth, listen to other women's stories, see what themes are shared, and discover that the personal is political—you are not alone."[7] In a world scarred by racial violence, and in an academic community confounded by identity politics, the foundational project of naming shared themes has become increasingly complex. Though Steinem's early writing is punc-tuated with language that describes her sense of standing upon a his-toric threshold, to a reader whose reading practice is informed by multiculturalist, postmodern, and/or poststructuralist philosophies or perspectives, or to one who is inclined to ask, Which personal? and Whose politics? such rhetoric might seem to bespeak the confidence of a bygone era.

Endlessly indebted yet reluctant to claim certain aspects of second wave legacies, I am simultaneously spurred on by Steinem's activist writing and thwarted by her discursive practice. As an emerging femi-nist academic interested in the spaces in which feminist theory, popular culture, and social activism intersect, I find myself mining Steinem's life and text, critiquing her rhetoric even as I find in her words the inspiration and the courage to embrace the challenge of moving feminism, as a political movement without the fixity of a single feminist agenda, into the next millennium. Steinem ends the final essay of *Outrageous Acts and Everyday Rebellions* with a call for action: "We are all organizers, and no organizer should ever end a meeting or a book or an article without ideas for practical action. After all, a movement depends on people moving. What *are* we going to do differently when we get up tomorrow?"[8]

Though Steinem posed this question fourteen years ago, and though it meant something quite different for her and her audience in 1983 than it does for me and mine in 1997, I sense that in many respects this is the defining question for many feminists of my generation: What are "we" going to do differently? Elizabeth Fox-Genovese's recent book *Feminism Is Not the Story of My Life* is but the latest in a series of popular texts intended to explain, as her subtitle promises, "how today's feminist elite has lost touch with the real concerns of women."[9] In light of contemporary debates about necessary sites for feminist activism, discrepancies in assessments of progress made and work left undone, and disputes over the status of a shared feminist vocabulary, the question of how *my* generation might continue to tell the story of women's movements—and make feminist history—takes on increasing significance.

Given that conservative pundits and some representatives of the mainstream American press have prematurely pronounced ours a "postfeminist" era, the need to continue to make feminist history—and to establish affinities within and between waves along the way—becomes increasingly urgent. If the writing of history is itself a form of historical intervention, that is, if historiography is, as Susan Stanford Friedman suggests, an act in the present on behalf of the future, then it becomes necessary to interrogate the ways in which historiographic discourse is used as a power play in current feminist debates.[10]

Feminism's Dissenting Daughters

In what follows, I will explore the epistemological, ontological, and ethicopolitical assumptions, or the meaning-making apparatus, that inform the works of some of feminism's prominent (published) daughters. As Nan Bauer Maglin and Donna Perry make clear in the introduction to their recent anthology *"Bad Girls"/"Good Girls": Women, Sex, and Power in the Nineties*, ideas popularized by Camille Paglia, Naomi Wolf, and Katie Roiphe have contributed to individualistic and depoliticized portrayals of power and victimization.[11] What has yet to be interrogated, however, are the ways in which historiographic discourse is used as a power play in such portrayals.

Positioning themselves as daughters of second wave feminist legacies, twentysomething "pop" authors Naomi Wolf, Katie Roiphe, and Rene Denfeld interrogate their inheritance and incite their age-peers to "reclaim" feminism for the 1990s. Though they differ in the tones they adopt, as well as in the strategies they advocate, these third wave historiographers share the common mission of reclaiming feminism by converting confused or otherwise misguided readers to "good" feminist practice. I have chosen to juxtapose these three populists of American feminism because their tracts are in many ways intertextual and because all three have received substantial media coverage. Denfeld's book *The New Victorians: A Young Woman's Challenge to the Old Feminist Order* has been dubbed the sequel to Roiphe's *The Morning After: Sex, Fear, and Feminism*.[12] Both Denfeld's and Roiphe's texts echo, in some respects, Wolf's *Fire with Fire: The New Female Power and How to Use It*.[13]

Though Wolf and Roiphe have sparred publicly on the pages of the *New York Times*, both are motivated by the desire to reinvent a viable feminism of their own. Dissenting feminist voices participate in a much needed intergenerational conversation at the very moment in which feminist discourses within and outside the academy have taken a self-reflexive turn. Yet the historiographic readings of a social movement that these particular authors produce are severely limited, in that the authors' desires for mastery overwrite any attempt to keep a dialogue moving. In their incorporation of a rhetoric of repossession, in their masterful articulation of "good" feminism, and in their righteous condemnation of a monolithic "bad" feminism, Wolf, Roiphe, and Denfeld make feminist history the story of a product rather than that of a process. In the interest of affirming the difference of the third wave, many third wave narratives assume a metonymic view of the second wave, in which a part of second wave activity is substituted for the whole. If intergenerational dialogue among feminists is to move forward, however, it must move beyond narrative scripts in which a monolithically constructed second wave necessarily becomes the bad mother, for such scripts can only result in paralysis.

Before examining the rhetorical markers of the products that Wolf, Roiphe, and Denfeld label feminism (good and bad), I would like to consider how a young feminist historiographer might, instead, read, write, and make feminist history as process, or, for that matter, might understand feminist history as perpetually in motion. In the spirit of inter- and intragenerational movement, honoring the moment when Steinem introduced the image, I return for a moment to the rhetoric of Steinem's riverbank of 1978 to address some of the generational, political, and philosophic concerns I have with the way in which writers such as Wolf, Roiphe, and Denfeld are reproducing a historiographic method of a previous generation of popular feminist writing. Steinem's landscape is problematic for many of feminism's daughters (as well as for many of Steinem's own diverse age-peers) in at least three regards. First, whereas Steinem understands the 1970s as an epiphanous era for many white, middle-class, heterosexual women, for either a non-white, non-middle-class, nonheterosexual woman or a relatively privileged woman of my generation—that is, one who has benefited from some of the institutionalized gains of previous generations of women's organizing—Steinem's historicizing question ("Who were you before this wave of feminism began?") may be somewhat difficult to answer. Moreover, for someone for whom these institutionalized gains remain irrelevant—that is, for a young (or aged or aging) woman living within the confines of a dark room who has yet to see not simply the sun of feminist consciousness but the advent of truly liberating systemic political restructuring—this question may be inapplicable, if not presumptuous and, perhaps, ironic.

Second, whereas Steinem expresses a faith that "[i]n this wave, words and consciousness have forged ahead, so reality can follow," today we ask, Whose consciousness? and Which reality? Steinem's epistemology, then, might pose problems for a feminist daughter who is of a poststructuralist and/or multiculturalist perspective, or, again, for one who is inclined to ask, Which personal? and Whose politics? If one recognizes the poststructuralist argument that all accounts of history are ideologically informed and discursively formulated, that all historicizing is narrativizing, then it becomes impossible to objectively locate a monolithic "real" called "this wave of feminism." Or, as Katie King persuasively argues, "Feminists too easily believe 'we' already know the 'history' or even histories of feminism even in the U.S. What is taken as history are some privileged and published histories of feminism, which have been all too quickly naturalized."[14] Because feminism speaks itself differently at different times and in different locations, narrative chronologies that say "in this wave" tend to erase the heterogeneity of feminisms at any given moment. Indeed, any historical narrative that collapses the diverse activity of a period or a movement to make generalizations about "this period" or "this movement" necessarily results in a reductive portrait. The question of whose story gets told is particularly loaded for women, whose stories historically have been excluded from the master narratives of history. Today's feminist historiographers in particular, then, must be wary of exclusions and omissions when writing their own histories.

A third and related reason that a young woman today might stutter in response to Steinem's question is that it is difficult for this third wave of feminism to speak of "who it is" in a moment when the universal feminist "I" of humanist discourse has been called into crisis.[15] In "Disarticulated Voices: Feminism and Philomela," Elissa Marder speaks to the difficulties that inhere in speaking "as a feminist" at this particular juncture in academic history:

> In speaking "as a feminist," I am beside myself. The term "feminism" always speaks in the plural; not only is feminism itself plural (there are many different "feminisms" under the name "feminism") but when one speaks "as a feminist," in the name of the feminist project, one must say "we." If feminism posits this "we," it is because its necessity, its reason for being as discursive praxis, is as political response.[16]

If, following Marder's lead, a third wave feminist historiographer recognizes both the violence and the necessity of a feminist "we," she is indeed beside herself. Today's historiographers, then, might face up to the challenge of current feminist theory and practice as informed by poststructuralist, postmodernist, and multiculturalist modes of thinking. We might begin to confront the challenge of negotiating between the discursive destabilization of the humanist notion of "a" feminist self and the historic mobilization of a politically engaged feminist "we." That is, we must recognize that there can be no single representative subject of feminism, while, at the same time, we must continue to speak in a collective voice that articulates political demands on behalf of a group called "women." This is the paradox that faces women of my generation: It is not easy for "third wave" feminists to say "we," yet we must.[17] Similarly, inasmuch as we need to problematize the writing of history so as to avoid the re-creation of master narratives, we must nevertheless continue to make history through the very act of making historiography.

I return, then, to the works of Wolf, Roiphe, and Denfeld, three third wave popular historians who self-consciously position themselves as authors of interventionist accounts of what and where feminism has been, where it is, and where it should be going. When I look up *wave* in my deskside *Roget's College Thesaurus*, I find myself drawn instead to the next word, *waver*, which means, "vacillate, fluctuate, hesitate, sway, tremble, totter. See DOUBT, OSCILLATION." Although many of us identify with the feminist label, other third wavers waver. To speak of, about, and to the feminisms of my generation, a third wave historiographer would need to extend Marder's caveat to acknowledge the feminisms of pro-woman women who, for whatever reason, do not identify with the "f" word. My understanding is that many women of my generation reject the "f" word for at least two reasons.

In 1983, Alice Walker coined the word *womanist* to refer to, among other identities, a feminist of color:

> Womanist 1. From *womanish*. (Opp. of "girlish," i.e.,
> frivolous, irresponsible, not serious.) A black feminist or feminist
> of color. From the black folk expression of mothers to female
> children, "You acting womanish," i.e., like a woman. Usually re-
> ferring to outrageous, audacious, courageous, or *willful* behavior.
> Wanting to know more and in greater depth than is considered
> "good" for one . . . .
> 2. *Also:* A woman who loves other women, sexually and/or
> nonsexually. . . . Traditionally universalist, as in: "Mama, why
> are we brown, pink, and yellow, and our cousins are white, beige,
> and black?" Ans.: "Well, you know the colored race is just like a
> flower garden, with every color flower represented." . . .
> 4. Womanist is to feminist as purple to lavender.[18]

In this context the rejection of the label "feminist" is often code for a rejection of an elitist practice perpetuated by some of feminism's middle-class, heterosexual, white female founders (and their daugh-ters). Here the refusal of the label is a politicized gesture critiquing a feminism that restricts itself to the discussion of a singular idea of oppression derived from the perception of sexual difference as its primary cause. In another context, however, the rejection of the label bespeaks a conservative or perhaps reactionary fear of the radical-lesbian-man-hating-militant stigma, as in, "I'm not a feminist, but I support women's right to social, political, and economic equality." Although there remain, no doubt, multiple and varied rationales for the rejection of the "f" word, Wolf, Roiphe, and Denfeld maintain that the primary reason young women flee from the term today is because the feminist movement has gone seriously awry. The problem? "We feminists" has come to mean, unilaterally and unequivocally, "we victims."

Armed with this explanatory device and inspired by the mission of recuperating feminist agency for the good of all, these three dissenting daughters set out to reclaim the label "for the majority."[19] In their campaign against the "victim mythology" that they argue pervades current organized feminist activism, Roiphe and Denfeld appropriate the phrase "taking back" feminism, a parodic play on the "Take Back the Night" rallies organized by campus rape crisis centers in the 1980s.[20] Although Wolf takes Roiphe to task for her ethically irresponsible coinage of the term "rape-crisis feminism" and for her shameless mockery of the feminist perspectives informing the "Take Back the Night" events, Wolf herself was one of the first to coin the now infamous term "victim feminism." Though they differ in the degree to which they see this "victim" paradigm at work within the ranks of establishment feminism, Denfeld, Wolf, and Roiphe maintain that the regressive obsession of today's feminist leaders with women's victim status is turning young women away from feminism in droves, as is evident in the following representative excerpts from their respective texts:

> Today's feminists are remarkably similar to Victorians in significant ways [such as the way they embark on a moral and spiritual crusade and advocate political helplessness], and not only in their vision of sexuality. This is clear through an examination of several different causes and trends in today's movement that, if anything, are a complete reversal of the movement's progress during the seventies. This is the New Victorianism. And this is why women of my generation are abandoning the women's movement. (Denfeld, 11)

> In *Fire with Fire*, I will argue that we are at what historians of women's progress call "an open moment." Twenty-five years of dedicated feminist activism have hauled the political infrastructure

into place, enough women in the middle classes have enough money and clout, and all women now have enough desire and determination to begin to balance the imbalance of power between the sexes. But three obstacles stand in our way: Many women and their movement have become estranged; one strand of feminism has developed maladaptive attitudes; and women lack a psychology of female power to match their new opportunities. . . .

I will also point out that victim feminism is obsolete because female psychology and the conditions of women's lives have both been transformed enough so that it is no longer possible to pretend that the impulses to dominate, aggress, or sexually exploit others are "male" urges alone. (Wolf, xvi–xviii)

At the most uncharted moments in our lives, we reach instinctively for the stock plots available to our generation, as trashy and clichéd as they may be. In the fifties it was love and marriage, or existentialism and Beat poetry in smoky bars. Now, if you're a woman, there's another role readily available: that of the sensitive female, pinched, leered at, assaulted daily by sexual advances, encroached upon, kept down, bruised by harsh reality. Among other things feminism has given us this. A stock new plot, a new identity spinning not around love, not marriage, not communes, not materialism this time, but passivity and victimhood. This is not what I want, not even as a fantasy. (Roiphe, 172)

Call it "power feminism," call it "babe feminism," call it "feminism for the majority," today's populist feminists are rejecting the "obsolete" and "maladaptive," the "Victorian" and the "stock plot fantasies" of their feminist foremothers—and their progeny.

Though they indeed dissent from some of their (mainstream, white) feminist forebears in the content of their various arguments, a close reading of passages such as those preceding reveals the extent to which this next generation of feminist historiographers make some of the same problematic assumptions as did their predecessors. Like Steinem, these authors position themselves as harbingers of a new order, a new order, that is, for middle-class, heterosexual, white women. In contrast to Steinem's heavy reliance on images of revelation, however, the texts of the next generation are infused with a righteous anger and a fundamentalist zeal. This time around, the populist feminist mission is not consciousness-raising but consciousness-changing.

The final section of Wolf's *Fire with Fire*, for instance, bears the heading "What Do We Do Now? Power Feminism in Action." Denfeld includes her own recommendations for action (which, incidentally, include a recommendation to "dump women's studies programs") in a closing chapter entitled "The Final Wave: Reclaiming Feminism." Though I may (and do) profoundly disagree with many of the strategies and changes they advocate, I applaud these writers' efforts to incite a resurgence of feminist activism in an era that badly needs it. (Whereas Roiphe's and Denfeld's impassioned critiques are often uninformed and somewhat appalling, some of Wolf's recommendations are well researched and tremendously appealing.)[21] What is immensely troublesome, however, is the way in which these historiographic diatribes are marketed and received as representative of an entire generation.

Never mind that Roiphe's book grew out of her experiences as a student at Harvard and Princeton, two of the nation's most elite academic institutions. One has only to look at the title of the paperback edition to understand that Roiphe's claim now extends the walls of campus culture. Whereas the original hardcover edition bears the subtitle *Sex, Fear, and Feminism on Campus*, the subtitle of the 1994 paperback edition (which also includes a new introduction) reads, *Sex, Fear, and Feminism.*[22] Further, Roiphe translates her own transparent, "real" experience ("what I see") into historical evidence without genuinely acknowledging the ideological pitfalls of a historiography based on experiential evidence.[23] She relies heavily on personal anecdote, and the result is an uneasy mix of research and reminiscence, a limitation to which she pays lip service in the introduction:

> This book is not a scientific survey of campus life, measuring the immeasurable with statistical certainty. This is not a comprehensive, encyclopedic sociological analysis. It is not a political polemic. I am not a camera. . . . I cannot offer the objective truth, unfiltered through my own opinion. I have written what I see, limited, personal, but entirely real. I have written my impressions. (6–7)

In spite of this disclaimer (which is somewhat troubling in and of itself, as Roiphe goes on to generalize from her admittedly limited "real" experience to the Real of history), Barbara Presley Noble celebrates *The Morning After* as "one of the books that defines the Zeitgeist" in an interview with Roiphe published in the *New York Times*.[24] As is evident in the new introduction, in public appearances, and in magazine interviews, Roiphe herself increasingly has come to see her dissenting position as representative of a majority silenced within a supposedly "liberal" feminist society virulently intolerant of dissent. Not surprisingly, Roiphe's celebrants include right-wing commentators such as George Will, who honors what he calls "a bombshell of a book" with a personal endorsement in the preliminary pages of the paperback edition.[25]

Though not yet made into fodder for a growing and hungry Right, Denfeld's book, ripe for the picking, has been similarly lauded in mainstream American publications as a welcome new voice of contention. In a March 1995 review of *The New Victorians* published in the *New York Times Book Review*, Michelle Green heralds Denfeld as "one bold writer" who "[l]ike others of her generation . . . is appalled by extremists who neglect real-life issues in favor of bashing men, worshipping the Goddess, battling porn-mongers and denouncing heterosexuality." Green goes on to promote Denfeld as an emergent commander of young feminist troops:

> The author's bravery and passion . . . will inspire most readers to
> cheer her on. An amateur boxer, she has a feisty, street-smart edge
> that is a bracing contrast to the smugness of the women she
> brands the new Victorians. Ms. Denfeld's book is a powerful call
> to arms for women of her generation; let's hope she stays on the
> front lines until her radical elders give up the ghost.[26]

As a targeted comrade who fundamentally disagrees with the vast majority of Denfeld's claims, I want out of her army. Whereas Wolf's recommendations for a continued feminist future may be genuinely "new" (albeit elitist—hence, old), there is nothing particularly new about Roiphe's and Denfeld's respective challenges to the "old feminist order." The issues may be different, but the condemnation of a burlesqued "feminist order" is the same. The rhetoric with which many of Denfeld's and Roiphe's advocates praise their work is boringly familiar: these two young soothsayers bravely condemn those "smug" (read shrill) "extremists" (read radicals), those "porn-mongering" (read bra-burning) "male-bashers" (read lesbians) who are perpetually angry and embarrassingly sexually repressed. Though today's scary demons have new names—the New Victorians, the victim feminists, the rape-crisis feminists (George Will, take your pick)—those speaking in the name of taking back feminism seem merely to be reproducing a stock antifeminist plot, one that would deliver us all back to a prefeminist past.[27]

Good Feminism, Bad Feminism

I might respond to the popular reception of and response to these self-identified feminist authors in any number of ways.[28] Yet any response I might offer may be readily countered with the cry that I am merely arguing from the standpoint of an ideologically rigid advocate of victim feminism. Any attempt to engage genuinely and critically with the issues these authors raise may be met with the countercritique that I am merely a smug New Victorian crying backlash. Though these rebellious pundits declare that an entity called "the feminist establishment" is increasingly intolerant of dissent, we seem to be at a deadlock on all sides.[29] Thus, in the hope of creating a space for a genuine inter-generational and *intra*generational dialogue in a moment when the status of feminism is being interrogated within and outside the academy, from the Left and from the Right, I would like to explore the contours of the new—yet old—terminology and rhetoric adopted by these "new" historiographers. Fighting the urge to be equally dismissive, that is, suppressing my desire to wander down to the proverbial riverbank and sling some not-so-proverbial mud, I am really quite interested in the names being called, for name-calling is never a neutral act—politically, ontologically, or epistemologically.[30]

In their attempts to master (and bury) the would-be past of feminist history, Wolf, Roiphe, and Denfeld create sensational, fictional accounts of a demonized feminism to satisfy a "progressive" narrative structure that might be summarized (pace each author's respective rhetorical flourish) as, "Down with the 'bad' feminism and up with the 'good!'" Their critique of the "bad" is often based upon a presupposition of a preexisting ideal of a public sphere that claims to represent all women and thus can be criticized and made answerable for its failure to do so, as is evident in the following passages:

> There are, in essence, two different women's movements alive today. One is a cultural movement, reflected in women's magazines such as *Glamour* . . . and expressed in the independent actions of thousands of feminist-thinking women who fight for equality in their lives—such as [Shannon Faulkner, of Citadel fame, and Dallas Malloy, an amateur boxer fighting for women's right to the ring]. . . . But this movement lives primarily in the hearts and minds of women: It isn't organized, and most of its members do not call themselves feminists. That's because that word refers to the *other* women's movement—the organized, ide-

ological form of feminism represented by groups such as NOW, women's studies courses, and feminist leaders. It is this organized women's movement—which defines the feminist label—that is the focus of this book. (Denfeld, 6)

I'll show that there are and have always been two different ap-proaches within feminism. One—"victim feminism," as I define it—casts women as sexually pure and mystically nurturing, and stresses the evil done to these "good" women as a way to petition for their rights. The other, which I call "power feminism," sees women as human beings—sexual, individual, no better or worse than their male counterparts—and lays claim to equality simply because women are entitled to it. Victim feminist assumptions about universal female goodness and powerlessness, and male evil, are unhelpful in the new moment for they exalt what I've termed "trousseau reflexes"—outdated attitudes women need least right now. (Wolf, xvii)

When I got to Harvard in the fall of 1986 . . . I found something called feminism that was unfamiliar to me. The feminism around me in classrooms, conversations, and student journals was not the feminism I grew up with. The Take Back the Night marches and the sexual harassment peer-counseling groups were alien, and even sometimes at odds with what I thought feminism was. All of a sudden feminism meant being angry about men looking at you in the street and writing about "the colonialist appropriation of the female discourse." (Roiphe, 4–5)

In their reconstruction of a precritically conceived past (and present), Wolf, Roiphe, and Denfeld compose cartoonish caricatures of contem-porary feminists and reduce the terms of contemporary feminist debate to the old rhetoric of equality versus difference.[31]

The major flaws of these books, and their greatest danger, is that they set up an image of an atomistic difference-feminism as their straw woman, and although they cogently argue against that image, they fail to realize that what they are advocating in its place is a straw woman with a new hat marked, "Agency! Power! Equality!" (Hey, grrrls—isn't it about time we all get out of the cornfield?) All three argue against what Denise Riley has termed the effeminization or overfeminization of feminism, that is, the emphasis on women's essential weakness or victim status. Writes Michelle Green, for example, in her review of *The New Victorians*, "Like Naomi Wolf in her book *Fire with Fire*, Ms. Denfeld maintains that her contemporaries are weary of being cast as maidens in distress."[32]

Repackaging Wolf's "victim feminist" by dressing her up in Victorian garb, Denfeld argues that an "antimale sentiment has led to what amounts to victim mythology, a set of beliefs that promote women as the helpless victims of masculine oppression" (12). As both Victorianist scholar Gertrude Himmelfarb and feminist commentator Katha Pollitt suggest in their respective analyses of Denfeld's book, Denfeld's representation of Victorian culture is historically inaccurate (Himmelfarb) and politically out of vogue (Pollitt).[33] Similarly, Denfeld's descriptions of what she repeatedly refers to as "the feminist school of thought" are, like many popular descriptions of feminist positions, simplified and overstated. Caricaturing feminism (in the singular) as a naive movement that has not much changed since the early 1970s, Denfeld and her cohorts fail to note the complexity and the diversity of current feminist modes of thinking.

It seems odd, given their search for an alternative to "victim feminism," that these authors do not more carefully acknowledge and build on the work of feminist theorists such as Linda Gordon, a historian known for her resistance to a "victim" paradigm of women's history and for her advocacy of a complicated notion of social control that promotes the analysis of ways in which women maneuver within the specific constrictions they face.[34] It seems equally odd, given their commitment to reclaiming feminism for the majority, that they do not acknowledge and build upon the work of African American historians and literary critics such as Hazel Carby and Barbara Christian, who document ways in which African American women historically have retained a tremendous sense of agency from within multiple matrices of oppression. These omissions are not surprising, however, given the fact that all three historiographers are eager to differentiate their work from a demonized straw woman named feminist theory.

Attacking academic feminisms, which she lumps together under the nicknames "club feminism" and "insider feminism," Wolf blames feminist academics for being irresponsibly irrelevant:

> The prose style of the best feminist academic thinking ensured
> that the most fashionable and influential ideas would be drained
> of relevance to the real world of politics and action, and would
> be couched in what, to the millions of women and men outside
> the ivied gated who had not incentive to master an exclusive and
> elaborate professional jargon, amounted to pig Latin. (125)

Whereas Denfeld clumsily blames New Victorians for having "climbed out on a limb of academic theory that is all but inaccessible to the uninitiated" (5), Roiphe parodically nicknames her feminist seminars "The Mad Hatter's Tea Party" (114). According to all three, theory is the refined instrument of feminist fascism; theory exists in, of, and for itself; theory exists independently from actual feminist movements and causes, that is, feminism rallied around specific, "real-world" actions and claims.

It is, of course, misleading for Wolf, Roiphe, and Denfeld to market their historiography as free of "theory" and "ideology." Yet they do. In the promotional blurb from the *National Review* that graces Roiphe's book, the reviewer markets the book as "Unpretentious [read theory-free] . . . a fast, entertaining read. Hooray for Katie Roiphe!" Like Roiphe, Denfeld dispenses the obligatory disclaimer to those who would take her observations as "scientific" analysis, but she then proceeds to generalize from her experience and to theorize about the needs and wants of a generation: "Throughout this book, you will hear voices from other women of my generation. . . . I sought these women out in a variety of places, and I make no claim that I conducted anything even remotely resembling a scientific survey. But I do think these women speak for many" (21). Though these authors may claim otherwise, science-free does not mean theory-free or methodless.

In defense of the multiple sites, forms, and functions of theorizing, as bell hooks and Katie King argue from their different academic contexts, theory (pretentious and unpretentious) takes many forms. In her analysis of how academic machinery often privileges theory made by certain individuals and leaves others uncredited or unacknowledged, King theorizes a warning against a metonymic view of the production of theory that seems relevant to the discussion at hand, and thus worth repeating in full:

> An error feminists make over and over is to mistake the *part* of a
> particular theoretical reading, especially a published reading, for
> the *whole* of the many forms theorizing takes: active thinking,
> speaking, conversation, action grounded in theory, action produc-
> ing theory, action suggesting theory, drafts, letter, unpublished
> manuscripts, stories in writing and not, poems said and written,
> art events like shows, readings, enactments, zap actions such as
> ACT UP does: or for that matter, incomplete theorizing, sporadic
> suggestiveness, generalizations correct and incorrect, inadequate

theory, images and actions inciting theoretical interventions, and
so on. It's not that all human actions are equivalent to theorizing,
but rather that a particular product of many forms of theorizing
should not be mistaken for the processes of production itself.[35]

Though they voice a genuine (and justified) concern that theory, as a
democratic tool, should be accessible to many, by engaging in the uni-
lateral and ever popular sport of theory-bashing, Wolf, Roiphe, and
Denfeld play into an anti-intellectualism that banishes theory as something "they"—not "we"—do.

In an essay entitled "Theory as Liberating Practice," hooks argues that critical thought predicated upon "lived theorizing" closes the
gap between theory and practice.[36] Though she acknowledges that not
all theory is "inherently liberatory, or revolutionary" and that theory
"fulfills this function only when we ask that it do so and direct our
theorizing towards this end," she nevertheless acknowledges the possibility that theory can function as (lived) critical intervention. According to hooks, theory can be the act of "making sense out of what [is]
happening," a sanctuary where one might "imagine possible futures, a
place where life could be lived differently."[37] Theory takes multiple
forms and often transpires in unlikely places. In their passionate embrace of my question on the back of the restroom door, for instance,
the women of the undergraduate library were practicing—and living—
theory.

Although Wolf, Roiphe, and Denfeld profess an interest in thinking and living the feminist life differently, it seems that the energy behind these texts is deconstructive (in the sense of destructive) rather
than reconstructive, with Wolf's how-to manual being an important
exception. Roiphe closes the body of her text on a note of rejection:
"This is not what I want, not even as a fantasy" (172). If Roiphe
spends 180 pages denouncing rape-crisis feminists, Denfeld devotes
a full 279 (not counting the last 14 pages of recommendations for
action) to a full-force demonization of the New Victorians. In the introduction to *The New Victorians*, Denfeld specifies the "organized
women's movement," the one that "defines the feminist label," as the
focus of her book, yet one wonders why she does not foreground instead the exemplary actions of the so-called silenced majority—that is,
"the independent actions of thousands of feminist-thinking women
who fight for equality in their lives," the unorganized movement that

"lives primarily in the hearts and minds of women." In the closing paragraph of her book, Denfeld (smugly?) pouts, "If there were a movement that addressed [young women's] concerns, we would gladly call ourselves feminists"(279). To this I might reply, there exists such a movement. Young women, adding their voices to those of their fore-mothers, are continuing to imagine feminist futures—on restroom doors and elsewhere.

What's Love Got to Do with It?
Tolerating Dissent versus Engaging Difference

> Readers may be surprised to see that I appreciate on some pages thinkers or publications with whom I argue on others. Let this book be read with the thought in mind that drove me to write it: dissenting with another's ideas is a form of honor, and taking a critical look at one's own cherished movement is an act not of sacrilege but of love. (Wolf, xii)

> Young women, supposedly, have tuned into Channel Backlash, and for that reason we hesitate to call ourselves feminists. . . . Using the cry of "backlash" whenever current feminist trends are criticized, New Victorians have effectively muzzled discussion within the movement—and, it would seem, outside the move-ment. (Denfeld, 4, 19)

> In the pages of this book, devoted to the idea of women taking responsibility for their actions, I am writing against the grain. Moral and legal responsibility are not in vogue for anybody these days—it is never our fault or our responsibility, it is always low self-esteem or social oppression or our family or patterns of abuse. . . . Tolerating dissent simply means that we sit with for-eign ideas, the way we might with foreign people, long enough to hold a conversation, long enough for the difference between us to rise and expand, fully clarified and articulated. Tolerating dis-sent is allowing for the give-and-take, push and pull of intellec-tual conflict; it is the willing suspension of disbelief in order to allow ideas that are not our own to sharpen our perceptions. . . . Intolerance [of dissent] breathes life into words like "the back-lash." Words like this force a confrontation. They offer a choice: embrace the article or book or book review in question as truth or dismiss it entirely. . . . As the conversation opens up to more and varied voices, I hope there will be room for the jostling of ideas, for nuances and complexities, for speculations and rumina-tions, not just for the sound and the fury. (Roiphe, xiv-xv, xviii, xx, xxiii)

As is evident in these passages, all three young historiographers antici-pate a hostile reception from those who disagree with their controver-sial theses. Yet if Roiphe's model for "sit[ting] with foreign ideas" in the same way we "tolerate" foreign people is any indicator, we are sorely in need of more imaginative paradigms for living with difference, for *engaging*—rather than merely dismissing, tolerating, or caricaturing—ideas (and people) that are different from our own (from us).

In her analysis of a published debate between feminist historians Joan Scott and Linda Gordon, Friedman argues that the exchange be-tween these advocates of two fundamentally different views of historic agency demonstrates "the oppositions between agency and its cri-tique, between the will-to-empowerment and resistance to the will-to-power."[38] It would seem that the terms of this particular exchange are somewhat replicated, albeit in simplified form, in the unspoken (be-cause unspeakable?) exchange between Wolf, Roiphe, or Denfeld and a reader who does not agree that "victim feminism" (in the singular—a closed, monolithic ideology, a united front) is an accurate descriptor of the diversity of feminisms that exist today. As one who understands feminism as a perpetually changing and potentially varied movement, I argue that it is in fact the New Historiographers who are stifling de-bate. Yet "they" leave little room for such a critique. If I still think that women are victimized by systemic injustice, it's because I'm resisting the will-to-power. If I cry backlash, it's because I'm ideologically rigid. If I don't agree with you, it's because I'm intolerant of dissent. So what's an academic feminist—that is, one who yearns for liberating feminist praxis that bridges academic, political, and discursive sites of activism—to do?

Current debates about the issues of identifying with feminism and the identification of feminism posit a homogeneous appearance of feminism in spite of its factual heterogeneity. How, then, might one continue to write feminist interventionist historiographies—to make feminist history—in a way that allows for an engaged notion of dif-ference, a recognition of oral as well as written forms of theorizing, an honoring of conflict? In my quest for a methodology for producing history in a way that Katie King might condone, I am reminded of Dominick LaCapra's call for the creation of spaces within the academy in which dissenting voices within and outside the academy may engage in dialogic encounter:

> The virtue of traditional historiography at its best has been an ability to join meticulous research with a form of critical rationality in the investigation of the past. I in no sense want to abandon that virtue. Instead I would like to see it emerge fortified through a confrontation with contemporary challenges that may be interpreted to indicate the need—both in the historical profession and beyond it—for a conception of reason open to certain contestatory "voices." . . . One thing an institution should be is a setting for a dialogic encounter in which limiting norms necessary for life in common are put to tests that may strengthen or transform them. Indeed a humanistic discipline remains vital to the extent it is possible within it to engage points of view that pose fundamental questions to one's own. The difficulty is to create the material and intellectual conditions in which such an exchange is possible.[39]

Though the creation of such material and intellectual conditions may indeed be difficult, the result would no doubt be a new sound in the world. Cacophonous discord is sometimes more exhilarating than stagnant silence, and the clamor of individuals stuttering more euphonious than the symphony of a master narrative. This is, in fact, one instance in which I find myself in agreement with Roiphe, who states that "If feminism is going to be a vital movement, then it is going to have to be able to sustain critiques . . . that are unsettling, critiques that shake us. By definition true dissent is disturbing, uncomfortable . . . but without it we can never get to a place where our exchange of insults becomes an exchange of ideas" (xxi–xxii). Fueled by a commitment to move feminism into the next millennium, third wave praxis ultimately depends upon the work of theory that strives to reimagine the differences that exist between us as a vital space of feminist encounter.[40]

Postscript: A Posting from the Outpost of the Postfeminist Frontier

Though I may indeed stutter, I will conclude by venturing some historiographic remarks of my own. It is important to understand the historic context in which the texts (and titles) in question are consumed by frequenters of the nation's general bookstores.

In June 1994, a review of five recently published books assessing and critiquing women's movements in the United States, playfully entitled "Sisterhood Was Powerful," is published in the widely distributed newsmagazine *Newsweek*.[41] On December 22, 1994, PBS airs William

F. Buckley Jr. hosting an edition of *Firing Line* wishfully entitled "Resolved: The Women's Movement Has Been Disastrous."[42] Popular feminists appear on TV talk shows responding to the question "Is feminism dead?" The publication of *Fire with Fire*, *The Morning After*, and *The New Victorians*, then, roughly coincides with the pronouncement by the mainstream media and by conservative pundits that we are living in a "postfeminist" era.

I place the term "postfeminist" in quotation marks intentionally, for I am afraid of the popular connotations, and the ideological implications, of this trendy little neologism. When invoked in the popular press, "postfeminist" most often describes a moment when women's movements are, for whatever reasons, no longer moving, no longer vital, no longer relevant; the term suggests that the gains forged by previous generations of women have so completely pervaded all tiers of our social existence that those still "harping" about women's victim status are embarrassingly out of touch.[43] Like Friedman, who notes that "The Montreal massacre of fourteen women gunned down as 'feminists' because they were women in an engineering class hammered home the message that women, as women, are not safe, because they are women," I insist that this world is emphatically not beyond the need for feminisms.[44]

In an October 1993 interview published in *Glamour*, reporter Judith Stone asks Roiphe whether she sees the oppression of women as part of the fabric of American life. Roiphe responds, "No. I don't choose to, maybe. I don't think it's constructive. There are parts of this society in which it is true, but I'm talking about the people *I* know."[45] Aside from the fact that Roiphe's sense of social justice and equity is unconstructively elitist and devastatingly naive, she is not alone in her adoption of a classist historiographic method. Roiphe's statement echoes Wolf's claim that "enough women in the middle classes now have enough money and clout," that "all women now have enough desire and determination to begin to balance the imbalance of power between the sexes," that "twenty-five years of dedicated feminist activism have hauled the political infrastructure into place," and that "power feminism" is the way to go (xvi). Although Wolf's model of "power feminism" may be a hope for the future that can be readily practiced by privileged women today, I find myself questioning Wolf's belief that a feminist infrastructure is currently firmly in place. Is it really time to say "enough"? The tone of current debates about welfare reform, teenage pregnancy, and affirmative action would suggest that there is still quite a long way to go before we can ethically say "enough."

Denfeld echoes both Roiphe and Wolf when she argues that because some gains have been institutionalized for the already enfranchised, we no longer have a need for the word *victim*; what the matter really comes down to, according to Denfeld, is choice:

> We have it much better now than our mothers ever did. . . .
>   For women of my generation, feminism is our birthright. While sexism may still permeate society, we know what it is to live without excessive confinement. We are the first generation to grow up expecting equal opportunity and equal education, as well as the freedom to express our sexuality. We are the first to assume what feminists had to force society to accept against its deeply ingrained prejudice: that we are the equals of any man. This belief may translate into the pursuit of a career or it may mean demanding respect for raising children—women of my generation believe in the right to choose. (1–2)

To whom, I ask, are "we" referring?

Desperately needing to read beyond these premature (and presumptuous?) calls (and wishes?) for "the end" of "victim feminism," I find myself in the position of wanting to reclaim the term "victim." Although Wolf, Roiphe, and Denfeld would drain claims to victimhood of any semblance of agency, the radical act of pronouncing oneself victim to systemic inequity does not necessarily amount to a defeatist confession of utter weakness. In many instances, to name oneself "victim" is an articulation of strength, for to give a name to the injustices that continue to oppress is to adamantly refuse victim status. A feminist philosophy or theory that advocates such naming actions is not operating from the confines of a victim paradigm. In my desire to break through the racist, classist, sexist, heterosexist, ageist ties that continue to bind, I am not a "victim feminist." I am a feminist activist who actively refuses to be a victim.

I cannot tolerate the thought of those purporting to "take back" feminism taking it back from me, for feminism was never mine alone to begin with. Feminists of different stripes must stop jockeying for control and ownership, must cease mistaking each other for the enemy, must begin to forge links with their feminist predecessors, if movement is to continue moving forward. As a young woman committed to the continuation of feminist revolution within and outside the academy, I am both inspired and burdened by the knowledge that there is so much moving left to do, so much history left to make. I feel the weight of generations upon me, and I wonder, with increasing urgency, just how "we" are going to find the words, and the movements, to make it.

Notes

1. Gloria Steinem, *Outrageous Acts and Everyday Rebellions* (New York: Holt, Rinehart and Winston, 1983), 169.

2. Steinem's writings of the 1970s and 1990s are punctuated with acknowledgments of a "pre-" and a "postfeminist" consciousness: "Most of us have a few events that divide our lives into 'before' and 'after'" (*Moving beyond Words: Age, Rage, Sex, Power, Money, Muscles: Breaking the Boundaries of Gender* [New York: Simon and Schuster], 1994, 266); "a lot of the work I published prefeminism was schizophrenic" (*Outrageous Acts,* 15); "immediately post-consciousness, [I] . . ." (*Outrageous Acts,* 20); "Once this feminist realization dawned, . . ." (*Outrageous Acts,* 113); "After feminism arrived in my thirties to show me that women had a right to every human choice, I began conscious resistance to all that" (*Moving beyond Words,* 256); "Since feminism I've . . ." (*Outrageous Acts,* 69). For other such narratives of feminist awakenings of the 1970s, see Rachel Blau DuPlessis, "Reader, I Married Me: A Polygynous Memoir," 97–111, and Leslie W. Rabine, "Stormy Weather: A Memoir of the Second Wave," 211–25, in *Changing Subjects: The Making of Feminist Literary Criticism,* ed. Gayle Greene and Coppelia Kahn (London: Routledge, 1993).

3. Steinem, *Outrageous Acts,* 160.

4. Ibid., 158.

5. Ibid., 360. In one respect the numerical descriptors of feminism's waves reflect a generational chronology. Steinem numerates "waves" of feminism in a 1979 essay entitled "Words and Change":

> Feminism was international—and antinational—during its last massive advance in the nineteenth and early twentieth centuries. (If we call that "the first wave," it's only because we live in such a young country. The feminist revolution has been a contagious and progressive recurrence in history for thousands of years.) The last wave won for many women of the world a *legal identity* as human beings, not the possessions of others. Now we seek to complete that step for all women, and to gain *legal equality,* too. But there will be many more waves of feminism before male-supremacist cultures give way (ibid., 181)

Some feminists of color employ the term "the third wave" to name a feminism that has grown out of the challenge to white feminism posited by women of color. See Kayann Short, "Coming to the Table: The Differential Politics of *This Bridge Called My Back,*" *Genders* 20 (1994): 3–44. I will herein use the term "the third wave" to connote the diversity of feminisms articulated and practiced by contemporary young women.

6. My critique here focuses on popular feminist texts written by three relatively privileged women who understand "most women" today to be "walking in the sun." For a sampling of current writing by third wave feminists who explore the multiplicity of women's conditions, see Barbara Findlen, ed., *Listen Up: Voices from the Next Feminist*

Generation (Seattle: Seal, 1995); and Rebecca Walker, ed., *To Be Real: Telling the Truth and Changing the Face of Feminism* (New York: Doubleday, 1995). For earlier articulations, see Paula Kamen, *Feminist Fatale: Voices from the "Twentysomething" Generation Explore the Future of the "Women's Movement"* (New York: Fine, 1991); and Nadia Moritz, ed., *The Young Woman's Handbook: A Publication of The Young Woman's Project* (Washington, D.C.: Institute for Women's Policy Research, 1991).

7. Steinem, *Moving beyond Words*, 270.

8. Steinem, *Outrageous Acts*, 354.

9. See Elizabeth Fox-Genovese, *Feminism Is Not the Story of My Life: How Today's Feminist Elite Has Lost Touch with the Real Concerns of Women* (New York: Doubleday, 1996).

10. Susan Stanford Friedman, "Making History: Reflections on Feminism, Narrative, and Desire," in *Feminism beside Itself*, ed. Diane Elam and Robyn Wiegman (New York: Routledge, 1995), 11–54.

11. Nan Bauer Maglin and Donna Perry, eds., *"Bad Girls"/"Good Girls": Women, Sex, and Power in the Nineties* (New Brunswick: Rutgers University Press, 1996).

12. Rene Denfeld, *The New Victorians: A Young Woman's Challenge to the Old Feminist Order* (New York: Warner Books, 1995); Katie Roiphe, *The Morning After: Sex, Fear, and Feminism* (Boston: Little, Brown, 1995). Subsequent references to these sources appear parenthetically in the text. See Gertrude Himmelfarb, review of *The New Victorians*, by Rene Denfeld, *Washington Post*, 2 April 1995. Katha Pollitt similarly refers to Denfeld's book as a "Roiphesque tract" in "Subject to Debate," *Nation*, 10 April 1995, 481.

13. Naomi Wolf, *Fire with Fire: The New Female Power and How to Use It* (New York: Random House, 1993). Subsequent references to this source appear parenthetically in the text. See Anna Quindlen, "And Now, Babe Feminism," *New York Times*, 19 January 1994, OpEd section, p. 21.

14. Katie King, "Producing Sex, Theory, and Culture: Gay/Straight Remappings in Contemporary Feminism," in *Conflicts in Feminism*, ed. Marianne Hirsch and Evelyn Fox Keller (New York and London: Routledge, 1990), 83. Addressing her concerns about the reproduction of a totalizing history, King writes:

> What I've just produced here is a series of overlapping—in time and space—historical "moments," what I've sometimes called conversations in feminism. . . . One can locate examples documenting each statement I've made in a place and time, but as periods in feminism they actually overlap, since they also describe different realities for slightly different political unities shifting over time. Also they describe *kinds* of events which might have happened in some places in different times than at other places. This may not be *your* historical memory, but maybe that means you are overhearing, eavesdropping on a recentered history. (83)

15. For works that explore feminist theorizing after poststructuralism, see Susan Stanford Friedman, "Post/Poststructuralist Feminist Criticism: The Politics of Recuperation and Negotiation," *New Literary History* 22 (1991): 465–90; Tania Modleski, *Feminism without Women: Culture and Criticism in a "Postfeminist" Age* (New York: Routledge, 1991); and Gayatri Chakravorty Spivak, *Outside in the Teaching Machine* (London and New York: Routledge, 1993).

16. Elissa Marder, "Disarticulated Voices: Feminism and Philomela," *Hypatia* 7, no. 2 (spring 1992): 163. Marder concludes that "we" is a necessary fiction, a performance: "I would argue that the feminist 'we' can and paradoxically must continue to

speak as a 'we' as long as that 'we' does not believe in its own concrete identity. Our collective 'we' only has force as long as we collectively refuse to accord that 'we' status as a knowable, identifiable category" (153). For a consideration of "we" as a temporary social space, see Elin Diamond, "The Violence of 'We': Politicizing Identification," in *Critical Theory and Performance*, ed. Janelle G. Reinelt and Joseph R. Roach (Ann Arbor: University of Michigan Press, 1992). In the introduction to their anthology *Feminism beside Itself,* Diane Elam and Robyn Wiegman ask, Must "we" always be a utopian collective, a vehicle for a collective merger? (1). In "Making History," Susan Stanford Friedman pointedly states the potential limitations of such attempts: "The political problem with endless problematization of the ground on which we stand is the elimination of any position or standpoint from which to speak, organize for social change, or build coalitions based on common objectives. This applies as well to history writing as a form of feminist activism" (26).

17. As the youngest employee of the National Council for Research on Women in 1991 (the year that Anita Hill took the stand, Susan Faludi wrote *Backlash*, and Wolf published her first book, *The Beauty Myth*), I participated in numerous intergenerational and cross-cultural conversations with council staff and affiliate members. Convinced of young women's (my own) need for a forum in which we might (1) explore ways to constructively critique, transform, and extend the feminist legacies we have inherited, and (2) discuss possibilities and strategies for continued political activism, I, along with a sister council staffer, spearheaded a network of one hundred young women, twentysomething to thirtysomething, employees all of social and feminist organizations based in New York City. Documents of this network, the New York City Young Women's Network, are archived at Radcliffe's Schlesinger Library. During the two years of its existence, the network held monthly meetings, coordinated book groups, distributed a newsletter, facilitated sexual harassment workshops at local high schools, organized support for various local and national pro-choice efforts, and worked in coalition with local and national women's organizations to sponsor citywide events, including a panel discussion entitled "An Intergenerational Conversation among Feminists."

Although the loosely organized New York City Young Women's Network eventually disbanded, some of its members went on to found an organization now known as the Third Wave Direct Action Corporation. Backed by the Ms. Foundation for Women and personally endorsed by Gloria Steinem (who is, incidentally, godmother to cofounder Rebecca Walker), the Third Wave continues to address issues of racism, classism, and elitism within women's movements. Rebecca Walker, a publicly biracial, bicultural, bisexual feminist writer and activist, continues to serve as a spokesperson for this diverse generation—my own. Interestingly, and perhaps ironically, the Third Wave is not a grassroots membership organization that makes decisions by consensus, but rather a "direct action corporation." In an interview in *On the Issues* (Bonnie Pfister, "Communiques from the Front: Young Activists Chart Feminism's Third Wave," *On the Issues*, Summer 1993, 23–26), Walker responds to the critique that her organization replicates a hierarchical (patriarchal) model of activism with the claim that consensus feminism is outdated: "The Third Wave is not a membership organization. That is something we said at the beginning. We do projects. . . . This way the base is broader. You don't have to construct a party line that members have to maintain. . . . I had the same kind of vision: That we would all sit around in a circle and decide things. But it doesn't work, which is sad" (24).

18. Alice Walker, *In Search of Our Mothers' Gardens: Womanist Prose* (New York: Harcourt Brace Jovanovich, 1983), xi–xii.

19. "We must reclaim the feminist label and return it to the majority of women"

(Denfeld, 277); "Power feminism can, without compromising its principles, be reclaimed by the majority" (Wolf, 23).

20. Another prominent advocate of "taking back" feminism is Christina Hoff Sommers, the author of *Who Stole Feminism? How Women Have Betrayed Women* (New York: Simon and Schuster, 1994) and a leader of the newly organized Women's Freedom Network (WFN). In her popular book, which was funded by right-wing foundations, Sommers argues that feminists in the academy have taken feminism too far. According to the *WFN Newsletter* (fall 1994), at the WFN's first national conference, entitled "Taking Back Feminism,"

> the conference was distinguished by the diversity of the participants who were united by their independently achieved conclusions that: intelligent life can not [*sic*] continue under the presumption that all men are beasts and all women helpless victims and 2) journalists seeking commentary on gender issues require a third alternative to the radical feminist PC Left and the far-out Phyllis Schlafly Right.

21. Wolf's recommendations for putting "power feminism" into action include the following:

> I'll propose specific strategies, such as using ad campaigns, consumer clout, 900 numbers, health clubs and sororities, charity dollars, and women's magazines, to make prowoman action in this decade, and into the next century, something that is effective, populist, inclusive, easy, fun, and even (forgive me Karl) lucrative. Rather than relying on "converting" mainstream women into a subculture that can sometimes feel like it is for activists only, this approach brings the movement smoothly into most women's—and men's—everyday activities." (xviii–xix)

Although her recommendations are inventive and appealing, one must nevertheless question the assumption that "most women" belong to health clubs, sororities, and charities, buy women's magazines, and have money to call 1-900 numbers. Wolf's model of "power feminism" is feasible only for those who have some degree of power to begin with.

22. Wolf's subtitle also underwent a transformation from the first to the second edition. Whereas the original subtitle reads, *The New Female Power and How It Will Change the Twenty-First Century*, the revised version reads, *The New Female Power and How to Use It*. If the alteration in Roiphe's title signals an expansion of the claims recorded within the pages of her book, Wolf's new title places additional emphasis on the reader's agency (and responsibility) to practice what Wolf preaches; the new title suggests that this is, indeed, a how-to book.

23. For discussions of the ideological elements of experience, see Susan D. Bernstein, "What's 'I' Got to Do with It? Confessing Feminist Theory," *Hypatia* 7, no. 2 (spring 1992): 120–47; Linda S. Kaufmann, "The Long Goodbye: Against Personal Testimony, or An Infant Grifter Grows Up," in her *American Feminist Thought at Century's End* (New York: Blackwell, 1993), 258–77; and Joan W. Scott, "Experience," in *Feminists Theorize the Political*, ed. Judith Butler and Joan W. Scott (New York: Routledge, 1993), 22–40.

24. Barbara Presley Noble, "At Lunch with Katie and Anne Roiphe: One Daughter's Rebellion or Her Mother's Imprint?" *New York Times*, 10 November 1993, C1.

25. In the introduction to the paperback edition, Roiphe expresses condescending disgust toward those critics who have warned her that "the enemy doesn't read for ambiguities . . . [but] for simple messages it can use for its own dark purposes" (xxii). She writes: "Intolerance of dissent disguises itself most convincingly in the argument that

a book like this one might 'fall into the wrong hands.' Countless people have raised the concern that this book will be 'used by the enemy.' This anxiety is based on the assumption that the Rush Limbaughs and Ronald Reagans and Pat Buchanans of the world need a book like mine to justify their ways. They don't" (xxi). Maybe not, but they sure get excited about an unabashedly feminism-bashing book that does their dirty work for them. The paperback edition also features an endorsement from the *National Review*.

26. Michelle Green, "The Feminine Mistake," review of *The New Victorians*, by Rene Denfeld, *New York Times Book Review*, 19 March 1995, 9. Green's battle metaphors are inspired by Denfeld's prose. Writes Denfeld, "Combined, they [today's leading feminist causes and trends, such as male-bashing and goddess worshiping] have almost killed feminism. It is their collective force that has redefined the meaning of feminism for women of all ages. And it is their sum total that has caused women of my generation to abandon the movement, leaving it without troops and without a future" (16).

27. In her discussion of a "postfeminist" ideology, Tania Modleski suggests that "what distinguishes this moment from other moments is the extent to which it [backlash] has been carried out not *against* feminism but in its very name" (*Feminism without Women*, x).

28. For critiques of these texts, see Susan Faludi, "I'm Not a Feminist but I Play One on TV," *Ms.*, March/April 1995, 31–39; Katha Pollitt, "Subject to Debate"; and Anna Quindlen, "And Now, Babe Feminism." In addition, the publication of Roiphe's "Date Rape's Other Victim" in the *New York Times Magazine* (13 June 1993) precipitated a flurry of angry letters to the editor. See, for example, letters by Naomi Wolf and Sonya Rasminsky, "Date Rape Debate," *New York Times*, 4 July 1993, Magazine Desk, 4; Diane Welsh, "Date Rape's Other Victim," *New York Times*, 11 July 1993, Magazine Desk, 8; Susan Brison, "Date Rape's Other Victim," *New York Times*, 25 July 1993, Magazine Desk, 8; and Mary P. Koss, "Date Rape's Other Victim," *New York Times*, 15 August 1993, Magazine Desk, 6. Responses in support of Roiphe included letters by Charlotte Price and Holly York, "Date Rape Debate," *New York Times*, 4 July 1993, Magazine Desk, 4; and Linda Faigao-Hall, "A Feminism for All," *New York Times*, 15 December 1993, Living Desk, 8.

29. Note Roiphe's critique of absolutism: "The cliché about the war between the sexes has, like all clichés, its grain of truth: this war has its propaganda and its blind patriotism. When the maps and alliances and battle lines are drawn, loyalties pledged, sides declared, all ambiguities, doubts, and subtleties seem to disappear. This is a war of absolutes" (xiii).

30. For an account of feminist name-calling in an academic context, see Marder, "Disarticulated Voices."

31. Though the word *difference* has taken on multiple and nuanced meanings within feminisms since the early ERA debates, when difference referred to difference from men, these authors foreground gender difference.

32. See Denise Riley, *Am I That Name? Feminism and the Category of "Women" in History* (Minneapolis: University of Minnesota Press, 1988); and Green, "Feminine Mistake."

33. Himmelfarb, review; Pollitt, "Subject to Debate."

34. See Friedman, "Making History," 32.

35. King, "Producing Sex, Theory, and Culture," 89.

36. Bell hooks, *Teaching to Transgress: Education as the Practice of Freedom* (London and New York: Routledge, 1994), 61.

37. Ibid., 70.

38. Friedman, "Making History," 35. The debate, published in *Signs* 15, no. 4

(summer 1990), comprised the following: Joan W. Scott, review of *Heroes of Their Own Lives: The Politics and History of Family Violence*, by Linda Gordon (848–52); Linda Gordon, "Response to Scott" (852–53); Linda Gordon, review of *Gender and the Politics of History*, by Joan Wallach Scott (853–58); and Joan W. Scott, "Response to Gordon" (859–60).

39. Dominick LaCapra, *History and Criticism* (Ithaca and London: Cornell University Press, 1985), 141–42.

40. See Gloria Anzaldúa, *Borderlands/La Frontera: The New Mestiza* (San Francisco: Spinsters/Aunt Lute, 1987).

41. Laura Shapiro, "Sisterhood Was Powerful," *Newsweek*, 29 June 1994, 68–70.

42. Panelists included Camille Paglia, Elizabeth Fox-Genovese, Betty Friedan, and Helen M. Alvare of the National Conference of Catholic Bishops. For extended documentation of media pronouncements that ours is a postfeminist era, see Faludi, *Backlash: The Undeclared War against American Women* (New York: Crown, 1991). See also Patricia Mann, "On the Postfeminist Frontier," *Socialist Review* 1–2 (1994): 223–41.

43. When invoked in the academy, "postfeminist" also refers to the challenges of current feminist theory and practice as informed by poststructuralist, postmodernist, and multiculturalist modes of analysis.

44. Friedman, "Post/Poststructuralist Feminist Criticism," 469.

45. Katie Roiphe, "Sex, Rape, and Second Thoughts," interview by Judith Stone, *Glamour*, 19 October 1993, 177.

CHAPTER FOUR

HUES Magazine: The Making of a Movement

Tali Edut, with Dyann Logwood and Ophira Edut

Hello, my name is Tali . . . and I was an addict. You see, once upon a time I had this problem. I just couldn't stop myself from subscribing to magazines for women and girls "just like me." I confess that I was a victim of the ill mainstream media; the glamorized trappings that amounted to just about every "ism" in the book. If a product was being pushed, in all its brightly colored wrapping, I was zealously tearing off the bow. Though I now publish a magazine that encourages intelligence and self-sufficiency "for women of all sizes, ethnic backgrounds, and lifestyles," it was my lifelong battle with the pressures and the standards of "successful" women's magazines that motivated me to collaborate with my girls to create *HUES* magazine.

While growing up, I learned a lot from women's magazines. I learned how to apply just the right shade of lipstick to get that "special guy" to (not) notice me. I learned that all the stretching, pulling, and lifting in the world couldn't make me pencil thin like the teenage models I was *supposed* to look like. Beauty, success, and coolness, they taught me, were reserved for an illusory circle of pale-skinned, prom-perfect ultrafemmes with tiny features and unchallenged minds. No matter how outstanding I was on my own, these glossies assured me that life was never really complete without a man by my side.

By the time I graduated from *Seventeen* into *Cosmopolitan*, I had mastered the art of picking apart my body like a twenty-piece chicken dinner. My 1970s collection of board games such as Fashion Plates and Barbie's Dream House had been shelved for a new activity—"The Mirror Game." Locked in the family's bathroom, I wasted precious teen hours staring at my reflection, wondering why I had been cursed. Everything was too big. My nose with the bump in it was a trademark of my Jewish lineage (which I hated as a result). As for my full lips, the orthodontist had pulled my mother aside to suggest we consider the option of surgically reducing them, along with my nose (my teeth were "finally perfect"). My body, which one might call Rubenesque, was all wrong to me. I wasn't gangly and long, and I didn't have a gap between my inner thighs. My round butt never sustained a comb in the back pocket as I skated around the roller rink in a tight pair of designer jeans. The only part of me I could stand were my eyes— although I would have preferred them to be a dramatic violet instead of hazel. But, I figured, since I wasn't exactly a nominee for home-coming queen, no one would really want to look in them anyway.

I was constantly comparing myself to the girls in my magazines. I would open to the article "Thinner Thighs in Thirty Days" and per-form leg lifts in front of the mirror while my eyes darted between the model on the page and my reflection. As for my schoolmates, I felt every girl was prettier, cooler, sexier, and so on, than I was. Amid the Black, White, and "other" students at my working-class high school, even my upbringing in an Israeli household set me apart from my peers. I felt like a modern version of Barbra Streisand's "funny girl," the klutzy, misfit Jewess whose survival depended on a good sense of humor.

To add to the situation, I was an identical twin, so when I got sick of looking in the mirror, I shared much of my life with someone who looked, gestured, and thought a lot like the much-hated me. Fam-ily and strangers alike were forever comparing us, with no thoughts of how their unsolicited candor would make us feel. "I think Ophi is a bit thinner than Tali," people would remark. Or, "Tali has a clearer com-plexion than Ophi, but aren't they i-den-ti-cal?" As insecure teens, we took the comments to heart. Although we were the best of friends, we also developed a twisted support network. If one of us fretted or cried over someone's rude comparisons, the other would comfort and reas-sure her. But we also began picking at each other, doling out self-hatred in the form of "constructive criticism." She would suggest I pig out a little less after school, and I would rip out Stridex magazine ads for her.

At fifteen, with my family's unwavering support, Ophi and I started the "Dee-troit Diet," the first of a series of low-cal, fat-free ob-sessions. Although I was smart enough to pass calculus with a solid A, the equation I knew best was the one that multiplied fat grams by nine and divided that number by the calorie count. After school, Ophi and I would rush home for a couple of hours of aerobicizing with five-pound ankle weights. At the time, being thin was the only thing that mattered to me as much as getting a boyfriend. At least if my body looked more like a model's, I rationalized, maybe guys would ignore the imperfection of my face.

Like most people, I wanted to be liked and accepted. My circle of friends were cool and fun, but they weren't necessarily what you would consider popular. So at fifteen, when the tips I'd learned from "How to Snag That Perfect Boy" finally paid off, I shamefully dissed my girls, to hang with HIM (and ONLY HIM). I looked to HIM as my one-way bus ride from the reject asylum. HE was my salvation from ugliness (hey, I could get a *man*) and my ethnic cleanser (just because my name was Tali Edut didn't mean I was a "foreigner" like my parents), and he was Joe Average enough to counterbalance my artsy style. Suddenly I was double-dating, staying out until midnight, and doing all the things I'd read that a teen girl was supposed to do.

When I wasn't working out, dying my hair a brassy bottle-blond, or hanging with HIM, I was doing one of two things: studying my way into college (and the hell out of Oak Park, Michigan) or reading. Scouring the shelves, I never found, nor expected to locate, a magazine with women and girls in it who were much like me. So, after sifting through each month's delivery of *Teen* and *YM*, I would lose myself in books. I actually found books that didn't constantly remind me of how uncool I was, and they gave me something to dream about besides the prom. In retrospect, I wish I would have found Toni Morrison's *The Bluest Eye* when I was in high school. Although the character Pecola is Black and I am Jewish, I relate to her as someone who grew up feeling valueless because her appearance and ethnicity set her apart from the mainstream.

In our first year of art school at the University of Michigan, I finally reached my limit. I gained the dreaded "freshman fifteen," whereas Ophi became unnaturally thin from eating too little. Stress from late-night projects destroyed my dieting efforts. As luck would have it, I wound up with an aspiring model as a roommate, which did nothing to keep me from occasionally wolfing Pillsbury cookie dough and then sticking my finger down my throat. I had numerous failed crushes on guys whom I now would consider total losers. (My "perfect" high school boyfriend had dumped me for a sexually available local girl ten minutes before I left for school.) I had even cut down on hanging with Ophi, because I was so afraid of being called "the bigger twin." I felt alone and depressed, and I knew that something had to change.

This saga of my teen angst is not a cry for sympathetic greeting cards or a plea for a guest spot on a daytime talk show. Rather, it's an attempt to make a point about how miserable a girl's life can be when she tries to follow the manifesto of the mainstream media. I felt hopelessly inadequate when I was trying to reach a standard that for me was impossible (at least, without peroxide, colored contacts, liposuction, rhinoplasty, and enrollment in a WASP training academy). This standard wasn't just something I pulled out of a hat, either. It surrounded me—not only on billboards and in the pages of my monthly magazines, but in the minds of the majority of America's female population.

Almost every woman I knew could draft a sizable list of the things she wanted to change about herself. And I'd place bets that if there were ten items on that list, eight of them would refer to her physical characteristics. *Ummm, I'd like a slim-waist platter, along with a side of perky breasts. Oh yeah, and can you make my skin a little more . . . alabaster, please?* I now know that I could no more have gotten rid of those outer-thigh curves that one fitness-obsessed magazine writer referred to as "saddlebags," than Kate Moss could expect to runneth over the cups of my 36D bra. The point is, women shouldn't be expected to live up to any look-of-the-day other than the one we can naturally achieve through an emotionally and physically healthy lifestyle.

The saddest part about the image-obsession craze is that it keeps women so preoccupied with feeling bad about our appearances that our minds and souls become secondary. Instead of investing money in mutual funds or taking night classes, the only numbers we're interested in crunching are the ones on the scales at Jenny Craig. The struggle for self-esteem is ongoing for many women. It's undeniably easier for a woman to find outlets for self-hatred than to find ones that tell her to feel good about who she is. All she has to do is pick up a magazine. If she doesn't know that airbrushing is the only real answer to cellulite, she might believe the hype.

When we were nineteen years old, Ophi and I met Dyann Logwood. She had been sitting in the dorm room of a mutual friend when Ophi walked by, and Ophi (as she said later) was just drawn in. The two of them wound up having such an amazing conversation that they actually forgot about the guy they had each come to visit. I was introduced a couple of days later, and we soon became an inseparable trio. It was odd that we got along so well, because our backgrounds were really different. Dyann was African American, the daughter of a Pentecostal preacher. Her upbringing had been strict and somewhat conservative, in a religious sense. Although we all came from integrated schools, Dyann was among a significant population of African American students. Ophi and I were two of possibly twenty Jews in our school district, and the only Israelis. Although Jewish traditions such as holidays and seven years of Hebrew school were upheld, our family tended to be more liberal about daily life. In high school, Dyann was well known for her public speaking abilities and was nicknamed Jesse Jackson for her pro-Black speeches. Although Ophi and I were known for winning writing contests and making crazy, artistic clothes, we were more on the outside fringe. We tended to be more closeted about our Jewish heritage then, preferring to blend instead of making any grandiose political statements about ethnicity.

In spite of our differences, our friendship was both medicinal and educational. Our late-night talks over pizza and vending machine snacks were like group therapy sessions and basement political meetings. (And you wouldn't believe how good junk food tasted after years of oat bran and frozen yogurt.) It was from these talks that we gained a perspective into worlds beyond our own doorsteps.

Dyann was the first woman the two of us had ever met who didn't constantly put herself down. She wasn't afraid to take pride in the things she did well. In her mind, if you didn't believe you were "all that," no one else would, either. At sixteen, she had decided that she didn't want to go through life hating herself. She enlisted the help of a few daily affirmations, wherein she would look in the mirror and tell herself she was beautiful and strong. She swore by it as a confidence booster. That was such an odd concept for me and Ophi. We could hardly fathom looking in the mirror and saying, "You look okay, I guess." But beautiful? That was a whole new ball game. The three of us were all shaped similarly—short and thick. The difference was that in Dyann's community, being skinny was considered unattractive and "having some meat on your bones" was actually a sign of beauty. As a teen, Dyann had felt an uncomfortable urgency to sprout some curves, whereas Ophi and I had worked obsessively to diminish ours. Although Dyann had felt less impact from teen girls' magazines (the permanent absence of Black models and issues had dulled her interest), she had been unduly affected by the industry's by-product—what she referred to as "the Black Barbie syndrome." The Black woman with light skin, green eyes, and long hair (which, I learned from Dyann, is sometimes hard for Black women to grow)—essentially the Whitest-looking Black woman—was touted as the most beautiful. Whereas a lot of Jewish girls Ophi and I knew were constantly dieting, blow-drying the curl out of their hair, and occasionally spending spring break at the plastic surgeon's, Dyann was acquainted with Black women who spent hundreds of dollars getting their hair permed straight, popping colored contacts, even buying over-the-counter skin bleach.

Getting to the stage of believing she was a strong, beautiful woman wasn't easy for Dyann, though. In spite of Hollywood's portrayal of hard-core Black women who didn't take any shit, Dyann recalled regular sermons about a woman's role being to support her man at all times. She also remembered the girls at her church being commanded to "keep their legs closed." Although the women she grew up around had a strong presence, they rarely challenged the church-prescribed role of wife and mother. Similarly, although no one was directly insisting that Ophi and I become stereotypical, overbearing Jewish mothers, we always felt pressured to find that "nice Jewish boy" to make our lives complete. For all of us, growing beyond the prescribed definition of womanhood demanded a good deal of work.

While we were chowing down, we talked about a lot of things besides physical image. We'd all had interracial friendships prior to college, but they had tended to be more color-blind (you're aware of surface differences, for instance, but you choose to ignore them for fear of bringing up possibly unpleasant issues). Whether it was the self-actualizing aura of college life or the fact that we were suddenly awakening to the ills that surrounded us, the three of us couldn't seem to have a conversation that wasn't political. We talked about *everything*: How people in Dyann's classes often assumed she was there only because of affirmative action. How futile it was for Blacks and Jews to debate the significance of slavery versus the Holocaust. How sad it was that a man's influence could quash a woman's dreams. How our teachers had rarely encouraged us toward big-money careers. How hard it was to decide whether Judaism was a race or a religion. How annoying it was that our peers assumed we were sellouts or wanna-be's because we didn't hang exclusively with people inside our cultures.

From those talks a new cross-cultural guideline emerged: don't tiptoe around the issues, but also be prepared to shut up and listen. Initially we were all somewhat clueless about each other's cultures, and, I won't pretend that we disbelieved every stereotype. (We cracked up when Dyann revealed that someone had once told her that the word *Jew* came from *jewelry*, because Jewish people owned all the jewelry stores.) It took a little while before we were able to admit that we weren't always liberal ambassadors with innate understandings of every cultural truth and faux pas. After hanging out for a couple of weeks, we reached a comfortable understanding that if someone said something ignorant, another could correct her without ending the friendship, and that if someone asked a "stupid" question, we would try to answer it without jumping down the other's throat. Above all, we learned to listen and learn from each other's experiences. I had once believed that racism had been eradicated along with the Jim Crow laws. Dyann's life stories helped me and Ophi see that we still had a lot of privileges on the basis of our paler features. And, after the three of us decided to be roommates, we saw firsthand how many apartments suddenly became "unavailable" when Dyann walked into the rental office.

By the time we figured we knew *everything* there was to know about Black and Jewish cultures—as if—we got the idea that our talks might be a good basis for bringing more women together across cultural "boundaries." We knew we weren't the only three women in the world who had been affected by an era of heroin-addicted models and Martha Stewart-like supermoms. We were especially concerned with the impact on women like ourselves, who were considered "cultural others."

While we were waiting for inspiration on the perfect way to unite all women, I got my first behind-the-scenes look at women's magazines. I was back at home on summer break, thumbing through my little sister's *Sassy* magazine. At that time, *Sassy* was arguably the closest thing to a teenage feminist publication that existed. Of all the teen and women's magazines on the shelves, it was the one publication with a voice that I could sort of relate to. The writers were frank and opinionated, rather than prissy and NutraSweetish. So, when I arrived at the page announcing that *Sassy* was having a "Reader-Produced Issue Contest," my interest was stirred. Essentially, *Sassy* was offering teenagers the opportunity to "replace" its entire staff for one issue. I had always had an interest in both the media and New York City (where

Sassy was located), so, with the technical skill I'd gained from a couple of computer graphics classes at the University of Michigan, I decided to try for the role of art director. A few weeks later, Neill, then the real art director of *Sassy*, phoned with the unbelievable news that I would be taking his place for the month of August.

At *Sassy* I joined the other contest winners—a small but amazing group of young women from all over the United States and Canada. After five minutes, I felt my transformation from a midwestern hopeful to a cosmopolitan diva begin. We were all hyped to try out a few revolutionary ideas, as we were under the impression that we could "recreate" this issue. I, for one, wanted to put some of my own political awakenings into action in this mag. Unfortunately, the reader model winners had already been instructed that to enter, they had to fit the standard dimensions (at least 5′8″ tall, size seven clothes). Still, amid the "goth" fashion shoots (heavy black eyeliner, dyed black hair), a few of the more political contestants and I managed to slip in a little consciousness. We included a basic piece about feminism and an article by the Filipina reader-editor about growing up as a "minority."

We learned our first big lesson when we chose a Black girl and a Filipina girl to model for the cover. When we met with the publishing board to discuss our potential cover design, we expected a briefing on basic concerns, such as which articles to make into headlines and the best ways to pose the models. Instead, talk turned, uh, political. We were told that if we wanted to use these two models, we also had to include a White girl in the picture. According to the publisher's supposed expertise and marketing data, a cover without a White girl would alienate a tremendous number of readers at the newsstand. The South, after all, was an important area, and they didn't want to lose any subscribers. Although the publishers never came right out and said it, the message was clear: *Sassy* was yet another magazine strictly concerned with the number of White people reading it.

Looking back, I realize that there were other tears in the fabric of *Sassy*. The hip editorial staff was constantly at odds with the number-crunching publishing board. Writers were not allowed to touch certain subjects, such as abortion and homosexuality, at the risk of losing lucrative makeup ads. The fashion department at *Sassy* was made up of beautiful and stylish women, but few had the anorexic proportions of the models they chose month after month. Gone were my notions of some insidious White man picking seven-foot girls from an uberwaif lineup. I saw firsthand how easily the status quo image of female beauty was perpetuated—and by women, at that! Here were women who actually had the power to reduce the damaging pressures on teen girls—pressures that are directly linked to eating disorders and poor esteem among girls and women; yet they were unwilling to take the risk. Their claim was that fashion companies made sample clothing in size seven only. (Perhaps at the heart of this brainwash is a group of fashion designers giddy over the yards of fabric they have saved during the thin-is-in craze.) Still, I wondered, if *Sassy* was able to use its influence to bring offbeat fashions such as combat boots to American teen girls, then how hard could it really be to rustle up a pair of pants in a size fourteen? The old *Sassy was* an "alternative," in the sense that encouraged more independence than its boy-crazy competitors, such as *Teen* and *YM*. Nonetheless, it never dethroned the Anglo beauty queen—even if she was wearing Doc Martens.

I returned from my *Sassy* summer to the University of Michigan feeling both jaded and inspired. On the one hand, I had acquired some incredible new knowledge. Not only had I peeped the inside track of the magazine industry, but I had also gained a fairly comprehensive understanding of what went into producing a national publication. On the other hand, I had learned that what goes on behind the scenes of the media is not nearly as glamorous as what's seen on the pages.

That semester, Dyann, Ophi, and I enrolled in an introductory women's studies class. Part of the curriculum included a semester-long "action project" that involved working with women's issues in some capacity. Inspiration struck while we were musing over ideas for the assignment: why not try to create our own women's magazine and distribute it on campus?

We were in unanimous agreement that we wanted this project to be not just a magazine but a movement that would bring women together across "boundaries." We envisioned a sort of sisterhood, which we defined partly in reference to our own friendship, being played out on the pages. We saw the need for greater loyalty among women. Among our peers it was often considered cooler to be "one of the guys" than "one of the girls." Sisterhood to us meant having a support network strong enough that a woman could stand up for herself without feeling crazy or alone. It also meant having a greater sense of loyalty between women, so that, for example, we would believe each other if we said we were raped, not go after our best friend's boyfriend,

stand up for the girl who gets called a slut, not feel threatened by someone we think is "prettier," and so on. Beyond that, we wanted to encourage a new style of communication among women that was more
direct than conflict-avoiding. The three of us were able to accept each
other's differences without feeling hostile or competitive because we
had an in-your-face, no-holds-barred approach to communication. We
wanted to see more women talk to each other instead of about each
other when dissension arose, which we felt would diminish much of
the hostility that often goes on between women.

Because a conscious magazine for young women hadn't been
printed to date, we didn't have a model on which to base ours. Although this made our task a little harder, it also allowed for greater
creativity. Our ideas definitely diverged from the mainstream periodical
selection. The publication would have to be a women's magazine of a
different kind, one that would include rather than exclude. It would
speak to women's intelligence, promoting self-esteem and sisterhood.
It would be fun and serious, intellectual and raw at the same time. It
would highlight women's experiences and direct readers to resources.
It would encourage solution-oriented positivity rather than hopeless
frustration. Above all, it would give women a new, real standard to
look to, rather than the unattainable gloss of other women's magazines.

One of our major concerns was to provide a movement that
would include women who are traditionally excluded from the mainstream—not only as participants but also as cocreators. We'd had
enough of the typical women's organizations that planned their agendas with a mostly White board and then wondered why they couldn't
seem to get any "women of color" to participate in their struggles. I
remember feeling disgusted after the three of us attended an open
planning meeting for a women's conference. Under the presumption
that the meeting was going to be run democratically, we instead butted
up against a "good old girls network"—a group of established self-
proclaimed feminists who had a prescribed set of right and wrong answers for all women. Although the discussion participants insisted that
they wanted to draw in "women of color," they were opposed to trying
anything beyond setting up a special "women-of-color" booth in the
waiting area and bringing in one Latina professor to speak. The meeting ended up being just another illustration of the constant marginalization of non-White women into the category of "other." (I mean, if
non-White women get to be "women of color," then do White women

have exclusive rights to the word "women"?) This happens so often among "well-meaning" feminist groups. They claim that they want to include all women, but they want to control the quantity and the quality of women's participation.

The three of us wanted to see multiculturalism finally done right in a women's movement. It wasn't about hand-holding and singing cheesy songs. And we weren't trying to pimp "diversity" as a cover-up for token representation or do some overhyped Benetton we-are-the-world thing. Rather, we were looking for a forum wherein women of different cultures and classes could come together without losing their identities. We envisioned a successful modern women's movement in terms of the old patchwork quilt cliché. Each square would represent its own identity, but the pieces would be inextricably sewn together.

It was important to us that women of all cultures and classes be properly represented in our magazine. We agreed that a code of self-representation was the best way to handle this. If a story was to be told, we wanted it straight from the source. So, there wouldn't be any term-paper-cum-news-story on an American woman's fourth-hand experience with female circumcision; but there might be a story by a woman who had undergone the process, or there might be three women's stories. The way we figured it, the truth was best when it was undiluted by an outsider's inferred understanding. It was also important to us that we illustrate the diversity that existed within a single culture. To break down the stereotypical notion that all Asians, lesbians, single moms, and so on, think in the same way, we wanted to highlight a variety of thoughts within each community.

After much brainstorming, we decided to name our magazine *HUES*, which conveniently shaped itself into an acronym for "Hear Us Emerging Sisters." It seemed like a word that could translate into more than just the obvious multicultural innuendo. *HUES* represented to us the varying shades of womanhood. It was inclusive (rather than simply *HUE*), and, best of all, it wasn't some frou-frou beauty reference like "mirabella" or "allure."

With the name decided upon, we posted flyers and E-mail across campus and soon assembled a small—but truly multicultural—group of women. The *HUES* collective—which included a bisexual Black TA, a Filipina political science major, a Nigerian-born art major from the South Bronx, a single mother attending community college, a White woman who worked with the mentally ill, a Puerto Rican–Chinese photographer, and a Jewish pre-law major—spanned an even broader range of experiences than we'd expected. Still, believe it or not, there was rarely any tension. The women who came to spend Wednesday evenings eating pizza in our living room were a lot like the three of us—open-minded and willing to listen and learn. It didn't hurt that we all seemed to have good senses of humor, too. There were plenty of laughs as we sat around planning the new world order.

Before the presses rolled, the *HUES* collective took time out to assess the status of our generation of women. Would they be receptive to a new women's movement? At the time we were planning our first issue, the movie *Disclosure* (in which a male exec has an extramarital encounter with his female boss, then wins a sexual harassment case against her) was on its way to the box office, and "politically correct" was fast becoming America's favorite dirty word. The trend seemed to be toward gender neutrality rather than separatism. Not only did many women seem to fear the idea of joining together with other women, but also a lot of them saw no practical need in it. Their lives had been only covertly touched by sexism, and they were uneasy with the idea of rocking the boat.

We decided that the general attitude of our generation could be summed by the catchphrase "fear of a feminist planet." A lot of poor and non-White women associated feminism with privileged, middle-, and upper-class Whites who wanted to control their struggles and mediate their issues. In many instances the absence of non-Whites from women's groups confirmed this suspicion. Then there were the countless clueless, who still believed that pro-woman equaled anti-man. In the end, a lot of these young women wound up being feminists by default.

So, we asked ourselves, how could we package feminist ideals such as sisterhood and empowerment in a way that would speak to more than just a small segment of the female population? We started with terminology. Instead of directly calling *HUES* a feminist magazine, we subtitled it *A Woman's Guide to Power and Attitude*. We felt this allowed women to choose how they wanted to define themselves in the realm of the women's movement, be it feminist, womanist, pro-woman, or something else. Meanwhile, we focused on what we felt were the most pertinent issues. Body image, self-esteem, sisterhood, cross-cultural relations, and education topped the list. To make these issues digestible, we felt it was important to write articles in a sisterly tone and to add some humor to the lineup. It was like spoon-feeding feminism to the fearful, as opposed to ramming it down people's throats. We preferred to show through personal anecdotes rather than preach from some political pulpit. And, to keep a good balance of heavy and lighter pieces, we decided that *HUES* should highlight various facets of pop culture, from conscious fashion to music reviews to interviews with well-known women. We saw these pieces as an opportunity to give important press coverage to talented women who might be overlooked in other magazines.

Because we knew Gen-Xers were used to sensory overload, articles would have to be complemented by appealing graphics and photos. We would use models of all sizes, looks, and ethnic backgrounds throughout the entire magazine, reinforcing the idea that *HUES* represented *all* women. Unlike the "concerned" women's magazines that, for example, printed a "shocking" exposé on anorexia, only to follow with a Kate Moss fashion spread, *HUES* had to have a nonhypocritical balance between content and image.

Our aim was to make *HUES* look as well designed as any other publication on the shelves. Of course, it took a few tries to get to that point. When we finally published the first issue of *HUES* in April 1992, it was actually a half-size, black-and-white 'zine. We had raised enough money to print one thousand copies through receiving a few donations from campus groups and by throwing a few hip-hop parties around town. Articles included a piece called "Why Feminists Need Men," a piece on female rappers, and the story of a Filipina rape survivor.

The response to the premier issue was overwhelmingly positive. We got E-mail and letters from women thanking us for producing something aimed at making women feel good about themselves. Of course, there were a couple of annoying responses along the way, such as the one from a man angry about our editorial "No Justice, No Piece . . . Down with John Wayne Bobbitt." But we remained unfazed by our critics. Over the next two years, we pumped out three more issues. With each magazine we improved the quality of our contents and upgraded the "look." Our fourth issue was full size and printed on glossy paper. We added more resource-oriented articles that would connect women with helpful and proactive organizations. We finally had a good set of regular one-page columns on which to structure future issues. And, through fund raisers and the sale of ads to local businesses, we had enough money to do our first color cover and eight inside color pages.

What amazed us most was how *HUES* seemed to travel on its own. Because a lot of students brought *HUES* home from school with them, the magazine crossed state lines. We started getting calls from people across the country who loved *HUES* and wanted to subscribe. During the summer of 1994, after our fourth issue, we got a call from *Ms.* magazine, which published a one-page article about our magazine. Soon after that, the *Chicago Tribune* called. We had no idea how either publication had found *HUES*, but we realized that with our "sisters" we had created something that obviously appealed to women beyond Ann Arbor, Michigan.

At that point Ophi and I had graduated from college, and the three of us figured it was high time we took *HUES* to the next level. When we decided on our national launch in early 1995, we were pretty starry-eyed. We connected with a few national distributors who promised to shelve *HUES* in chain stores and newsstands from New York to California. We decided to complement sales with big promotional drop-offs at colleges across the country, which would also help get out the word about *HUES*. We were interested in selling ad space to companies that didn't objectify women or sensationalize culture. With the money from ad sales, we planned to make *HUES* more visible, create self-esteem workshops, and spread the message of sisterhood. Everyone—ourselves included—was *sure* that hordes of big corporations would be pouring their dollars into *HUES*. We approached companies that had advertised in other women's magazines. It seemed logical that companies would want to invest in a magazine that targeted *all* women instead of just a select handful. We boasted promising newsstand visibility, positive press write-ups, and piles of letters pouring in from women telling us that *HUES* was what they'd been waiting for all their lives.

Still, the big-money players weren't ready for us. Advertisers of universal women's products unabashedly told us that *HUES* "wasn't their audience." Even supposedly "alternative" companies such as charitable long-distance services gave us the same line. One ad agency actually told us that "ethnics don't sell." To another we were "spreading ourselves too thin with the multicultural, multisexual thing." Then we were informed that "college women don't spend enough to make them worth our ad dollars." To us, these rejections added up to one thing—

society was still uncomfortable with the idea of an intelligent, self-empowered woman. Advertisers counted on women having low self-esteem in order to sell more "nighttime cellulite cream." A magazine that encouraged women to use their minds threatened the very premise many companies clung to. *What would happen if she figured out that our gym shoes aren't going to give her the body of an aerobics instructor? If she realized that our totally smudge-proof mascara won't bring her Prince Charming? Hmmm . . . let's keep her misinformed, guys.*

We also discovered that in big time publishing, a lot relies on who you know (and whether or not you are a Time, Inc., publication). Being an independently owned magazine was another strike against us. In many cases it prevented us from even getting a foot in the door. But getting rejected by everyone from Nike to Kotex was actually a blessing in disguise. It gave us an opportunity to reevaluate our goals. We had always been firm in our desire to keep *HUES* a resource for women, including women business owners. We decided to make *HUES* into an affordable network for more conscious companies to reach conscious consumers (i.e., *HUES* readers). And we had to learn a thing or two about creative financing. Although Dyann, Ophi, and I had honed the art of organizing young women into a productive unit, we had to start thinking like businesswomen as well. Dyann created a college marketing department from which college professors began ordering *HUES* for use in course curriculum, as well as an internal sales network for feminist bookstores.

We were also blessed to have families who believed in us enough to co-sign a start-up loan from a local bank. With that extra boost, along with revenues from some smaller advertisers, we launched our first national issue. It sold beautifully on the newsstand, and soon our 1-800 number was ringing with subscribers, the press, and people wanting a *HUES* woman to come speak at their conference. After that we did manage to sell a four-page ad to Levi's Jeans for Women for our second national issue, and we hoped that perhaps that would give us an edge with a few other clothing companies. Since then, we've connected with some awesome publications that share our mission, such as *New Moon: The Magazine for Girls and Their Dreams*; *Teen Voices*; and *Hip Mama*. In the spirit of true sisterhood, our four publications are forming an umbrella organization to support each other and share resources.

Today, Dyann, Ophi, and I are scrambling around trying to finalize the last-minute details of our eighth—and fourth national—issue, which is due to go on press in (aaaghh) only two weeks. There are articles that need to be dropped into layout, and filler columns to write and edit, not to mention that a few companies are still deciding what size ad to run. Even after five years of publishing, there is still the hectic buzz of uncertainty and instability. Still, we remain confident that *HUES* is what women need; we just may be a few years ahead of our time. In creating a publication that is not just a magazine but a movement, our goal remains to create a new standard of self-acceptance for women. And, whether or not *HUES* becomes the "femme-pire" of our dreams, we do hope the ideals—such as promoting sisterhood and including a diversity of women—will somehow translate into other women's magazines. A reporter recently asked me if I thought a magazine like *HUES* could ever move into the mainstream and be as big as, say, *Glamour.* I guess that one is up to the women of the world. For now, it still feels good to be a part of a new movement that truly includes *all* women.

THE THIRD WAVE AND REPRESENTATION

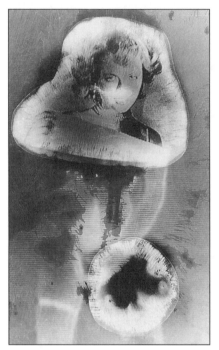

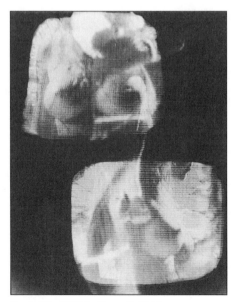

THE THIRD WAVE AND REPRESENTATION

Representation is a very general term that we make particular use of here. Recent theory has focused on the multiple ways that forms of media don't just represent life or the "real world" but, rather, help to create it. Theorists of the mass media such as Jean Baudrillard go as far as to say that "reality" is a "simulacrum"—that is, contemporary culture is media saturated, dominated by simulations that shape our world and our perceptions of that world. Simulations aren't a cheap imitation of a "real" thing—they *are* the real thing (like Coke ads, which claim to be "the real thing" in relation to other kinds of cola).[1] Given the ways in which the mass media have impacted the subjectivities and practices of third wave activists, and the ways the deployment of the term *feminism* in the mass media has functioned recently to hinder activism, it is clear that, as W. J. T. Mitchell writes, "representation . . . can never be completely divorced from political and ideological questions."[2] In the context of this section, representation is perhaps primarily a political and ideological question.

The essays featured here tackle the question of the third wave and representation from three different angles. Leigh Shoemaker's "Part Animal, Part Machine: Self-Definition, Rollins Style" articulates the complicated relationships between the self-representation of a media figure such as Henry Rollins, who explicitly offers himself as a figure of identification for the twentysomething generation; the psychological and spiritual malaise characteristic of some members of that generation; the cultural forces—such as widespread unemployment and complicated gender politics—that give a figure like Rollins cultural clout; and the contradictions of that clout for gender activists. Jennifer Reed's "Roseanne: A 'Killer Bitch' for Generation X" argues that the creation and deployment of alternative femininities by one performer—Roseanne—offers new subjective spaces or possibilities for third wave self-representations, which makes her performance political. Carolyn Sorisio's "A Tale of Two Feminisms: Power and Victimization in Contemporary Feminist Debate" examines the circulation of mass media representations of the term *feminism*, charting how the conservative feminism currently most widespread relies on the misrepresentation of feminist histories to make its claims and to shape—negatively—the future of feminism.

Read together, Shoemaker, Reed, and Sorisio suggest that potential third wave feminists may come into being and be motivated by the contemporary context of cultural conservatism and the media play it is given. In some of the most crucial ways, the political battles fought today are battles of representation, struggles for control of the mass media, definitions, and terminology. As the site where third wave identities are most actively forged, the activism that most engages the question of representation will be definitive.

Notes

1. See Jean Baudrillard, *Selected Writings*, ed. Mark Poster (Stanford: Stanford University Press, 1988).

2. W. J. T. Mitchell, "Representation," *Critical Terms for Literary Study*, ed. Frank Lentricchia and Thomas McLaughlin (Chicago: University of Chicago Press, 1995), 15.

CHAPTER FIVE

Part Animal, Part Machine: Self-Definition, Rollins Style

Leigh Shoemaker

A few years ago, sometime around 1991, I was traveling with a girlfriend to a small college town to see another friend's struggling band play one of its first shows. My girlfriend had the Rollins Band cassette *Do It* (1988) in the stereo, and we were cruising along shouting out the lyrics to "Turned Out" with pure sincerity: "I don't know you. . . . I know my enemies, They show themselves to me with honest eyes. . . . They hate my guts but at least it's the truth. . . . I'll trust 'em just as far as I can throw 'em off a roof. . . . YEAH!" And oh, how I had been turned out . . . by authority, by friends, by lovers, by individuals I admired, by years of growing up female in the backlash–Reagan-era 1980s. Trust? Ha!

When the cassette had played itself out, I expected silence and the inevitable click-whirr as the tape turned itself over and the other side began its sonic assault. However, my friend had a little surprise tacked onto the end of the tape. A strong, calm, deep voice began a deliberately paced monologue, and my head cleared miraculously as I began to concentrate on the speaker—Rollins himself. He spoke, and I identified with every word that came out of those cheap, tinny speakers. I was transported to a plane of togetherness and focus and clarity. The monologue turned out to be a poem called "I Know You" from Rollins's book *Black Coffee Blues*. It sounded like it came straight from my personal journal: "You don't trust people. You know them too well. You try to find a special person, someone you can be with, someone you can touch, someone you can talk to, someone you won't feel so strange around. . . . You find out that they don't really exist" (1992b, 140). It was all in there—the anger, the depression, the rejection, the solitude—so real, so very, *very* real. I knew that it was real because Rollins had been there, still was there—he was no showboat, no trained entertainer, no fake, no poser.

Something happens to a person when her feelings are articulated so well, especially when she feels inadequate to express them herself. The knowledge that she is not alone, that she is not the only one experiencing her death, is enough to fuel great passions, even if they are somewhat misdirected. This happens in politics, in religion, in every facet of our lives in which personal beliefs or convictions seem to require outside acknowledgment in order for us to feel legitimated, recognized, directed. At the time that I began to identify with Henry Rollins so strongly, and consequently began to look to him to legitimize my reactions to what was happening to me and to the world around me, I was a self-identified feminist, but a feminist who lacked the critical tools, knowledge, and awareness that might have caused me to pause and consider the object of my identification. I could march in pro-choice marches, I could argue vigorously for the advancement of women's rights at the conservative Christian college I was attending, I could vote for left-wing progressive candidates, but I needed the words of Henry Rollins to shake me awake, push me out of my lonely slumber, and get my ass moving.

It strikes me that perhaps this is a unique time in history, a time when it is perfectly acceptable for women and girls to look to certain types of masculinity as models of strength and clarity with which they can identify. Many women now desire to be strong, to be able to withstand the contradictory demands of a society struggling with its attitudes about gender, and to be able to achieve "greatness" with due recognition. Complicated by race and class positionalities, second wave feminism enabled the women of my generation to view themselves as capable, as possessed of great potential, and as worthy of the same societal reward and recognition as men. However, as second wave feminism was filtered through the conservatism of the 1980s to our young minds, that message from the women's movement became somewhat confused and diluted. In a sense, second wave feminism made it possible for us, as women and as future feminists, to choose male "role models" as examples of strength, as traditional ideas about masculinity—still entrenched—had made it apparent that we could not be both strong and female. Ironically, if we wanted to be "strong," some of us thought, we had to identify with men, with the strong images of masculinity (the Terminator, Rambo) presented to us during the

1980s. These images helped to lay the foundation for future feminist identification with supposedly alternative models of masculinity, such as Henry Rollins.

Feminists of my generation learned at a young age that we were girls and that we could do anything the boys could do (thanks to second wave feminism), but also that to achieve that goal, we could no longer be *girls* (thanks to 1980s conservatism). We could not admit to feminine qualities—to compete, we had to disavow "girly" emotions, responses, appearances. We had to be just as hard as the boys. We might have thought that we were making great strides for girls on the playground, but in fact, through valorizing masculinity and devaluing femininity, we were reaffirming the old, restrictive dualisms that we were trying so fiercely to rebel against. It is precisely this contradictory message—generated by the filtration of second wave feminism through the gender backlash characteristic of the Reagan years—that has created a generation of feminists who live with this same contradiction every day of our lives. We are still fighting to overcome our internalized images of the dualisms that shaped our young lives and our budding feminisms.

Many of my friends, both male and female, have identified strongly with Rollins at one time or another. Most of them have now moved beyond their love for the man, but I can remember a time when we traded his books and tapes and CDs with each other, plotted road trips to Rollins Band shows, and actually paid attention when the Rollins Band opened up the first Lollapalooza. At some earlier point in my life, it was exciting to hear that one of my friends had jumped onto the stage to sing with Rollins, and another had actually been able to smell Rollins's sweat from his position in the audience. We never really discussed his lyrics or books critically, never really questioned our identification too strongly (at least until we tired of his increasingly visible presence on MTV and other media venues and of what we considered the decline of the Rollins Band). Perhaps we should have, for to identify with Rollins is to admit to misanthropy (perhaps even misogyny); to a need for differentiation from all the other normal jerks in the world ("I'm a Freak, Touch Me!" a Rollins Band T-shirt reads); to feelings of inadequacy, isolation, depression, sharp anger; and to a need for identification without absorption.

Had my friends and I engaged in more critical engagement with Rollins and his texts, we would have found that a Rollins solution is a questionable solution at best, and we might have discovered that his supposedly "alternative" model of masculinity is not an unfamiliar one at all. As bell hooks says, "Even though the subject matter *appears* 'radical,' it doesn't necessarily *mean* it's radical" (1994, 220). In fact, we might have found that we were reaffirming and learning to portray a mode of being that is not at all unfamiliar to our society (both mainstream and underground), a mode of being that is and has been dangerous to my generation and to previous generations and that presents an interesting problem for third wave feminism. It is a fascist mode of being, and it currently exists as one solution among many for the deep malaise that seems to have shrouded many members of my generation, feminists included.

Henry Rollins and Fascism

While participating in a seminar on the male body led by Susan Bordo, I encountered a book by Klaus Theweleit called *Male Fantasies*, volume 2, *Male Bodies: Psychoanalyzing the White Terror* (1989).[1] I began reading this text as a foray into unfamiliar territory, only to discover that the pre-Nazi writings excerpted by Theweleit for his analysis of the German Freikorps (a fascist military group predating Nazi rule) were strangely familiar. It did not take me long to recognize the disturbing parallel between these fascist literary attempts and the works of Henry Rollins. Due to my and my friends' past close identification with Rollins, this troubling correspondence immediately struck a chord with me and urged me toward a critique not only of Rollins and his writings, but also of the culture that had prepared my friends and me for our past embrace of the Rollins Way. Why were we, supposedly progressive youths, so eager to accept a fascist model of masculinity, of humanity?

One of my primary lessons from Theweleit has been that "fascism" has many more insidious meanings and manifestations than I had previously thought—and I had thought that it was incredibly insidious. As a term, *fascism* is used almost thoughtlessly by everyone from experienced politicians to high school rebels who want justification for their defiance of authority. In light of this "familiarity" with the term, it becomes necessary to clarify the additional meanings that Theweleit brings to the word *fascism*. The ninth edition of *Webster's New Collegiate Dictionary* defines *fascism* as "A political philosophy, movement, or regime that exalts nation and often race above the individual and that stands for a centralized autocratic government headed by a dictatorial leader, severe economic and social regimentation, and forcible suppression of opposition." Coming from another, more psychoanalytic school of thought, Theweleit suggests that fascism is not so much a practice or an ideology one ascribes to later in life (like Republicanism or communism), but rather a style of being that one attains through certain crucial life experiences. To borrow from Simone de Beauvoir, one is not born a fascist; rather, one *becomes* a fascist. To quote Theweleit, "No man is forced to turn political fascist for reasons of economic devaluation or degradation. His fascism develops much earlier, from his feelings; he is a fascist from the inside" (1989, 380). These words, coupled with the similarities between early Nazi fascist literature and the literature of Henry Rollins, began to make me think that contemporary American culture is producing, wittingly or not, fascists from the inside. Additionally, I began to recognize my own rather contradictory complicity in this situation.

According to Theweleit, fascism is not simply a throng of sieg-heiling skinheads waiting with tight-lipped anticipation to pounce on their next victim. Rather, fascism is a mode of being that is outwardly manifested through violent, destructive behavior directed toward the "Other"—which is defined as any entity not aligned with the fascist "nation." The purpose of this destruction of the Other, and of the creation of an Other in the first place, is to enable the fascist to compensate for his lack of secure boundaries. This Other usually is expressed in the imagery of fascist literature as a "mass," a flowing, formless, organic miasma that threatens to engulf or absorb. The Other, or the mass, is often depicted as feminine, and must be controlled or destroyed for the fascist to gain a sense of boundary; the fascist is constructed in self-contained opposition to the mass, just as stereotypical masculinity is commonly constructed in opposition to stereotypical femininity. Although each of these constructions is dependent upon the other for its very definition, the interesting paradox for the fascist is that he dreams that his most complete existence is achieved through total destruction of the Other. His fantasy self occupies empty spaces—he is all there is. It could be said that fascism is in some ways a logical extension of male-dominant social structures, in which the "individual" is gendered masculine and the "community" feminine. Fascism is a more radical form of the same constructed dualisms that are part of our everyday lives, but its very radicality has led to the popular perception that it is an aberration that occurred only in World War II Italy and Germany. However, none of us is ever far from fascism's influence.

Rollins embodies a fascistic approach in both his physical appearance and his writings. To look upon the body of Rollins is to look upon the body of a man actively seeking differentiation from the world: his body is a wall of muscle and tattoo, impenetrable, hard, an organic fortress. His writings serve as attempts at differentiation as well, brimming with images of empty spaces created through annihilation and destruction of the Other, empty spaces that allow him to exist in the world safely, with full and unchallenged boundaries. Rollins constantly warns his readers of the dangers of the Other, of the softness that threatens the righteous: "People are pigs. They want to make you soft. They try to kill you with small talk. Death to the annihilators of time" (1992a, 90). People are rats and corpses that are decomposing and oozing toward Rollins with the threat of absorption and assimilation. They are "devouring women" who are threatening to engulf Rollins and force him to become one with them, thus destroying his boundaries, and to incorporate him as a part of the great, undifferentiated mass.

Rollins is at his pinnacle when he describes his solution to this threat, a threat he will have to overcome with "the iron mind, the iron will" (187). Annihilation and alienation are his security blankets in a world filled with the "crawling mess." For Rollins, "The destruction is the cure. . . . When you say annihilation, you've said it all" (121). Destruction of the pigs, for Rollins as for the Freikorps fascist, is what ultimately sets him apart from the rest of the unclean, impure mess that is humanity. Rollins is not safe in the world, his boundaries not firm and solid and impenetrable, until all threats have been systematically removed.

Rollins often refers to himself as "part animal part machine" (203). In an increasingly technological age, when bodies are described as intricate machines and technology is coupled with the organic to create more "complete" and fully realized human beings, this statement can be viewed as ambiguous, perhaps a statement of cyborg allegiance. However, viewing this declaration in the context of Rollins's literary fascism allows us the privilege of taking Rollins's statement as an assertion of another duality that all too often is recognized by, and serves as a source of frustration for, the fascist male. The animal part of Rollins is the miasma within, the threat to boundary that he must constantly fight, whereas the machine is the ultimate realization of the fascist dream: "the hard, organized, phallic body devoid of all internal viscera which finds its apotheosis in the machine" (Theweleit 1989, xix). The statement serves as a testimony to the fact that the fascist, in this case Rollins, is under construction and is incomplete as long as the animal is allowed to exist in conjunction with the machine. Rollins is still going through the process of construction that will result in his emergence as total machine. He must be reborn, but not of woman. He must erase her influence from his existence. He has yet to attain utopia.

Henry Rollins and a Generation of Separatists

In the epilogue of *Prozac Nation*, Elizabeth Wurtzel touches on a trend that she and other individuals have noticed among members of my generation, the generation that spent its formative years attempting to come of age during the backlash Reagan 1980s. For Wurtzel, who refers to present-day America as "one big Prozac Nation" (1994, 297), the focus is on "mainstreaming of mental illness" and increasing dependence on antidepressants as a solution to an inescapable, almost inexplicable, general malaise. Wurtzel refers to Hillary Rodham Clinton's descriptions of America's "sleeping sickness of the soul," "alienation and despair and hopelessness," "crisis of meaning," and "spiritual vacuum." She also cites statistics from a report published by the *Journal of the American Medical Association* that reveal an alarming trend toward depression among post–baby boomer generations: "Those born after 1955 are *three times* as likely as their grandparents' generation to suffer from depression" (298). Statistics on women and mental health show that women's risk for depression is twice that of men's, and that women attempt to end their depression through suicide more often than men (DiMona and Herndon 1994, 224). Why are we so bummed out? More importantly perhaps, how are we reacting to our misery, and how are we seeking to overcome it?

Many of my friends describe their experience of depression as existential rather than chemical; in other words, they are quicker to acknowledge that something is wrong with the world around them rather than with their own physical makeup. This implies a frustration and a dissatisfaction with present institutions and systems, and also implies the possibility of an external solution to the problem. There is a fear expressed through voicing one's depression in this manner, a fear that one will soon become part of the problem by being absorbed into the system and being forced to play by the rules of a cultural machine that is ultimately at the root of such deep and bitter angst (a fear not unlike Rollins's). This fear fuels the need for alternative models who will provide examples of modes of being in the world that simultaneously oppose existing power structures and offer clarity and focus for the confused and misdirected young progressive. It is a fear that demands action and incites many members of my generation to examine more closely the system that has shaped and continues to shape their most intimate ways of being.

However, this fear can also be dangerous in that it can possibly instigate us to engage in unexamined, reactionary behavior that ironically does not attack the system but only serves to uphold it. Society prepares us to seek immediate solutions to our problems rather than giving us the tools to undergo lengthy self-examination. A supermarket mentality pervades even the most progressive of minds, whispering that the answer must be readily available, wrapped and stacked and awaiting immediate consumer approval. What can happen, and often does, is that the confused and frustrated individual is offered a prepackaged "alternative" model that isn't alternative at all.

This confusion, depression, and fear becomes especially relevant to the young feminist who is aware that the current social structure holds little for her and that, in fact, may be in some ways responsible for holding her back physically and psychologically. It is imperative for her that she not allow herself to become a contributing member of this "norm." She may express her disdain for cultural conventions through external manifestations of difference: choosing a nontraditional or nongendered mode of dress, piercing strange body parts, accumulating tattoos, shaving her head in new and exciting ways, and so on. Visible bodily inscriptions such as these serve a dual purpose for the young feminist; she is asserting her difference while at the same time claiming her body as her own by physically defining its boundaries. But these manifestations of "difference" are readily co-opted into forms of cultural cool and become norms in themselves.

Unlike body markings, the source of frustration and depression may not always be apparent. Popular culture is the source of many mixed messages that become an integral part of our identities. Feminist cultural criticism can offer some insight into this process and supply a conceptual vocabulary. Reading Susan Faludi's *Backlash: The Undeclared War against American Women* (1991) has done a great deal to clarify for me exactly what messages I am receiving and how those messages uphold traditional gender roles and their extreme extension into fascism.

Quite frankly, much of the rhetoric used during the 1980s to put "uppity women back in their place" reeks of fascism. In her description of the nature of the backlash, Faludi states that "once a society projects its fears onto a female form, it can try to cordon off those fears by controlling women—pushing them to conform to comfortingly nostalgic norms and shrinking them in the cultural imagination to a manageable size" (70). In other words, when the boundaries between male and female (actually, between the constructions of masculine and feminine) become blurred, the backlash male (or female) fears loss of identity and boundary, and seeks to create a more rigid duality that he or she can then use to construct a self-identity. Just as in fascism, backlash masculinity is created in strict opposition to "femininity," which must be flowing, unstable, devouring, irrational—and always a threat. To stem the tide, men (the masculine) must be hard, solid, rational, and machinelike. Through this dualism, the mass (femininity, women) is easier to identify and control, and consequently, life is made safer and easier for the fascist. Existence for the "real man" is not possible without the creation of an Other for him to control and manipulate.

Faludi also points out that the imagery used to depict woman in times of backlash represents her as "silenced, infantilized, immobilized, or, the ultimate restraining order, killed. . . . She is 'the Quiet Woman. . . . She is Laura Palmer" (70). The best woman, from the perspective of the backlash and the fascist, is a dead one, just as the best mass is the annihilated one. The ultimate solution is the most violent and final solution. The message for the woman growing up during such periods is an incredibly confusing one—to live life as a good woman, she must live her life in ways that constrain and kill her Self, even as she is encouraged to develop that self to achieve great things. She must live in ways that perpetuate the system that keeps her from full realization of her life, even as popular rhetoric continuously reminds her of her limitless opportunity.

If the mass learns to control itself, the task of the fascist male is made easier. American culture, for one, has offered women, as members of the "dangerous mass," various ways to control ourselves both physically and emotionally. (Although the methods are different, the same may be said of other members of the mass—the working class, immigrants, nonwhites, etc.) Thanks to the second wave feminist analysis of beauty culture, we can see that fashion gives us corsets, hose, high heels, underwire bras; the "health and beauty" industry gives us paints, powders, dyes, silicon, liposuction; "nutrition" centers offer diets and other ways to become smaller and less present while remaining in continual states of paralyzing obsession; the mental health industry offers Xanax, Valium, and Ativan; and advertising tells us, "You've come a long way, baby," pretending to offer freedom but actually turning the key on a new form of imprisonment. Femininity now, as in the second wave and before, is about constriction.

Although the 1980s are history (timewise), virgin/whore dichotomies of control are still prevalent, truly rebellious women are silenced or killed, and outspoken women such as Madonna, Roseanne, and Courtney Love are focused on as never before when they enter into that state that still serves to define womanhood, even in the 1990s: pregnancy and motherhood. It is amazing how easy it still is for conservative representations to silence and subvert strong female models, reducing them to their biological functions with disturbing ease. *Vanity Fair* demonized the latest media "whore," Courtney Love, for her alleged heroin abuse during pregnancy (Hirschberg 1992, 230), whereas *People* exalted Madonna's straight and "grounded" lifestyle (no drink, no drugs) during the gestation of her infant (Schneider 1996). According to the representations in *People*, Madonna is "like a virgin" now that she has chosen to fulfill her "longing" and "feeling of emptiness" with a Baby (48). The whole "whore" thing, these representations assure us, was just an act—Madonna is really a purist, a true Woman with "natural" impulses that she must acknowledge and submit to. The lesson is clear: extremely successful women are neither successful nor fulfilled until they bow to their ultimate purpose in life, to the only way they can truly be satisfied—by filling the gaping abyss of the womb with potential life. Any other efforts or expenditures of energy are misdirected longings for motherhood and are not really what the woman is about. And what of the woman who becomes pregnant but does not accede to the demands of her natural duties (Courtney Love)? She must be exposed for what she "is"—the worst kind of woman, "unnatural," a whore through and through.

A young feminist can critically attempt to filter through all the bunk she will inevitably encounter about her female role models, or, succumbing to the backlash notion that strength and clarity are masculine traits, she can seek a three-dimensional male model, one presented as a real person capable of successes, contradictions, and mistakes. This model is not reduced to his biology or sexuality (unless he is gay) and serves as a point of focus and clarity that a female model surrounded by controversy cannot. One case in point is Henry Rollins's recent love affair with the media. Here is a white, heterosexual man who, despite his purported "alternativeness," has carved out his existence with the "father's tools": he is a successful entrepreneur, a self-made man, a Teddy Roosevelt kind of guy. Quite simply, white hetero men still receive media coverage that constructs them as whole entities, refuses to question their particular incarnations of masculinity, and ultimately assures the culture that identification with certain types of masculinity is not only acceptable but safe.

How, then, is identification with male models a reality for some third wave feminists, a reality they can't shake despite "knowing better"? Again, the answer can be found in the mixed messages that have recently characterized our culture. Images of masculinity that took over cinema screens from 1980 through 1988 were a significant part of the reinscription of traditional dualisms and constructions of gender. Stallone and Schwarzenegger became the prime examples of the hard-bodied masculinity that pervaded popular culture during this time. Susan Jeffords, in *Hard Bodies: Hollywood Masculinity in the Reagan Era* (1994), critically engages these bodily images and the resurgence of macho masculinity that they represented for a nation that seemed to be in the process of losing its proverbial balls. I will further argue that these hard bodies represented a resurgence of fascist imagery and identification, and readied my generation (men and women alike) for identification with the hard body and imagery of Henry Rollins and others like him.

According to Jeffords, the Reagan presidency was constructed in opposition to the feminized presidency of Jimmy Carter and was presented as a return to American "values" of "strength, labor, determination, loyalty, and courage," all values that could be visually represented in the "hard body" (24): "the Reagan America was to be a strong one, capable of confronting enemies rather than submitting to them, of battling 'evil empires' rather than allowing them to flourish, of using its hardened body . . . to impose its will on others rather than allow itself to be dictated to" (25). The Reagan America was to be a fascist America, constantly in the process of creating itself in opposition to some entity that threatened to engulf it (Communism, in particular). It would be capable of destroying Others.

Thus, the Reagan years became years of erecting and reaffirming boundaries, of creating a dualism between the strength and solidity of masculine America and the softness and fluidity of feminine third world nations. This was occurring at the same time that traditional ideas about women and femininity were reconstructed in opposition to men and masculinity. Popular culture helped some sectors of the American public identify with this hardened version of masculinity by playing on fears about diminishing American prominence and by presenting the fearful with glorified and heroic hard bodies such as Stallone's Rambo. Through this identification, the American public could see itself reflected in the hard body and could view itself as "masterful, as in control of [its] environments . . . , as dominating those around [it] . . . , and as able to resolve crises successfully" (27). In a statement that seems to echo the analysis of Theweleit, Jeffords quotes Antony Easthope: "The purpose of the masculine ego is to master every threat. . . . The castle of the ego is defined by its perimeter and the line drawn between what is inside and what is outside. To maintain its identity it must not only repel external attack but also suppress treason within" (27). This is a masculinity that constantly senses threat (real or imagined) and must be constantly vigilant to avoid confrontation and absorption by an undifferentiated feminine mass. This commonplace masculinity is very similar to the fascist masculinities Theweleit studies.

I was eight years old when Reagan was elected, and twenty when Clinton came to office. During most of those twelve years, I was just a kid trying to grow up and figure my life out, but with no idea of what was going on in the world around me, at least not on a very deep level. I was submerged by the conservative cultural turn and surrounded by its dominant media images, with parents who came of age not in the 1960s but in the 1940s and 1950s. I did not have the critical distance necessary to separate myself from the mixed messages that were thrust at me. By the time I hit high school, I knew that something was up, but I still did not have the ability to do the necessary filtering. In other words, when the shit hit the fan, I was right under it, and there was nothing I could do but get covered and hope for an eventual cleansing shower.

The Concrete Generation

One thing that the backlash did do for me, and for other female members of my generation, was to encourage rejection of all things feminine, as I learned to associate the feminine with women and with things that I did not want to become or to associate with—weakness, lack, obsessive behavior. Through my encounters with the media, my friends, and our parents' own internalized prejudices, I learned that the best way to deal with pain was to shut it out, to grit my teeth and persevere, and never, ever, to cry or show emotion. If the best woman was a dead one, then the second best woman was a man.

I would like to think that some budding feminist consciousness was trying to emerge in my determination to do everything that the boys did (and do it better), but my young rebellions and questionings became entangled with the regressive message I was receiving. As I mentioned earlier, the legacy of second wave feminism had taught me that, as a girl, I could do anything I wanted to do, but the backlash let me know that this was possible only as long as I wasn't a *girl*—as long as I wasn't soft and feminine and weak. I fell victim to the sort of dualistic gender essentialism that I have since learned to reject intellectually but that still makes me skeptical, on an emotional level, of anything that might involve my admittance of a stereotypically feminine quality.

So, in the 1980s, after repeated viewings of *First Blood*; *Rambo: First Blood, Part II*; and *Terminator*, I internalized a very clear image of the type of masculinity that I needed to look to in times of confusion. And, from the center of my confusion, depression, and misanthropy in the 1990s, I did just that. I looked to Henry Rollins as a representative of masculinity that could affirm my own feelings and that I could identify with and utilize as an image of clarity and control. I thought it was safe because Rollins was presented to me as an example of "alternative" masculinity: he hated the system, he was a punk during the Reagan era, he sang with Black Flag. The hard body and mind of Rollins became a reflection of the hardness and imperviousness that I had learned to desire as the only alternative to what I perceived as the softness and weakness of femininity. To draw again from Jeffords, "Such bodies assist in the confirmation of this mastery by themselves refusing to be 'messy' or 'confusing,' by having hard edges, determinate lines of action, and clear boundaries for their own decision-making"

(27). Rollins says in "Hard" (as if to confirm this), "I am because I'm hard" (Rollins Band 1990).

I argue that my generation's "privilege" of coming of age during the 1980s prepared us uniquely for potential identification with figures such as Rollins. Ironically, for the women of my generation, this identification would not be possible without the gains of second wave feminism. This is not to say that second wave feminism is to blame for our misdirection, but rather to acknowledge the fact that we were introduced to the accomplishments of feminism through a time period that reinterpreted and twisted its lessons. Second wave feminism taught us that women could be strong and that they could use their strength to challenge patriarchal power and to fight to overcome oppression. Traditional models of gender taught us that men were strong, that strength equals power in a patriarchal (fascist) society, and that women could not be strong or powerful and still be women. Somewhere along the line, some feminists of my generation interpreted this confusing message to mean that we could not identify with women as models of strength, that we needed a man to fill this role for us.

Thus, the confused and frustrated soul who feels as though she is looking down the barrel of a giant societal vacuum cleaner is able to find "relief" in the clarifying masculinity of Henry Rollins. To her fears of inevitable absorption into confusion, depression, and society, she responds by seeking to stand alone, apart, and above the mess, perhaps even desiring destruction of the system or mass that propagates and feeds homogeneity.[2] She may even feel that this destruction is necessary for her to be safe from the threatening and impending grasp of her fears. It is at this point that she seeks guidance, seeks an individual like Rollins who has seemingly attained the untouchable vantage point, who has seemingly placed himself within a solid enough boundary of scar tissue that the mass will never touch or reach him. He is offered to her as a savior, an alternative to the mass, but in fact *Rollins* is "the mass" that is the patriarchal status quo. He is the embodiment of this destructive system and its continual Othering of women and non-elite men. Yet he seems so far beyond its reach. His position, for the frustrated and confused, is an enviable one. He knows. He's been there. He's told me. Now I must learn. I would gratefully throw away my humanity, my vulnerability, if I could become steel, cement, impermeable, unchangeable—if I could stand clearly apart from the mass that is the source of my confusion, frustration, and pain.

Before I experienced Rollins as an entity unto himself, or as anyone other than just the lead singer for Black Flag, I wrote the following poem:

> i am concrete
> grated and cold and shaped
> by the atmosphere around me
> chipped and flaking
> but recognizable.
> my eyes are steel,
> calculating,
> far-off observers of reality.
> my smile is chrome,
> my teeth
> bright mirrors of industrial laughter.

When Rollins says, "I'm dead to the touch, dead to the words spoken meaninglessly on the streets, dead to the eyes I look through. . . . I see my reflection in cement" (1993, 9), I now know exactly what this means. It's a very edifying moment, for the concrete generation, when we see our feelings reflected so clearly in the steel mirror of Rollins.

A third wave feminist's identification with Henry Rollins is an ironic one indeed. As a feminist, she must actively seek to differentiate herself from patriarchal social structures. As a feminist who grew up during the backlash, she has internalized a tendency to identify her struggle for differentiation and focus with a type of hard-bodied masculinity that reflects the archetype of fascism and patriarchy. In her search for alternative models to look to during her times of crisis, she sometimes ends up choosing a model that represents the same old dualisms, the same old system, the same old poison that is at the root of her initial frustration. It is so easy to hear her struggles reflected in the voice of one who writes, "You're right in it, trying to separate yourself, just like me, trying to separate yourself. . . . I'll show you around these parts" (31). It is a contradiction for a self-identified feminist to find it easy and comforting to identify with a fascist model for responding to fears and concerns. However, it is a contradiction that must be acknowledged and dealt with lest we engage in an unwitting reinscription of the fascism that we are supposed to be fighting against.

One Truly Alternative Alternative

An interview with bell hooks recently appeared in *Re/Search* magazine in an issue with the theme "Angry Women." In the introduction to the interview, which is reprinted in hooks's *Outlaw Culture*, hooks points out that even this alternative media source (*Re/Search*) succumbs to the trivialization and two-dimensionalizing of women's efforts at reconstructing and reconfiguring popular culture:

> In our culture, women of all races and classes who step out on the edge, courageously resisting conventional norms for female behavior, are almost always portrayed as crazy, out of control, mad. . . . Set apart, captured in a circus of raging representations, women's serious cultural rebellion is mocked, belittled, trivialized. It is frustrating, maddening even, to live in a culture where female creativity and genius are almost always portrayed as inherently flawed, dangerous, problematic. (1994, 207)

It is equally frustrating to be a feminist who has internalized the message that the only alternative to this problematic female rebellion is to be found in a truly problematic masculine model the adoption of which only contradicts her feminism.

Within the interview, hooks presents what can be configured as a workable alternative to identification with a fascistic masculinity. Although it remains important for the third wave feminist to desire difference and nonconformity (to the male norm) and to challenge the dualisms that have been under construction for millennia and have recently been confirmed and reestablished by the backlash culture of the 1980s, it is also of crucial importance for the third wave feminist to remain constantly aware of the forces that shape and have shaped her and that ready her for responding in a dangerous manner to her need for differentiation. The interviewer for *Re/Search* touches on the problem when she addresses hooks with the following statement: "Things are so alienated, fascistic, polarized. . . . Everyone who really wants to change the world needs so much to be bonded together with our differences, instead of separated" (216).

Hooks responds by addressing the need to redirect some of the energy for differentiation into community building, but not a community built "in reaction to" what threatens us. The reactionary community is a community built on a fascist model of bonding together in the face of the Other in order to control or destroy it. Alternative communities are built through the intentional tearing down of boundaries, through empathizing with the Other and allowing identification with that Other. Hooks says that

> [This] understanding comes through our capacity to empty out the self and identify with that person whom we normally make

> the Other. In other words, the moment we are willing to give up
> our own ego and draw in the being and presence of someone else,
> we're no longer "Other-ing" them, because we are saying there's
> no space they inhabit that cannot be a space we can connect
> with. (219)

This is no easy solution—it is one that takes time and constant effort to achieve.

The model of rebellion that proposes understanding of and refusal of Othering is very different from rebellion that adopts a fascist model of Othering in order ultimately to define and destroy that Other. The fascist model involves complete intolerance of the Other and the creation of false dualisms that invoke the possibility of an Other. Hooks's model disallows the possibility of an Other, and so flies in the face of conventional dualisms that make a fascist or patriarchal model an option. However, the model of community may still cause a skeptical pause among my generation, as this brings to mind stereotypical associations with constructed femininity (empathy) and the soft, alternative, communal cultures of the 1960s. The desire to form community, to overcome fear of lack and confusion of boundary, is often missing in my generation. The desire to join together and to empathize with the constructed Other has been preempted by a drive to seal oneself off from the pain brought on by the mass. The urge to accept the patriarchal model of individuation and to stand tall and alone pushes one to accept isolation as proof of survival, of strength, of the ability to persevere. However, as I have learned through my own experiences in living in community with three other women for the past year, there is nothing soft about hooks's proposal. Attempting to shape a truly alternative model of living has taken considerably more time, effort, energy, and will than my identification with Rollins ever did. It is continually troubling to find that that old fascist model still holds appeal as an easier alternative to my present situation.

To deal with the internalized contradictions, frustrations, anger, depression, and confusion of this and future generations, third wave feminism must learn to adopt language, metaphors, and theories that acknowledge the reality of the conservative cultural backlash and the effects that conservatism has had on the collective cultural psyche of the nation. It must keep up with the new realities brought about by the information age and must recognize new urges for isolation and the possibilities for constantly shifting personas, appearances, bodies, and boundaries that can be realized through the anonymity provided communicating over the Internet. It must learn how to sift through the new contradictions that form almost daily, such as the expansion of global communications capabilities and the concurrent shrinking of global information networks, juxtaposed with an increasing desire for isolation, nationalism, and rugged self-determination. And it must demand a nonessentializing, dualism-denying, radical theory that addresses constructed dualisms without allowing for the possibility of their unwitting reinscription.

Most important, third wave feminism must be constantly vigilant, aware that it has been intimately shaped by backlash media and popular culture, and able to recognize the contradictions that fuel its desire for change and differentiation. It must be willing to constantly engage in criticism of the models it chooses. This process will last a lifetime for the third wave feminist theorist and will offer none of the quick solutions offered by fascism and patriarchy. Bell hooks speaks of this as being a period of change, a process that leads to denial and a resultant sense of loss of self, despair, and pain. If her analysis is accurate, and if my generation is so miserable because it is experiencing severe growing pains and the agony of evolution, then her advice holds wisdom and hope for the third wave feminist: "There's one way you can look at this: it's like having a sickness in your body that gets more and more fierce as it is passing on to wellness. We don't have to view that period of intense sickness as an invitation to despair, but as a sign of potential transformation in the very depths of whatever pain it is we are experiencing" (242). The transformative potential of pain is something with which most "concrete generation" feminists can identify.

Notes

1. The seminar was held at the University of Kentucky, spring 1995. See Bordo's "Reading the Male Body" (1993), and her forthcoming book on the same subject.

2. In an early piece, Andreas Huyssen (1986) argues that the modernist movement early in the century had the same fear of the "feminized mass" and constructed its tenets at least partially according to that fear.

Works Cited

Bordo, Susan. 1993. "Reading the Male Body." *Michigan Quarterly Review* 32 (fall): 696–737.

diMona, Lisa, and Constance Herndon, eds. 1994. *The 1995 Information Please Women's Sourcebook.* Boston: Houghton Mifflin.

Faludi, Susan. 1991. *Backlash: The Undeclared War against American Women*. New York: Crown.

Hirschberg, L. 1992. "Strange Love." *Vanity Fair*, September, 230–33.

Hooks, bell. 1994. *Outlaw Culture: Resisting Representations*. New York: Routledge.

Huyssen, Andreas. 1986. "Mass Culture as Woman: Modernism's Other." In *Studies in Entertainment: Critical Approaches to Mass Cutlture*, 188–207, edited by Tania Modleski. Bloomington: Indiana University Press.

Jeffords, Susan. 1994. *Hard Bodies: Hollywood Masculinity in the Reagan Era*. New Brunswick, N.J.: Rutgers University Press.

Rollins, Henry. 1992a. *Art to Choke Hearts and Pissing in the Gene Pool*. Los Angeles: 2.13.61 Publications.

———. 1992b. *Black Coffee Blues*. Los Angeles: 2.13.61 Publications.

———. 1993. *Now Watch Him Die*. Los Angeles: 2.13.61 Publications.

Rollins Band. 1988. *Do It*. Texas Hotel compact disk TXH.13.

———. 1990. *Turned On*. 1/4 Stick Records compact disk QS0002CD.

Schneider, Karen S. 1996. "And Baby Makes Three." *People Weekly*, 29 April, 46–51.

Theweleit, Klaus. 1989. *Male Bodies: Psychoanalyzing the White Terror*. Vol. 2 of *Male Fantasies*. Minneapolis: University of Minnesota Press.

Wurtzel, Elizabeth. 1994. *Prozac Nation: Young and Depressed in America*. Boston: Houghton Mifflin.

CHAPTER SIX

Roseanne: A "Killer Bitch" for Generation X

Jennifer Reed

In an interview in the *Advocate*, the longest-running national lesbian and gay magazine of American culture, Roseanne marks herself as a cultural worker who speaks to Generation X feminists. Like many Generation X women (women who grew up with the second wave of feminism), Roseanne eschews the label "feminist" and says she prefers instead "killer bitch." She goes on: "It's women's self-hatred that doesn't allow us to be fighters or artists. It's the same way for black people and gay people."[1] Not only does Roseanne make explicit connections between sexist, racist, and heterosexist oppressions—a project central to third wave feminist organizing—she positions herself as an unequivocal, if irreverent, feminist activist. Although Roseanne is not a part of the Generation X age group, her work exemplifies and shapes third wave feminist sensibilities. Although Generation X feminists have been represented as the logical inheritors and creators of third wave feminism, Roseanne demonstrates that third wave feminism can be described as a discourse, a sensibility, and a politics that transcends strict generational lines. Roseanne, then, is a third wave feminist who speaks to and offers herself to Generation X feminists.

Roseanne's third wave cultural work, not to mention her irreverence, owes a debt to a solid history of feminist organizing, theorizing, and activism. She is not doing the reparative groundwork that earlier feminists had to do—the work of proving women's humanity. So much of that early activism concentrated on developing a cultural conversation that had to begin with defining and articulating "the problem." Early second wave feminists carried the weight of establishing a discourse, a burden that shaped their focus on reclaiming women's identities, re-searching histories, validating perceptions, and creating forums for emerging voices. Roseanne takes that work as her foundation and runs with it. Roseanne's anger is also the legacy of second wave feminism. Twenty-five years of feminist activism have raised expectations among women, and we are often disappointed. Roseanne voices the inevitable rage that comes when the knowledge created by feminist thinking and action encounters the intractability of oppressive forces. This encounter between feminist progress and ongoing feminist struggle in the context of backlash constitutes third wave feminist subjectivity.

Roseanne has made her reputation in mass culture as a loud, aggressive, overweight, working-class woman who always says what is on her mind, who will not be pushed around, who tells her own uncomfortable truths. She is particularly known for exposing the secrets of the bourgeois family by telling her own story and making public her own healing process. In her most recent autobiography, *My Lives*, published and publicized in early 1994 (and which already seems outdated), Roseanne discusses the parental abuse she suffered as a child and the enormous toll it has taken on her life.[2] As an explicit and articulate feminist, she is extremely critical of (among other things) the Hollywood establishment, the business of television, and the mainstream press. Her book is at least in part a response to journalists' portrayal of her as a woman impossible to work for and explosively moody, capriciously firing employees from her show and suing her closest associates. *My Lives* did not endear her to those who already hated her, because it is strongly and unambiguously worded, it is a direct confrontation of those who have hurt her, and it offers an unapologetic version of her own vision and truth.

Since the publication of her book, Roseanne's life has changed dramatically. In the publicity following her divorce from Tom Arnold, her subsequent marriage to her one-time chauffeur Ben Thomas, and the birth of their child Buck, Roseanne's image in dominant culture became increasingly precarious, even (maybe especially) among feminists. Some of my friends and I jokingly lamented that Roseanne was getting more difficult to hold up as a feminist icon. She didn't seem to mind. It is clear that Roseanne is in charge of the creation, if not the reception, of her image. In many ways she is a second wave poster girl living a second wave feminist success story: she is financially independent, makes her own choices and relationships, does the work she loves, and controls that work in ways unprecedented for women. Roseanne creates her own life in a very public way, although not as a role model for anyone. She says she has no interest in being a role model. In fact, she has this to say about role models in the *Advocate* interview: "That's such a bogus concept. People use role models to not get off their asses. If you have to find somebody to copy, you have a serious problem."[3]

This sentiment points to Roseanne's third wave sensibilities. For third wave feminists, there is no one right way to be: no role, no model. One of the strengths of third wave feminism is its refusal of a singular liberal-humanist subjectivity. With no utopic vision of the perfectly egalitarian society or the fully realized individual, third wave feminists work with the fragmentation of existing identities and institutions. If third wave feminism distinguishes itself from the second wave in any definable way, it is in its emphasis on making room for contradictions. We struggle to accommodate the differences and conflicts *between* people as well as *within* them. Third wave feminism looks for, ferrets out, and defines our contradictions—which ones we can live with, which ones we cannot, in ourselves, in our society—and these depend on the context. If we are trying to figure out how to use differences dynamically, creating alternative families and connections, surviving a capitalist society without exploiting others, minimizing our own exploitation and that of other women and men, we can take our role models only from the audacity and tenacity we see modeled in a world that makes no room for us. Roseanne models the courage we need.

It is through the discourses produced by and about third wave feminism—those discourses that encourage the exploration of the complexity and ambiguity constituting cultural productions—that Roseanne's work can be read as transgressive. If the third wave has learned nothing else from the work of the second wave of feminism, it has come to see the limits of the politics of purity. There is no clear line demarcating the inside and outside of hegemonic culture or differentiating the "oppressor" from the "oppressed." Roseanne's interventions into the construction "woman" embody the crucial insight, gained only through the political and cultural work of second wave feminism, that to make any transgressive move at all is to somehow already be part of hegemonic constructions of reality. Her work is a constant negotiation of hegemonic and counterhegemonic discourses based on the knowledge that there is simply no way to step, untainted, out of the hegemonic. The cultural work Roseanne does speaks to Generation X feminists in its recognition of the contradiction, ambiguity, and partiality that constitute the postmodern culture we grew up in, with, and as.

Throughout the second wave and so-called postfeminist years, Roseanne has created her selves in direct confrontation with oppressive forces—as a woman, as a poor woman, as a Jewish woman, as a mother, as all of these combined and more. Roseanne has many incarnations: the Roseanne of her enormously successful sitcom, the Roseanne who appears on talk shows, the Roseanne of her autobiographies, and the Roseanne of her other stage work. In this essay I concentrate on her work for the stage, and on a 1992 piece in particular, *Live from Trump Castle*,[4] but it is important to note that this choice is almost incidental in terms of the cultural work Roseanne does as a particular cultural icon that crosses several media and venues.

The personas Roseanne creates in *Live from Trump Castle* are similar, but not identical, to the ones she has created elsewhere in mass media. Certainly, a live performance in a large nightclub with a relatively small audience sitting at tables and drinking, allows her to be even more outrageous than she can be on national television. This performance was made for video, as well as for the live audience, but not for network television. Roseanne stands alone on the stage and speaks directly to an audience, rather than playing a character interacting with other characters. Roseanne has a full hour and an entire stage to tell us what she thinks, and she does.

After her "favorite husband to date" Tom Arnold warms up the audience, Donald Trump drives Roseanne onto the stage in a shining classic car. In a reversal on the classic "exchange of women," Roseanne is central and in charge, while two men service her, working to make her show happen. Trump helps Roseanne out of the car and she poses like a diva, looking strikingly elegant in a long red dress, a white boa, big silver earrings, and perfectly done makeup, hair, and nails. Roseanne, though, creates an immediate dissonance in what otherwise would look like an uncontested performance of stereotypical femininity. (In)famous for her working-class housewife persona used in her other stand-up and her sitcom work, her pervasive image cannot be dismissed or separated from this appearance. What we see first is the Roseanne we already know, dressed in high femininity. Her parody of femininity works for her in part because she is so well known in so many other media as "Roseanne." She takes that parodic dissonance and works with it and beyond it. Inflected by "Roseanne's" class positioning, this performance's critique of femininity through parody works within a third wave strategy of transgression. Roseanne's use of parodic dissonance enacts the ambivalent relationship to inside/outside distinctions that marks a third wave sensibility. Even as she plays with that ambiguity though, she also carves out a clear confrontation of a misogynist culture.

At the very least, her performance onstage offers alternatives for women. Within the formalized, staged situation where this "unruly" woman is enacted,[5] Roseanne offers different ways for women to envision themselves and their positions, alternatives for their own performances of gender. Natalie Davis suggests that the performance of a different kind of gender, through what she calls "woman-on-top" images of transgressive women, not only offers women the possibility to question the "natural order of things," such as gender and family arrangements, but also could stimulate new ways of thinking about established power relations and inspire women to "exceptional action."[6] As Davis makes the point, the transgressive performance of the unruly woman always holds the possibility of offering *some women* ways to think about change, different ways to conceptualize reality and their own lives. Transgressive performances might inspire those women who are looking for other ways to see.[7]

Davis also points out that these types of performances can reinforce prevailing social relationships by allowing temporary release from their pressure—the safety valve function—but such performances are also always "part of the conflict over efforts to change the basic distribution of power within the society." Like other third wave feminists, Roseanne's power to subvert existing power relations comes from connecting her outrageousness with the "everyday circumstances outside the privileged time of carnival and stage-play."[8] The point is not just that Roseanne is outrageous, but that she is an outrageous housewife, speaking within and about heterosexuality, nuclear family life, and her everyday life. As Davis argues, outrageousness is presented as an option for "ordinary" women living within heterosexual nuclear families. Roseanne is Davis's "ordinary woman," showing and telling other ordinary women how to be disorderly within their positions as wives and mothers, questioning and recreating these roles. Roseanne speaks as a "domestic goddess,"[9] a goddess certainly, but domesticated nonetheless, laughing (all the way to the bank) at all of it through parody, distancing herself through masquerade, transgressing through the performance of grotesque, but still speaking mainly to other people in similar positions. Having gained fame and fortune precisely by being the disorderly yet domesticated woman, Roseanne speaks to, and perhaps for, dissatisfied, rebellious, unruly, "ordinary" heterosexual women.

Roseanne's transgressions work for her because she is the creator of this image and because it is so well known in popular culture. Kathleen Rowe argues that Roseanne's sitcom character derives much of her power from the fact that Roseanne is the author: "Perhaps her greatest unruliness lies in the presentation of herself as *author* rather than actor and, indeed, as author of a self over which she claims control. Her insistence on her 'authority' to create and control the meaning of Roseanne is an unruly act *par excellence*. . . ."[10] The sitcom character "Roseanne" is based on the character she developed as her stand-up persona. She has waged an almost continuous battle with male network executives to retain and sustain her authority over the voice and vision of "Roseanne." *My Lives* includes the most recent and comprehensive chronicle of her fight to maintain control of her character.

Another example from this performance illustrates how Roseanne's strategies of parody, excess, and masquerade work together. Roseanne sarcastically asks the audience to take one minute from their lives to contemplate world peace, and she calls Tom onto the stage to help her onto the piano while they do. The piano plays a suspenseful, drumroll sound as Tom successfully hoists her onto the piano; the audience cheers and Tom limps offstage as though he has a hernia. Roseanne, comfortably sprawled on the piano, leans back to tell a story about a time in the early 1970s when she lived on an Indian reservation and met a man named Billy Jack. She can hardly keep from laughing as the piano lightly plays the theme from the movie *Billy Jack*. She then breaks into the song: "Now the valley cried with anger. . . ." She sings louder and more off-key, jumps off the piano, and keeps singing until she is shrieking the song. She has violated most of the rules of feminine decorum by foregrounding her fat body, treating her husband as her servant, and singing off-key in a voice well beyond the bounds of the acceptably feminine. She has used her body and her words to take up more space than "woman" is allowed. Excess is the most obvious strategy Roseanne uses to transgress femininity.

Roseanne uses the element of masquerade equally effectively in her performance of an unruly or disorderly woman, and she employs sarcasm to do so. During this part of the performance, she takes shots at some of the naive assumptions of the 1960s and 1970s that *Billy Jack* exemplifies. When she has finished singing the *Billy Jack* song, the piano music switches to the tune of "What the World Needs Now." With this juxtaposition, Roseanne talks about how the world does need love and peace, as the ideals of the 1960s told us: "For if we were all holding hands, no one could push the button. And if we all had a great big dick in our mouths, no one could speak ill of another. Let's start by holding hands." As her words make fun of the era of peace and love, it is even more apparent in her sarcastic tone and facial expressions that nothing is sacred. From exaggerated femininity to the ideals of the 1960s, Roseanne plays the distance from the qualities and sentiments she enacts: she makes clear that none of this is essentially her, or essentially true.

Roseanne's performance strategies distance her from an essentialized woman, whether feminine or feminist, and create a third wave subjective space. Not only does she illustrate that "woman" can be put on, and thus taken off, she is the one in charge of when and how to use various signifiers of femininity and feminism. The entire project is about creating herself, making herself and her desires and perceptions out of the materials she has to work with. Her stance is not quite oppositional, but rather indifferent to the audience. She is not seeking approval, from us or anyone else. She plays a woman who has created herself and lives and speaks on her own terms. At one point when she is receiving applause, she says to the audience in a sardonic tone, "Thank you, thank you. I feel your love and I bask in it. Trust me."

In keeping with a third wave sensibility, Roseanne's performances embody multiple subjectivity. Even though Roseanne does not play multiple characters in *Live from Trump Castle*, she still represents a version of Sue-Ellen Case's "collective subject,"[11] in that there is no single, unified self onstage. Roseanne presents a number of selves, selves that often conflict with each other and none of which she seems to take very seriously. In other words, Roseanne has enough distance from all of her selves so that she laughs at them with the spectators. Our identification and our pleasure in watching come from the multiplicity and contradiction that she enacts. Spectators identify with the experience of having fragmented selves, selves that are not in agreement, are often in direct conflict with each other, and do not constitute a coherent, seamless whole. Through the refusal of a naturalized, unified, completely rational and understandable self, and the assertion of a desiring body, along with the exposure and foregrounding of bodily processes, Roseanne *complicates* female identity rather than defining it. The parody of femininity, along with the performance of excess, works to undermine dominant ideological constructions of the human subject in general and of "woman" in particular. Roseanne's performances continue the feminist body-image activism of the second wave in an irreverent and skeptical third wave style.

As I have noted, excess is Roseanne's signature transgressive strategy. Roseanne's fat body is among the most immediately visible and radically destabilizing forces she uses. Rosalind Coward makes the point that in dominant U.S. culture, the ideal feminine body is that of an adolescent, a slight and immature body that connotes powerlessness. In contrast, Coward writes, "Fat women can be extremely imposing. A large woman who is not apologizing for her size is certainly not a figure to invite the dominant meanings to which our culture attaches to femininity."[12] By performing her fat body unapologetically, Roseanne breaks one of the cardinal rules of "woman." In the words of Rowe, "For women, excessive fatness carries associations with excessive willfulness and excessive speech."[13] Roseanne does not hope we do not notice her fat body. She foregrounds her body throughout the show, drawing attention to her weight with jokes that are not at all self-deprecating or apologetic. She doesn't try to explain away her weight, she doesn't make the jokes at her own expense, she doesn't use them for pity, she doesn't use them to say that she is not attractive, and she doesn't allow a fat body to desexualize her. By talking about her fat body, she refuses to erase it or hide it.

Early in the show, in a medley of old jokes, Roseanne says, "Well, I'm fat. I thought I'd point that out." She then gives an example of how fat people think differently than thin people, by imitating how a fat person would give directions. All of the markers in the directions are fast-food restaurants, ending with, "It's that chocolate brown building over there on the left, you can't miss it." In another bit, about gay men, she says, "I thank God for gay men. If not for them, us fat women would have no one to dance with." Comments about her fat body are interspersed throughout the show and combined with a sarcastic, unapologetic, loud style that links fat voice to fat body. She swears and she uses incorrect grammar. Her voice is uncontrolled, unmodulated, often shrill. She yells and screeches with abandon. Such bigness of both movement and speech is integral to the unruly woman's performance.

Sandra Lee Bartky writes that "women are far more restricted than men in their movement and in their spatiality."[14] Feminine movement and gesture are confined and constricted. Women learn to take up as little room as possible, staying within a narrow range of distance from the body's center, moving tensely and carefully. In contrast, Roseanne plays the "loose woman." Bartky writes, "The 'loose woman' violates these norms: her looseness is manifest not only in her morals, but in her manner of speech and quite literally in the free and easy way she moves."[15] Clearly, Roseanne plays the "loose woman" in every sense of the term, but two moments in particular illustrate the ways in which she combines that style with explicit social and political critique. Speaking about how "men only want one thing," she says: "Can you imagine what it was like, that meeting that men had to decide what that one thing that men want out of life was going to be?" In a very gruff voice, she takes on the persona of the man in charge of the meeting: "All right, listen fellas, I call this meeting to order. Can I have your attention? Shut up. All right. I got two votes over here for power tools. The chair recognizes Hiram." Now, as Hiram, in a gentle, lilting voice: "What if the one thing we wanted out of life was to nurture the life force in every living thing?" As the chair: "Yeah, uh, the chair says Hiram is a fag and doesn't deserve to have a penis. The chair recognizes Tony." As Tony, spitting on the floor and grabbing his crotch, burping, and snorting: "All right, now this may sound a little old-fashioned, guys, but what if the one thing we wanted out of life was pussy?" As chair: "Well, the chair likes pussy. All those in favor say 'aye.' . . . All right, so whaddya say, guys, we all get outta here, we go try to find some pussy, and if we can't find any, we come back here and beat the shit outta Hiram?"

Especially in her enactment of Tony, Roseanne here performs the excess of bodies: it is excessive because most often in hegemonic culture, we are trained not to notice anything about the body that calls attention to itself. Just as Roseanne does not allow her own body to be invisible, she does not allow other bodies or bodily processes to be erased, and she plays an exaggerated male body so as to make an oppressive masculinity visible. As Rowe says, "Her body epitomizes the grotesque body of Bakhtin, the body which exaggerates its processes, its bulges and orifices, rather than concealing them as the monumental, static 'classical' or 'bourgeois' body does. . . ."[16] In both her performative style and her narrative text, Roseanne foregrounds corporality, critiquing bourgeois norms as well as the limits imposed on femininity.

In the same vein, she performs a lengthy piece on women's experiences of menstruation. She says, "It's hard being a woman. . . . It's harder for us than it is for you men. Maybe it would be easier for us if we were only one woman, but no, we have to have that twenty-eight-day cycle, and during that twenty-eight days, at least that many personalities come and inhabit your body, and you're helpless." Roseanne goes on to enact, in an exaggerated manner, several of the personalities she experiences as part of her "normal" cycle. She uses her face, voice, and body in an uninhibited way to express her hostility and moodiness, her desire for control of her life, and her ambitions to be better and to work out. She becomes the exhausted woman who feels guilt for not taking good enough care of the kids, the woman who is awestruck by life itself, and the horny woman who says, "I just want to be and get fucked. I want it one time in the morning to open my eyes, then I want it one time at night just to close 'em. Then I want it one more time during the day, just 'cause I know he don't want to. And then I want . . . chocolate." She becomes the self-pitying woman, the victim, the eager-to-please woman, and the angry woman.

Both of these multiplicity monologues exemplify Roseanne's exposure of bodily processes, by enacting them and talking about them, as a strategy not to be "gross" or "crass" for its own sake, but to make larger political points. In the first monologue she confronts heterosexual, heterosexist, and homophobic assumptions of a masculinity that objectifies women, abhors what and who it labels "feminine," and embraces violence as a form of self-expression. And in the second, she makes visible and audible and funny a common women's experience, one that historically has been taboo to mention and, thus, instilled with shame and embarrassment, or that has been the object of misogynist derision, dismissal, and derogation. Roseanne talks about menstruation here like she talks about fat: it is a biological fact that requires no apology, embarrassment, or explanation. This piece in particular demonstrates Roseanne's use of the multiplicity and fragmentation of her selves to *describe* her experience of herself. And by making her own fat and her own menstrual cycle visible in her own words, she works to wrest female bodies from the control of misogynist discourse that makes fatness and menstruation shameful for women.

Roseanne marks herself as an unruly or loose woman through her performance of excess, her loud voice, her aggressive posture, her working-class syntax, her nonconstricted, abundant body, and her observations and opinions (that is, what she says). Mary Russo would call Roseanne's performance that of a "grotesque body," because she does what is particularly dangerous for women: she "makes a spectacle of herself." For a woman, Russo writes, this has "to do with a kind of inadvertency and loss of boundaries. . . . [Such women step] into the limelight out of turn—too young, too old, too early or too late—and yet anyone, any woman, could make a spectacle out of herself if she was not careful."[17] Russo argues that the grotesque woman, marked by a performance of parody, excess, and gender masquerade, is a potentially productive strategy for feminist intervention into the category "woman." It offers the possibility to go beyond the critique of what-is-always-there, "woman," to a counterhegemonic re-performance of gender, a radicalization of heterogender.

Negotiating the possibilities and limitations of gender roles has been a particularly accessible strategy for the third wave, and is a luxury provided by the groundwork done by second wave feminists. That work created the space for the irreverence, parody, dissonance, and irony that Roseanne uses to create a new subjective space for women. This, then, is a subjective space that negotiates the ambivalence inherent in the use of these strategies. This construction of "woman" both parodies and embraces glamour, the trappings of high femininity, and the very performance of gender and of heterorelating. In other words, it is a construction committed to working with the contradictions and the irreconcilability that constitute any attempt at carving out subjective space for women. This is one of the primary offerings the third wave makes to feminism.

Notes

1. Roseanne, "Her Life as a Woman," interview by Peter Galvin, *Advocate*, 24 January 1995, 54.

2. Roseanne Arnold, *My Lives* (New York: Ballantine, 1994).

3. Roseanne, "Her Life as a Woman."

4. *Roseanne Arnold: Live from Trump Castle*, written and produced by Roseanne Arnold and Tom Arnold, directed by Roseanne Arnold and Louis J. Horvitz, 55 min., Columbia TriStar, 1992, videocassette.

5. Kathleen K. Rowe, "Roseanne: Unruly Woman as Domestic Goddess," *Screen* 31 (winter 1990): 410. *Unruly* is a term Rowe uses to identify Roseanne (Arnold's) am-

bivalence and power. Her power comes from her position as "unruly woman," a woman who transgresses "woman." The unruly woman is a woman who steps out of the lines demarcated for femininity: "Through body and speech, the unruly woman violates the unspoken feminine sanction against 'making a spectacle of herself.' I see the unruly woman as prototype of woman as subject—transgressive above all when she lays claim to her own desire."

6. Natalie Davis, "Women on Top," in *Society and Culture in Early Modern France* (Stanford: Stanford University Press, 1975), 124–51. Davis is writing particularly about the performances of gender inversion in early modern Europe, not about contemporary performances. Her insights apply here to the possibilities offered by such performances, as basic gender arrangements still apply.

7. See Marilyn Frye, *The Politics of Reality* (Freedom, Calif.: Crossing, 1983), 170–71. Frye writes about the ways in which "phallocratic reality" shapes what we can see and what we cannot see. Part of seeing new possibilities for ourselves involves finding ways to see beyond or around or through phallocratic reality.

8. Davis, "Women on Top," 131.

9. Rowe, "Roseanne," discusses Roseanne's use of "domestic goddess" as a name for herself as an act of self-definition, "telling a truth that in her case is both ironic and affirmative" (412).

10. Ibid., 409–10.

11. Sue-Ellen Case, "From Split Subject to Split Britches," in *Feminine Focus: The New Women Playwrights,* ed. Enoch Brater (New York: Oxford University Press, 1989), 143.

12. Rosalind Coward, *Female Desires: How They Are Sought, Bought, and Packaged* (New York: Grove, 1985), 41.

13. Rowe, "Roseanne," 410.

14. Sandra Lee Bartky, "Foucault, Femininity, and the Modernization of Patriarchal Power," in *Feminism and Foucault,* ed. Irene Diamond and Lee Quinby (Boston: Northeastern University Press, 1988), 66. Bartky, building on a Foucauldian analysis, makes the point that feminine bodies are produced by a myriad of modern cultural practices. The body constructed to be feminine is a body made to be deferential, subordinate. The feminine body's subordinate status is manifested in any number of narrowly defined behaviors. Feminine bodies must be small, thin, hairless, circumscribed in their movements, and decorated.

15. Ibid.

16. Rowe, "Roseanne," 413.

17. Mary Russo, "Female Grotesques: Carnival and Theory," in *Feminist Studies/ Critical Studies,* ed. Teresa de Lauretis (Bloomington: Indiana University Press, 1986), 213.

CHAPTER SEVEN

A Tale of Two Feminisms: Power and Victimization in Contemporary Feminist Debate

Carolyn Sorisio

We have heard the old tale—how Betty Friedan's *The Feminine Mystique* brushed against a generation of women's lips with a hard kiss, waking Adrienne Rich's dead. The feminist movement of the 1960s and 1970s brought tangible change. In my field of feminist literary criticism, the newly resurrected struggled for representation of women writers in the curriculum and a better understanding of women in history. Thinkers as diverse as Hélène Cixous and the team of Sandra M. Gilbert and Susan Gubar held one common assumption—"woman" was a category that merited serious scrutiny; it was a word with weight. Yet now we hear another tale. We are postfeminist. Women don't want to call themselves the "f" word. Heavily influenced by the Reagan-Bush years, young Americans "completely recoil at anything too militant, too angry, too extremist."[1] Worse yet, feminism is cast as a tragic hero crafting its own demise. A monolithic "we" considers women passive victims of male sexual and economic violence. "We" have deployed a "fem police" that regulates the thoughts, sexuality, and choices of women in the name of equality.[2] Our dogma is stale, our ideology rigid, our fashion tastes hopelessly passé.

Although by no means uniform, much of the criticism aimed at feminism in the media for the past several years focuses on a few points of contention. First, feminists are charged with prescribing "correct" forms of feminine behavior, especially in relation to sexuality. Sally Quinn, in the *Washington Post*, contends that feminist leaders are not able "to separate the work place from the bedroom" and want "to regulate people's behavior in their personal lives."[3] Second, white, middle-class feminists allegedly revel in their self-imposed status of victims. For example, Wendy Kaminer pauses before reviewing Katie

Roiphe's *The Morning After: Rape, Fear, and Feminism on Campus* to explain that the "expression of oppression" is a general rule in feminism. "Protesting their sexual victimization enables privileged, heterosexual white women to claim a share of the moral high ground ceded to the victims of racism, classism, and homophobia," she maintains.[4]

Even more severe sins are laid at academic feminists' feet. We are denounced as rigidly dogmatic and irreparably esoteric. Writers refer to a sinister "sisterhood" that controls dissent and, ever conspiratorial, wields unprecedented power. Daphne Patai claimed in 1992 that women of color controlled the women's studies department at the University of Massachusetts at Amherst, despite the fact that she was then its acting director. She writes in the *Chronicle of Higher Education* that "as if in compensation for past oppression, no one can challenge or gainsay their version of reality."[5] Christina Hoff Sommers, author of *Who Stole Feminism: How Women Have Betrayed Women*, caricatures women's studies as impossibly trite. Nonetheless, she accuses an allegedly potent feminist clique of manipulating information about rape, sexual harassment, gender bias, and other women's issues. "The steady stream of errors, myths and screw-ups are not accidental" she told a crowd of undergraduates.[6] Denying any common ground, she informed the *Washington Post* that "The thing is, we're not a tribe. We're not a class. We do not have a shared vision."[7]

If not downright conspiratorial, academic feminists are nonetheless characterized as out of touch, confining ourselves to a realm of theory with no tangible significance in either the political or the personal sphere. A columnist in the *New York Times* chides, "try telling a welfare mother or a harried secretary that they should worry about being a victim of the unconscious process of phallocentric language."[8] Naomi Wolf thinks American female feminists seize on poststructural French feminist thought, as if to prove that we are as complex as many male intellectuals. "Here's something of our own that's just as hard," she imagines academics reasoning. "We'll teach it to our own kids, and no one will know what *we're* talking about either."[9]

In the 1980s and 1990s, feminism has become a paradox. On the one hand, it is perceived as so powerful that it has initiated a backlash, as is evidenced by the now truly banal "political correctness" wars. In this framework, women and people of color are awarded far more power than they actually exert. On the other hand, Susan Faludi's *Backlash: The Undeclared War against American Women* (1991) reveals the somber truth that, contrary to perception, women in the 1980s suffered major economic, legal, and cultural setbacks.[10] In my field on a national level, women writers and writers of color are not being included, beyond a few tokens, in the majority of classes.[11] Is it possible that feminism has become Virginia Woolf's Mrs. Ramsay? Is it so ubiquitous as to be diffused?

This is a depressing conclusion. Unlike so many women of my generation who the media tells me have disowned feminism, I have always considered myself a feminist. And unlike the women who unwittingly depict themselves as victims of an allegedly victim-producing movement, I consider feminism a quest that we continually redefine, rather than a doctrine that seeks to confine me. The question translates, for me, into what feminist scholarship is doing for women in general. I take the charges against academic feminists earnestly. However, it is too facile to dismiss theoretical sophistication as irrelevant to women's progress, and to imply that feminism should somehow be anti-intellectual. The nineteenth century, for example, left us the legacy of Margaret Fuller, whose *Woman in the Nineteenth Century* is a very complex and often difficult feminist theoretical text. Yet it also gave us such reformers as Lydia Maria Child and Frances E. W. Harper, who attempted to reach as large an audience as possible, even if it meant creating a very different aesthetic than Fuller's. We are richer for all three. Movements can take many forms, and although theory may not translate directly or perceivably into material gains, it has a role to play. Nonetheless, I am concerned that academics all too often talk only within our own circle, and need to make a more concerted effort to participate as clearly as possible in cultural debate.

The charges against both academic and mainstream feminism deserve serious consideration. Three recently published books raise concerns that also surface in the media: Katie Roiphe's *The Morning After: Sex, Fear, and Feminism on Campus* (1993), Naomi Wolf's *Fire with Fire: The New Female Power and How It Will Change the Twenty-First Century* (1993), and Camille Paglia's *Sex, Art, and American Culture* (1992).[12] These three women obtained considerable attention in the 1990s, and all contribute to the debate about victimization, dogmatic rigidity, and theoretical obscurity. By examining the relationship between popular feminist critique and issues within contemporary feminist scholarship, I hope to help bridge the gap between the two and to suggest ways in which academic feminists can best serve contemporary causes.[13]

Katie Roiphe's 1991 *New York Times* column "Date Rape Hysteria"[14] set off a wave of media attention and spawned *The Morning After*. Roiphe argues that white middle- and upper-class feminists have exaggerated incidents of date rape and sexual harassment to secure precocious power through victim identity. Although she spends some space challenging statistics about the number of sex crimes on campuses, Roiphe is more concerned with evaluating rhetoric. Describing a "Take Back the Night" rally at Princeton, Roiphe concludes that "there is strength in numbers, and unfortunately right now there is strength in being the most oppressed" (44). She interprets educational materials as regressing to Victorian ideas of the passionless woman. "Again and again," she charges, "the rape-crisis movement peddles images of gender relations that deny female desires and infantilize women" (65). By overstating the prevalence of sex offenses, feminists debilitate women by fostering an environment of fear. It is not rape or harassment, but rather the feminist response to these practices, that frightens this young champion of individual agency. Likewise, it is not sexual harassment that creates a "chilly" atmosphere for women on campus, but rather feminist surveillance of professors' actions. She charges feminists with generating "an atmosphere of suspicion and distrust" that "can lead professors to keep female students at a distance" (92–93).

Like her younger counterpart, the self-proclaimed heir of the 1960s, Camille Paglia, also accuses mainstream feminism of wallowing in victimization:

> Never in history have women been freer than they are here. And
> this idea, this bitching, bitching, kvetching about capitalism and
> America and men, this whining—it's infantile, it's an adolescent
> condition, it's *bad* for women. It's very, very bad to convince
> young women that they have been victims and that their heritage
> is nothing but victimization. (274)

Also similar to Roiphe, Paglia expends her greatest energy on her analysis of feminism and sexuality, calling for a new kind of feminism "that stresses personal responsibility and is open to art and sex in all their dark, unconsoling mysteries" (vii). Paglia gained national media attention for her outlandish claims, such as suggesting that date rape was really the result of "white middle-class girls coming out of pampered homes, expecting to do whatever they want," and then crying victim when they are attacked (268). She also smacks of primitivism, portraying working-class and ethnic women as celebrating the rawness of their culture. "Everyone knows throughout the world," Paglia asserts in her characteristically sweeping way, "that many of these working-class relationships where women get beat up have hot sex. . . . Maybe she won't leave him because the sex is very hot" (65).

Paglia's attack on the academy contains similar generalizations. Repeatedly, she portrays women's studies as slapped together haphazardly, as a "disaster" that should be eliminated (281–82). Yet she fires her heaviest artillery at the French, particularly at Jacques Lacan and his "overpraised feminist propagandists Hélène Cixous and Luce Irigaray." In a front-page 1991 *New York Times Book Review* essay, Paglia rebukes American academics for being "down on their knees kissing French egos." Not one for wasting time on theoretical specification, Paglia assesses French theory: "Of course the French felt decentered: they had just been crushed by Germany." Ever the tourist in "exotic" cultures, Paglia juxtaposes the intellectually deadened French to African American culture, which, presumably in a sort of preintellectual libidinal state, is "alive and ecstatic."[15]

Although both Roiphe and Paglia critique victimization, they have opposite beliefs about the origin of gendered behavior. Roiphe does not want to reduce identity to biology. Therefore, her sharpest assault is on Catharine MacKinnon, whom she accuses of presenting essentialist notions of identity. In MacKinnon's worldview, Roiphe charges, "men and women are inexorably locked into their roles" (158). Paglia's work is informed by the antithetical belief; she contends that men are physiologically more aggressive than women. "Hunt, pursuit, and capture are biologically programmed into male sexuality" she argues (51). Complaining that no one wants to talk about nature, Paglia laments the "contempt for science" that is going on in the humanities and charges feminists with ignoring biological difference (258).

Wolf's *Fire with Fire*, which is better researched and better argued than Roiphe's and Paglia's work, also advocates "power feminism" rather than "victim feminism." Wolf concedes that the image of feminism generated by the male-run media estranges many women, but she concentrates on what she sees as alienating aspects within feminism itself (60). The secret to women's success—one she believes many feminists have ignored—lies in women knowing how to end their own victimization and claim power. "Women are suffering from much subordination for no more pressing reason than that we have stopped short of compelling it to end," she suggests in an optimistically willful way (50–51). The answer? Wolf urges women to do three things: "to fantasize political retribution for an insult to sex, to claim and use money, and to imagine and enjoy winning" (36).

Like Roiphe and Paglia, Wolf also maintains that feminism restricts sexuality, creating "an elaborate vocabulary with which to describe sexual harm done by men, but almost no vocabulary in which a woman can celebrate sex with men" (184). Wolf proceeds to "come clean" with her "subjective truth": "I am sick of the opposition trying to make me choose between being sexual and serious; and I am sick of being split the same way by victim feminism. I want to be a serious thinker and not have to hide the fact that I have breasts; I want female sexuality to accompany, rather than undermine, female political power" (185). Except for her references to Andrea Dworkin, who hardly speaks for all feminists, Wolf is never clear as to how her socially sanctioned heterosexuality has been silenced. Yet her "subjective truth" is still a serious accusation; the movement that embraced sexual liberation is now being accused of silencing, even policing, sexuality.

More important to Wolf's argument than her heterosexual confessions is her critique of Marxist feminism, which she depicts as pathetically 1960s. Although Marxism once usefully linked issues of gender, money, and power, its hangover now results in "victim feminism." "These attitudes, which are passé now almost everywhere else in the world, are foolish burdens to carry," Wolf explains (68). "Power feminism," as defined by Wolf, makes capital the primary means of solidarity among women: "It calls for alliances based on economic self-interest and economic giving back rather than on a sentimental and workable fantasy of cosmic sisterhood" (53). Claiming "there is no more 'radical' system imaginable than the one we have inherited," Wolf encourages women to expand American liberal democratic ideology (115). Capitalism and individualism can be radical, and women must learn "to ask for more, always more" (243). By rejecting what she calls the "sentimental" and endorsing capitalistic individualism, Wolf effectively dismisses any feminist critique of American national identity. This stance is particularly troublesome, as it ignores the negative impact on women in other nations when American women seek "more, always more" of the world's resources.

Wolf's dismissal of women from other classes and nations is typical of these works, which all ignore or trivialize class and race difference. As I have discussed, Paglia tends to characterize various ethnic and working-class people as "naturally" more sexual. As hooks suggests, Paglia "unabashedly articulates white cultural imperialist representations of her beloved neoprimitive darkies."[16] Although Roiphe does not directly denigrate the working class, she elides all serious discussion of race and class and opts, instead, to base her argument primarily on her personal experience at Harvard and Princeton. Likewise, rather than assessing feminist theory by evaluating some of today's most influential feminist thinkers, Roiphe crafts her discussion on her subjective response to graduate seminars. This hearsay analysis leads her to conclude, "This is a game I don't want to learn, this is a tea party without tea, and I have gone through the looking glass" (114–15). Yet it is illogical to assess feminism by examining such a nonrepresentative group of women. I can remember my own undergraduate years, and I still shudder at the way many of us translated complex feminist ideas into small bites that we could chew and spit out whenever convenient at campus events. Did we announce, and perhaps believe, some preposterous things? Certainly. But they were no more ridiculous than the arguments posed by the College Republicans or the Young Americans for Freedom, and it would be just as unfair to base a critique of "conservative" politics on what those young students had to say in the exhilarating yet deceptively fluctuating atmosphere of the college campus.

By refusing to name the feminist theorists she implicates or to analyze their ideas seriously, Roiphe creates an inaccurately monolithic portrayal of what is a very complex, dynamic, and contentious field. She repeats the common pattern of replacing specific people and arguments with the all-encompassing category "feminists." Wolf, a Yale graduate, is also suspect for her "subjective truths." Reading both books, I get the unsettling feeling that, much like the 1970s feminist work they implicitly rebel against, both Roiphe and Wolf extrapolate too readily from their personal experiences to comment on feminism in general. Contrary to what they imply, all of America does not follow the Ivy League.

Nonetheless, the challenges they pose must be addressed. The charge of "victim feminism" seems to have generated the most attention. To attribute this recognition solely to an antifeminist backlash ignores other aspects crucial to the debate. Let's be clear here. The language of "victimization," much like "political correctness" several years ago, has been co-opted for a political agenda that goes far beyond gender. Critiques of "victim feminism" appeal to the myth of rugged individualism, the belief that anyone can overcome obstacles and succeed in American society. Pouring historically exploited groups into one victimization mold enables some Americans to disclaim any debt we may have as citizens who greatly benefit from gender, class, and race inequity. It obscures the true dynamics of power and absolves responsibility.

Critics of "victim feminism," while targeting some problems of mainstream feminism that I will presently highlight, play all too easily into antifeminist hands. For example, George Will hailed Roiphe for challenging the "victimization sweepstakes" that the government and media allegedly award. He then pushed her argument to his own politically useful conclusion, arguing that Anita Hill was one more woman posing as a victim to please liberals and the media.[17] Likewise, *Forbes* magazine dedicated two pages to a harsh review of *Backlash*, in which Gretchen Morgenson accuses Faludi of proposing paranoid conspiratorial theories and damaging women by ruining their self-esteem. "People who feel sorry for themselves don't usually put forth maximum effort," Morgenson concludes.[18] It is hard, indeed, in this atmosphere of optimistic individualism, to find a way to discuss the means by which groups are oppressed or exploited without seeming to be yet another victim coming out with a personal narrative of pain.

Although what some are calling "victim feminism" is only one tendency in a multifaceted field, it has serious implications for feminism's future. In my area of feminist literary scholarship, the notion of women as universal victims resurfaced in the 1970s and lingers today. The 1979 publication of Sandra Gilbert and Susan Gubar's *The Madwoman in the Attic: The Woman Writer and the Nineteenth-Century Literary Imagination* best represents this trend. The authors begin by asking if the pen is a "metaphorical penis" and argue that nineteenth-century women writers faced tremendous anxiety about their work.[19] As more historical research is completed, however, we learn that Gilbert and Gubar's depiction is not the whole story, especially in America, where women participated in the popular literary marketplace and penned many of that century's best-sellers. Historical and biographical work on a wider selection of writers leads feminists to reconsider notions of victimization, identity, and power.

Gilbert and Gubar's emphasis on victimization stems in part from its "gynocritical" viewpoint, a popular mode of feminist literary scholarship in the 1970s. Historically, gynocriticism marked a move away from studying the works of male authors and scholars in a male-dominated canon. In this practice, women's works are analyzed in relation to one another in their own literary tradition.[20] Elaine Showalter defines "gynocriticism" in her 1989 introduction to *Speaking of Gender*, an anthology that marks a shift to examining both genders: "Women can differentiate their positions from any number of stereotypes of femininity, and define themselves also in terms of being black, lesbian, South African or working-class; but to deny that they are affected by being women at all is self-delusion or self-hatred, the legacy of centuries of denigration of women's art."[21] Showalter claims "woman" as a category of great importance to identity, one that a person can tailor to race, class, sexual orientation, and so on. As her description of gynocriticism implies, one common assumption is that "all writing by women is marked by gender."[22] Thus, even as other components of personality were theoretically investigated, some feminists were reluctant to give up gender as the primary means of self-identification. Additionally, not only was a text considered to be informed by gender, but gender was too readily linked with an assumption of women's subjugation. This approach made "victim" somewhat synonymous with "woman." It became a way of visualizing solidarity among disparate groups.

Perceiving gender as the primary identity marker led many scholars to ignore race, class, and cultural differences that are not incidental but absolutely essential to feminism. In a sense, Roiphe, Paglia, and Wolf correctly call "victim feminism" harmful. However, it is not for the reasons they explore. Rather, it is injurious because it allows white bourgeois women to inaccurately absorb others' experiences into their own, to force them into a rhetoric of "sisterhood" or a category of "woman" that may not adequately describe different women's experiences. Bell hooks makes this argument in her *Feminist Theory: From Margin to Center* (1984). She contends that bonding as victims allows white women to avoid confronting their responsibility for sexism, racism, and classism.[23] She maintains:

> A central tenet of modern feminist thought has been the assertion
> that "all women are oppressed." . . . Sexism as a system of domina-
> tion is institutionalized but it has never determined in an absolute
> way the fate of all women in this society. . . . Many women in this
> society do have choices (as inadequate as they are)[;] therefore
> exploitation and discrimination are words that more accurately
> describe the lot of women collectively in the United States.[24]

Hooks suggests that one of the reasons many black women do not identify themselves as feminists is the tendency of white middle-class women
to cling to a theory of common oppression. She argues that women who
are exploited or oppressed daily cannot afford to relinquish the belief
that they exercise some measure of control, however relative, over
their lives. It would be psychologically demoralizing for these women
to bond with other women on the basis of shared victimization.[25]

Hooks's critique of feminism is powerful, on the mark, and clearly
stated. Yet you won't find it—or any sustained, substantial analysis
of feminists of color—in Roiphe, Paglia, or Wolf.[26] These three foes of
"victim feminism" could remind feminists who might begin work with
an a priori assumption of oppression that not all women share the
same experiences. This, in turn, could lead us to intensify our interrogation of the relationship among gender, race, class, and nationality.
However, I am not hopeful that this will happen. Quite simply, these
books leave their implied white middle- and upper-class readers feeling
just too good about their own power as Americans. For them, victimization gets in the way of the relatively privileged. It somehow messes
up their access to the boys' world of sex and capital. This is not the direction that feminism should take.

Rather, we must continue efforts to become more refined in our
understanding of victimization and oppression. In my field, many have
already begun to formulate an enhanced conception of the power
wielded by women and various racial groups in the nineteenth-century
American literary sphere.[27] Additionally, scholars such as Carolyn L.
Karcher and Frances Smith Foster investigate the challenges that faced
cross-race and cross-gender political coalitions.[28] These scholars, among
many others, reject notions of victimization and strive, instead, to
understand the methods by which exploited and oppressed peoples
claimed voice and activated change. They recognize the complex dynamics of race, class, and gender, and attempt to articulate them in a
historically specific way.

Although aspects of "victim feminism" are important, another implication of the debate also needs to be addressed. Lurking behind all of these arguments is anxiety about the cause of gendered behavior. For Roiphe, this concern surfaces in her apprehension regarding prescribed sexuality. Her most sophisticated argument comes when she interprets the language of date-rape pamphlets: "The movement against rape, then, not only dictates the way sex *shouldn't be* but also the way it *should be*. Sex should be gentle, it should not be aggressive; it should be absolutely equal, it should not involve domination and submission" (60). Similarly, Wolf's "victim feminism" is really another way of discussing essentialism. What she objects to most forcefully is feminism that claims a universally passive, nurturing female nature. She describes this mode:

> Women are not hierarchical but egalitarian. . . . Men want to dominate and separate; women want to communicate and connect. Men—especially Western men—are individualistic autocrats; women are communitarian healers. Men objectify women while women want commitment. Men kill; women give life. (144)

Unlike Roiphe and Wolf, Paglia, as I have mentioned, insists that gender difference is physiological and natural.

Historically, it makes sense that all of these books focus on essentialism. Essentialism first took root in America early in the nineteenth century and remains a powerful force today. As women of all races and African American and Native American men and women fought for democratic rights in the relatively new Republic, scientists and social conservatives began to argue that non-Caucasians and women were innately different and inferior.[29] In the complex and turbulent years that have followed, an essential feminine nature has been asserted by both advocates and opponents of women's rights. What is disturbing about Roiphe, Paglia, and Wolf is not that they once again highlight essentialism, but rather that they seem to derive no benefit from the excellent historical and theoretical work that has been published on the issue. They indicate that academic feminists must intensify efforts to speak to the overall feminist community. Otherwise, we will constantly remain in the same place, reinvent the same wheel, and learn nothing from the past.

Let's return briefly to the charges Roiphe brings against feminists. She interprets date-rape pamphlets as replicating Victorian ideology and blames feminists for blindly reinforcing gendered concepts of human sexuality. However, Roiphe ignores the complex relationship between the women's rights movement and sexuality in the century that serves as her example. She does not analyze the intricacy of the anti-vice and antiprostitution movements that women led from the 1830s to the 1880s. Like the feminists Roiphe implicates, these women also reinforced notions of female passivity and male lust in order to hold men legally and economically responsible for their sexual power. However, through this movement, women gained significant access to the media and cultivated business, fund-raising, and leadership skills. Working within a restrictive ideology, they opted for what seemed best, and they reinforced notions of essentialism to facilitate short-term political gains that improved many women's private lives.[30] Each process of feminism is a stage, each moment another lesson in strategy. We have much to learn from early feminists' victories and defeats.

If we view essentialism as a tool employed by women for specific reasons in both the 1870s and the 1970s, we can begin to ask questions about both its effectiveness and its liabilities. Similarly, we can analyze poststructuralism as a methodology that comes from a distinctive historical moment and is exploited by feminists for definable gains. Unlike essentialism, poststructuralism offers an alluring theoretical escape from the bodies that are said to relegate us to a subordinate societal role. It is quite possible that poststructuralism lures some feminists into thinking of gender only as a construct, not as a tangible presence that must be dealt with politically. Perhaps, we muse in an imaginary liberatory space, our bodies are not ourselves. Tania Modleski aptly summarizes the attraction:

> Since feminism has a great stake in the belief, first articulated by Simone de Beauvoir, that one is not *born* a woman, one *becomes* a woman (for if this were *not* the case it would be difficult to imagine social change), thinkers like Lacan and Foucault have provided the analytical tools by which we may begin the arduous task of unbecoming women.[31]

Besides allowing us to comprehend femininity as constructed, poststructuralism also equipped us with another valuable device. Through theory, we were able to grasp the binary nature of identity. We learned that to have "woman," one must have "man." To have "black," one must have "white." Poststructuralism, either directly or indirectly, allowed many scholars to begin to question male and white identity. It took the white Western male out of the center, out of a seemingly natural state, placing him instead under the category of construct. He became a set of expectations, rather than a universal and fore-ordained tyrant.

Yet when taken to extremes, some theory can hinder claims made on the basis of group identity. Modleski cautions that the "once exhilarating proposition that there is no 'essential' female nature has been elaborated to the point where it is now often used to scare 'women' away from making any generalizations about or political claims on behalf of a group called 'women.'"[32] Likewise, Barbara Christian questions the timing of the so-called death of the subject:

> I see the language it creates as one which mystifies rather than clarifies our condition, making it possible for a few people who know that particular language to control the critical scene—the language surfaced, interestingly enough, just when the literature of peoples of color, of black women, of Latin Americans, of Africans began to move to the "center."[33]

As Christian points out, although identity is not necessarily essential, we do not want to theorize ourselves out of a position from which to act. Because of this paradox, feminist scholars must work with multiple consciousness. We must attempt to understand how theories, even our own, have been used against us in the past, and we must learn from both material and theoretical history to avoid uncomfortable appropriation. We must repeatedly move beyond the harmful paradigms placed upon feminism that give us just "two tales," and into a more nuanced understanding of history, power, and struggle.

In this sense, academic feminists have much to offer. Currently, we can place knee-jerk reactions to "victim feminism" in a historical framework. It seems as if some white, middle-class women want to claim victory before the struggle is over. They want to race into the (not quite) top echelon of society, grab the booty, and bask in their newfound power. Yet we cannot seriously challenge sexual exploitation and race and class oppression until we also interrogate unchecked capitalism and American individualism. As hooks points out, much feminist work already compels "feminist thinkers to problematize and theorize issues of solidarity, to recognize the interconnectedness of structures of domination, and to build a more inclusive movement."

Yet this work "risks being undone" by "young white privileged women who strive to create a narrative of feminism . . . that recenters the experience of materially privileged white females in ways that deny race and class difference."[34]

Roiphe gives away her hand when she says, "Even if you argue, as many do, that *in this society* men are simply much more powerful than women, this is still a dangerous train of thought. It carries us someplace we don't want to be" (89). We certainly do not want to be in that place. But we are there. Men do have more power—economically, politically, and culturally. So do whites. So do Americans. And all the denial we muster will not erase the ugly facts. A long and complex process has brought us to where we are. A long and difficult struggle will bring us out. But struggle has a history of its own. Feminist scholars can help provide a basic understanding of the way power works. However, just because we recognize the means by which women have been exploited does not mean we have to cling to the status of victim. If we understand feminist theory as intimately connected to feminist history, and if we look to past struggle for strategies of resistance, then we might find that we are indeed equipped to dismantle the master's house with the tools our own hands have wielded in a rich and varied history.

Notes

1. Paula Kamen came to this conclusion after conducting 236 interviews for her book *Feminist Fatale: Voices from the "Twentysomething" Generation Explore the Future of the Women's Movement* (New York: Fine, 1991). See Suzanne Gordon, "Don't Call Them Feminists," *Philadelphia Inquirer*, 19 February 1992.

2. Naomi Wolf describes how her friends joke, "Don't tell the Sisterhood," or, "Promise you won't turn me in to the fem police?" when they want to confide "unsanctioned sexual longings or 'frivolous' concern about clothes or vulnerability or men." Naomi Wolf, *Fire with Fire: The New Female Power and How It Will Change the Twenty-First Century* (New York: Random House, 1993), 62.

3. Sally Quinn, "Who Killed Feminism? Hypocritical Movement Leaders Betrayed Their Own Cause," *Washington Post*, 19 January 1992.

4. Wendy Kaminer, review of *The Morning After: Sex, Fear, and Feminism on Campus*, by Katie Roiphe, *New York Times Book Review*, 19 September 1993, 1.

5. Daphne Patai, "The Struggle for Feminist Purity Threatens the Goals of Feminism," *Chronicle of Higher Education*, 5 February 1992.

6. Christina Hoff Sommers, quoted in Marie McCullough, "Feminist Debate Comes to Swarthmore," *Philadelphia Inquirer*, 29 April 1994.

7. Christina Hoff Sommers, quoted in Megan Rosenfeld, "The Feminist Mistake? Christina Hoff Sommers Sees a Tyranny of the Sisterhood," *Washington Post*, 7 July

1994. Teachers for a Democratic Culture devoted the majority of its fall 1994 newsletter to critiques of Sommers. *Teachers for a Democratic Culture* 3 (1994).

8. Susan Jane Gilman, "Why the Fear of Feminism?" *New York Times*, 1 September 1991.

9. Wolf, *Fire with Fire*, 125.

10. Susan Faludi, *Backlash: The Undeclared War against American Women* (New York: Crown, 1991).

11. See Paul Lauter, *Canons and Contexts* (New York: Oxford University Press, 1991), 97–101.

12. Katie Roiphe, *The Morning After: Sex, Fear, and Feminism on Campus* (New York: Little, Brown, 1993); Wolf, *Fire with Fire*; and Camille Paglia, *Sex, Art, and American Culture: Essays* (New York: Random House, 1992). Subsequent references to these works appear parenthetically in the text.

13. bell hooks also links these three authors, criticizing them for advancing their careers through a combative, argumentative style and for erasing class and race difference. She comments that "without Paglia as trailblazer and symbolic mentor, there would be no cultural limelight for white girls such as Katie Roiphe and Naomi Wolf." bell hooks, *Outlaw Culture: Resisting Representations* (New York: Routledge, 1994), 86.

14. Katie Roiphe, "Date Rape Hysteria," *New York Times*, 20 November 1991.

15. Camille Paglia, "Ninnies, Pedants, Tyrants, and Other Academics," *New York Times Book Review*, 5 May 1991, 29.

16. Hooks, *Outlaw Culture*, 85.

17. George Will, "A Female Ph.D. Candidate at Princeton Is Giving Sexual Harassment a Second Look," *Philadelphia Inquirer*, 25 October 1993.

18. Gretchen Morgenson, "A Whiner's Bible," *Forbes*, 16 March 1992, 152–53.

19. Sandra M. Gilbert and Susan Gubar, *The Madwoman in the Attic: The Woman Writer and the Nineteenth-Century Literary Imagination* (New Haven: Yale University Press, 1979), 7.

20. In a 1979 essay, Elaine Showalter describes gynocriticism as the effort "to develop new models based on the study of female experience" and to focus on the "newly visible world of female culture." See "Toward a Feminist Poetics," in *The New Feminist Criticism: Essays on Women, Literature, and Theory*, ed. Elaine Showalter (New York: Pantheon, 1985), 131.

21. Elaine Showalter, "The Rise of Gender," in *Speaking of Gender*, ed. Elaine Showalter (New York: Routledge, 1989), 4.

22. Ibid., 5.

23. See bell hooks, *Feminist Theory: From Margin to Center* (Boston: South End, 1984), 46.

24. Ibid., 5.

25. Ibid., 45.

26. Hooks also comments in *Outlaw Culture* on this lack of representation, arguing that "Paglia never mentions the critical writing of any African American" (85); that Wolf's writing reflects a new kind of work by feminists that "completely ignores issues of race and class" (93); and that she (hooks) is disturbed by the "overall erasure of the voices and thoughts of women of color" in Roiphe's work (103).

27. For example, Jane Tompkins reassesses the place of the woman writer in the nineteenth century by questioning critical assumptions regarding sentimental writing. See her *Sensational Designs: The Cultural Work of American Fiction, 1790–1860* (New York: Oxford University Press, 1985). See also Jane P. Tompkins, "Sentimental Power:

Uncle Tom's Cabin and the Politics of Literary History," in Showalter, *New Feminist Criticism*, 81–104.

28. Carolyn L. Karcher's cultural biography of Lydia Maria Child investigates cross-race alliances, particularly in relation to Child's work with abolition and Native American rights. See Carolyn L. Karcher, *The First Woman in the Republic: A Cultural Biography of Lydia Maria Child* (Durham, N.C.: Duke University Press, 1994), 614. In her chapter on Harriet Jacobs, Frances Smith Foster explores the trials facing Jacobs, who intentionally wrote across the color line. See Frances Smith Foster, *Written by Herself: Literary Production by African American Women, 1746–1892* (Bloomington: Indiana University Press, 1993), 95–116.

29. For analysis of essentialism in relation to race, see George Fredrickson, *The Black Image in the White Mind: The Debate on Afro-American Character and Destiny, 1817–1914* (New York: Harper & Row, 1971). See also Reginald Horsman, *Race and Manifest Destiny: The Origins of American Racial Anglo-Saxonism* (Cambridge: Harvard University Press, 1981); and Robert E. Bieder, *Science Encounters the Indian, 1820–1880* (Norman: University of Oklahoma Press, 1986). Cynthia Eagle Russett, in *Sexual Science: The Victorian Construction of Womanhood* (Cambridge: Harvard University Press, 1989), offers an excellent summary of the rise of gendered essentialism in the nineteenth century.

30. For an analysis of the antivice and antiprostitution movements of the nineteenth century, see Carroll Smith-Rosenberg, *Disorderly Conduct: Visions of Gender in Victorian America* (New York: Oxford University Press, 1985), 77–164.

31. Tania Modleski, *Feminism without Women: Culture and Criticism in a "Post-feminist" Age* (New York: Routledge, 1991), 15.

32. Ibid.

33. Barbara Christian, "The Race for Theory," *Feminist Studies* 14, no. 1 (1988): 51–63.

34. Hooks, *Outlaw Culture*, 102.

PART THREE

THIRD WAVE NEGOTIATIONS

Copyright 1995 by Barry Baldridge

Courtesy of HUES Collective

THIRD WAVE NEGOTIATIONS

Essays in this section begin to map the implications of shifts in feminist thinking and feminist theorizing, such as the impact of poststructuralism, queer theory, masculinity theory, and gender studies. Negotiating the range of acts, identities, and beliefs within feminism, and taking this range as possibility's signature, these essays also transgress various "truths," whether mainstream, poststructuralist, or feminist, by making eclectic use of hybrids based on all of these and more. These essays negotiate, for instance, the struggle to find words and use words to change lives when we know words are perpetually inadequate.

Although we might long for one, we have no dream like Adrienne Rich's dream of a common language. However, as Lidia Yukman writes in "Feminism and a Discontent," the differences between words interrupt us, connect us, move us, so "we" have learned to keep ourselves interrupted. Carol Guess's "Deconstructing Me: On Being (Out) in the Academy" interrupts poststructuralist dismissals of identity politics and essentialism, but finds some aspects of poststructuralism useful to a lesbian activist project. In "Masculinity without Men: Women Reconciling Feminism and Male-Identification," Cox, Johnson, Newitz, and Sandell interrupt definitions of masculinity and femininity predicated on opposition or biology, choosing instead to express and theorize a feminist participation in masculine roles and male-oriented cultures that they find empowering, enjoyable, *and* problematic. "We" keep ourselves interrupted, sometimes uneasily. Third wavers attempt to negotiate selves and communities that open up new possibilities for political work, trying not to act as if these identities are natural, but acknowledging and making use of them when they do feel good, right, or necessary.

CHAPTER EIGHT

Deconstructing Me:
On Being (Out) in the Academy

Carol Guess

Am I a lesbian?

I've asked myself this question twice now, and answered it once. Some years back, a series of events and realizations led me to feel and think that *lesbian* might be the best word I could find to describe many of the most significant emotions, thoughts, and actions of my life. Those emotions, thoughts, and actions had consistently been a part of my way of being in the world; I had simply had no words with which to describe them, and no context in which to imagine that they might enable me to feel connected to other people, rather than alienated and "queer." Discovering the word *lesbian*—which for me meant discovering both individual women and a community, both a living culture and a complex history—enabled me to understand many things about my past: feelings I'd had, words I'd spoken and written and thought, things I'd done. More important, discovering the word *lesbian* enabled me to begin to envision my future, to start meeting and making connections with women whose view of the world was similar to mine, or whose differences inspired and educated me. This process of recognizing, exploring, and naming my experience was both exhilarating and immensely painful; as Marilyn Frye argues, "the event of becoming a lesbian is a reorientation of attention in a kind of ontological conversion. It is characterized by a feeling of a world dissolving, and by a feeling of disengagement and re-engagement of one's power as a perceiver" (1983, 171–72). The sense of a world dissolving was indeed what I experienced; reengaging with my own capacity for perception is an ongoing, and now considerably more self-conscious, process.

Beyond these abstract statements, the details of that first "coming-out story" aren't significant here. Rather, what I wish to examine is the

relation between that process and a more recent experience: my introduction to, immersion in, and reckoning with poststructuralist theory.[1]
Perhaps this experience too might be considered a "coming-out story"
of sorts; like the first, this second period of exploration has no finale: I
am still asking questions, still without satisfactory answers. At times
I've experienced a sort of schizophrenia in the tug of the questions, and
it's that sense of division that I wish to articulate here. I don't know to
what degree the issues I'm grappling with exist or matter outside the
academy; asking that very question is a part of the process I call "being
(out)": my attempt to maintain a claim to some version of the identity
category "lesbian" within an academic climate heavily influenced by
poststructuralist thought. I see my examination of this tension as characteristic of third wave feminist thought, because it involves both a
critique of academic power structures (a critique influenced by second
wave feminist work) and an acknowledgment of my desire to participate in those power structures.

I came out in an era (the late 1980s and early 1990s) caught in
the wake of a paradigm shift: a shift away from lesbian, gay, and bisexual identity politics and toward the queer movement. Although the
theories and social-sexual mores of lesbian feminism continue to influence the way lesbian identity is constructed outside the academy (in
nonacademic lesbian writing, in nonacademic lesbian organizations
and political events, and in the discourse and structure of some lesbian
communities), within the academy lesbian feminist models are often
tacitly, if not overtly, considered "dead." I use the word *dead* deliberately, for the "death of the lesbian" is but one in a series of "deaths"
that have been attributed to poststructuralist philosophy. The most
relevant here is the "death of the subject," the repudiation of humanist
notions of subjectivity. Arguing against the humanist belief in a stable,
coherent, essential self, poststructuralists (many of whom would not
classify themselves according to that term) posit instead a self that is
split, fragmented, or fluid, never whole, never knowable. Poststructuralist theorists' critiques of the humanist subject have thus expanded
and radically altered discourse surrounding the notion of identity, calling into question the efficacy of identity politics and, indeed, the value
of identity categories themselves. The poststructuralist deconstruction
of the lesbian differs from other shifts in the representational history of
lesbianism (for example, the move from a medical model to a lesbian
feminist model) in that it questions not who may be included in the

category "lesbian," but whether the category itself has any meaning—or any usefulness—at all.

In many respects, the move from humanism to poststructuralism has been beneficial for feminism, because the concept of an essential subjectivity has historically been used to oppress women. In combating the notion that the subject is inherently male, feminists themselves were partially responsible for breaking down traditional humanist understandings of subjectivity and thus paving the way for more intensive poststructuralist critiques. Lesbians have also benefited from the breakdown of traditional humanist conceptions of subjectivity. During the second wave feminist movement, lesbians, women of color, and/or poor and working-class women were often excluded by the movement's largely heterosexual, white, middle-class focus. These minority feminists argued against the humanist assumptions built into second wave feminism—assumptions that enabled heterosexual, white, middle-class women to assume that the subject of feminism necessarily mirrored their own interests. When minority feminists critiqued these biases, they were deconstructing the labels "feminist" and "woman," questioning the way in which such labels functioned within binary hierarchies and the way in which particular subject positions were excluded by such labels in order to reify the boundaries of each category.

Recent poststructuralist thought carries such redefinitions one step further. Rather than perpetually redefining a given category in order not to exclude any potentially applicable subject position from within that category, poststructuralists express skepticism about the validity of categories themselves. The process of perpetually redefining identity categories is self-defeating, they argue, for the act of self-definition depends on exclusion and thus on the construction of an "other," that which one must exclude and indeed reject in order to constitute oneself as a subject. Identity is therefore dependent on the very institutions and selves to which it sets itself in opposition. To define oneself as "lesbian" is potentially to reify hegemonic structures of power and knowledge on which that identity must rely in order to constitute itself qua identity. As Judith Butler argues,

> To write or speak *as a lesbian* appears a paradoxical appearance of this "I," one which feels neither true nor false. For it is a production, usually in response to a request, to come out or write in the name of an identity which, once produced, sometimes functions as a politically efficacious phantasm. I'm not at ease with

"lesbian theories, gay theories" [the subtitle of the book in which Butler's essay was published], for . . . identity categories tend to be instruments of regulatory regimes, whether as the normalizing categories of oppressive structures or as the rallying points for a liberatory contestation of that very oppression. (1991, 13–14)

For Butler, the category "lesbian" is inherently restrictive: it limits the potential meanings of the sexuality it supposedly encompasses, and works alongside (even as it purports to dismantle) the ideology of compulsory heterosexuality by defining female homoeroticism in opposition to normative female heterosexuality, thereby reifying the latter category in the process. The identity "lesbian" thus fails to function subversively, and possibly even supports hegemonic sexual ideologies. In addition, the very act of categorizing female same-sex sexualities as lesbian de-eroticizes them, for to name a sexuality is to deny what makes it most sensual and desirable: its vagueness, its lack of boundaries, its potential for change, reversal, and expansion. Thus, Butler asserts, "if the [sexual identity] category were to offer no trouble, it would cease to be interesting to me: it is precisely the *pleasure* produced by the instability of those categories which sustains the various erotic practices that make me a candidate for the category to begin with" (14).

My initial response to such writing was confusion: having struggled for years to acknowledge and act on my lesbianism, I felt betrayed by the thought that current philosophical trends in the academy mandated that I critique, even dismiss, this identity in order to be accepted as a professional theorist. Too, I felt reluctant to give up the pleasure of speaking and writing about the reengagements of perception that I experienced as a lesbian. If I felt invisible in the classroom before I read Butler, I felt doubly invisible after: as a young scholar eager to lay claim both to dominant academic discourses and to the community and history of lesbians I had only recently discovered, where was my place in the academy? Was my ticket to the academic and theoretical community (and ultimately to a degree and a professorial position) my repudiation of lesbian identity?

Importantly, in claiming the label lesbian I experienced the very changes, reversals, and expansions of desire and erotic power that Butler claims she experiences via her disavowal (or at least interrogation) of sexual identity. The word *lesbian* means, for me, an escape from the kind of narrow, hegemonic understandings of sexuality in which Butler fears the word itself is implicated; to speak about that identity means to reperceive the world around me, to critique dominant conceptions of sexuality and gender from a hard-won (and continually fought-for) position. This is not to say that I see my position as static: my understanding of what it means to be lesbian is continually shifting and changing. I simply don't see such shifts and changes as necessitating abandoning the category altogether. In fact, as I have argued elsewhere, I view the identity category "lesbian" as itself constructed through dissent and debate, and therefore always-already changeable and fluid; disagreements about who or what it signifies simply help constitute it qua identity.[2] In this sense, then, Butler and I agree: we both conceptualize sexuality as protean and find the erotic in instability, change, dissent, difference. I don't feel, however, that using the word *lesbian* consistently to refer to my altogether inconsistent, changeable, and expanding understandings of my own eroticism in any way limits those understandings. I find *lesbian*, like *Carol*, a useful, efficacious signifier, yet one that fails (like all words, and especially all names) to mean everything that I intend when I speak or write it. I see this as a "failure" inherent in language, one we can cure not by abandoning words but only by making more of them. To use the failure of language to fully express our meanings as a reason to abandon any given word seems illogical, because all words are inherently inadequate, and human communication is inevitably predicated on such inadequacy. Although Butler's musings are certainly of philosophical import, translated into practical terms they generate what I've heard referred to as "deconstructive paralysis," the absolute inability to take a position (in this case, to speak) because any and every move is imperfect, fraught with a potential misstep.

Although I almost inevitably espouse constructionist understandings of gender, sex, and sexuality, I find highly convincing Diana Fuss's argument that "in and of itself, essentialism is neither good nor bad, progressive nor reactionary, beneficial nor dangerous" (1989, xi). Essentialism has become an all-purpose enemy, routinely dismissed, routinely scapegoated. Yet the enormous anxiety surrounding any mention of essentialism within the poststructuralist classroom seems counterproductive, for, like any tacit taboo, it limits what can and cannot be said and thought, first and foremost limiting discussion of the uses and drawbacks of essentialism. The irony of this is that when I first began coming out, such essentialism was exactly what I needed and wanted. Although that is certainly not every baby dyke's experi-ence, neither is it altogether unusual. I needed to read stories about women who called themselves lesbians, women who practiced ecstatic loving and fucking and called it lesbian sex. During this period, I turned eagerly to Gloria Anzaldúa, the Combahee River Collective, Judy Grahn, Audre Lorde, Minnie Bruce Pratt, the Radicalesbians, Adrienne Rich, and Barbara Smith. Although the range of acts, identi-ties, and beliefs included under the single label "lesbian" was often as-tonishing to me, it did not lessen my desire to claim that label, nor did it diminish the power of that label to represent for me the particular ways in which I feel the label suits me. Without those models I would not have had the strength to resist the messages sent by the very world in which I live. Seeing a possible future for myself as a lesbian in print enabled me to make choices about my life that I might not otherwise have had the courage to make.

Within the academy, however, I sometimes experience pressure to deny my identity as a lesbian in order to affirm my (ostensible) non-identity as a poststructuralist. My response to writers such as Butler has been a performance in itself. In the classroom, I have found myself in the awkward position of wanting both to demonstrate my ability to "master" the language and concepts of poststructuralism, and to share thoughts on the identity, culture, and community I choose to claim. More often than not, professional pressure on me to perform as a post-structuralist wins out; too, I feel fairly confident that any mention of what might be called personal experience will automatically stop con-versation dead. For example, when discussing Butler's *Gender Trouble* (1990) in a seminar on feminism, I refrained from bringing in lived ex-amples of butch-femme and drag experiences precisely because such examples go contrary to the unspoken rules of the poststructuralist classroom. The effect of this silencing is not a neutral classroom at-mosphere in which all students feel equally empowered to speak because no one's experience is privileged; rather, it is a classroom at-mosphere in which dominant ideologies masquerading as neutral, objective, abstract theoretical discourse predominate, and where ca-nonical Western philosophy still contributes the accepted intellectual paradigms for thinking, writing, and speaking. Read under these con-ditions, queer theory is far from queer or subversive. Traditional as-sumptions about who can speak, when, and on what topics remain intact. I suspect that much of queer theory's ability to replicate dominant hierarchies of power and knowledge while appearing subversive is partly responsible for its success within the academy.

The experience of listening to a group of male, heterosexual, white, middle-class graduate students arguing about butch-femme lesbian sexuality as an abstract philosophical performative rendition of gender is amusing and enlightening but also alienating, because my lived understanding of lesbian sexuality is discounted as grounds from which to speak. Although I can spar in abstract terms as well as the rest, I'm not always sure that such discussions are inherently superior to discussions that include both abstract and experiential musings. I do not, of course, claim that male and/or heterosexual students should not, or cannot, discuss lesbian sexualities, or any other sexuality whatsoever, any more than I claim that I, as a white middle-class lesbian, cannot discuss African American and/or male subjectivity, Judaism, heterosexuality, or blue-collar lives. I feel that it is vital that all students feel free to analyze and interrogate whatever subject(ivities) classroom discussion generates. Yet the disciplining of queer theory in the academy has made it possible to discuss queer writing divorced from any experiential context, much as we discuss the placement of commas in our students' frosh composition essays.

A queer body is not a comma; a queer body, like a straight body, may be self-conscious, gleeful, AIDS-ridden, antsy, or lascivious. Gender may be a performance, but it is a fleshed performance, potentially painful or aware of its prowess. To talk about bodies that aren't one's own is a situation that needs to be understood differently from either the experience of voicing the same/similar or the experience of voicing abstract dicta. If experience and real life are verboten classroom topics, if poststructuralist anti-identity politics mandates that every student understands every subject position equally comprehensively, how can difference ever be genuinely interrogated? There is a difference between claiming that every student has an equal right to speak about every topic (which I firmly believe to be true), and saying that every student understands every topic equally well (which I firmly disagree with). Classroom debate can and should include all voices as equally as possible, yet the distinctions between the subject positions of the speakers should also be open to interrogation, and the relation between voice and subjectivity fully explored.

Poststructuralist and queer theories, which are so often touted as liberatory, have had, for me at least, the effect of forcing me back in the closet within myriad academic contexts. Let me clarify: it is not that I necessarily want, or think it productive, to bring personal experience into each classroom encounter. However, for any acknowledgment of autobiographical or biographical feeling, identity, or experience to be tacitly verboten in discourse ostensibly concerned with desire, sexuality, gender, race, and class seems counterproductive. It is also elitist: the abstract, nebulous vocabulary and cautious rhetorical structures borrowed from canonical Western philosophical discourse are revered at the expense of rhetorical strategies that stand on the margins of academic discourse and academic communities. If one is going to make trouble, must one begin with Hegel? Must writers whose language is highly poetic (such as Lorde) or non–jargon laden (such as Rich) or defiantly multilingual (such as Anzaldúa) remain "low" theorists because they do challenge and question the language, structures, and ideologies of white, male, Western philosophers? Moreover, it is difficult not to read as hypocritical the actions of queer theorists who publish, teach, and appear beneath the rubric "lesbian, gay, or bisexual," but who devote vast quantities of ink and paper to rejecting those very terms. So much of this academic work seems hollow and stale—such as yet another essay on why the lesbian does not exist, even as the author profits from the word *lesbian* on the book jacket.

One of the queerest consequences of this distrust of identity categories has been that my use of the word *lesbian* is sometimes criticized, even invalidated, on poststructuralist grounds. Such critiques might seem less queer if I did not experience them within a community of lesbian scholars whose own openly lesbian research is also routinely criticized and invalidated, often for oddly dissimilar reasons. For example, a friend and fellow lesbian scholar lives in Georgia, where sodomy is illegal and discrimination against gays, lesbians, and bisexuals is rampant and violent. She publishes and teaches within an academic department that is quite conservative (wary even of feminist research), and so she worries constantly, with good reason, about her lesbian projects. She is highly selective about which colleagues she discusses her work with, and has been warned that her job options will be limited by the work she has presented and published on lesbian theory. This woman is discouraged from using, and is often afraid to use, the word *lesbian* for fear of suffering academic and personal discrimination. Meanwhile, although I work within a liberal, nondiscriminatory academic environment, I too am often anxious about using the word *lesbian*, in my case for fear of being located within what Jacquelyn Zita calls a "modernist closet" (1992, 124)—the kiss of death for anyone seeking a position as a feminist scholar or literary theorist. At times I see the difference between the two versions of censorship; at times, frankly, I don't.

Part of what distresses me about the education I'm receiving is that it distances me from the personal lives of the nonacademic (and even academic) lesbians with whom I socialize. Let me relate another anecdote, experienced at a party attended primarily by lesbians in the local community. When someone asked me what I was currently studying, I explained that I was critiquing the philosophical position that lesbians don't exist. As expected, this was received with bemused laughter and summarily dismissed as "strange philosophy." Turning to the woman beside me, I asked, "So, what have you been doing lately?" Her response: "Fighting my ex-husband to maintain custody of my son." For this woman and for many others in the room, debating the "nonexistence" of lesbianism on philosophical grounds is a luxury, one that might seem educational until one loses a child custody case, a job, a home. Deconstructing identity does little to make the world seem safer at such moments.

Caught as academics are in the historically vestibular space between identity and shifting networks of desire, it seems worth remembering that the identity you're deconstructing may be someone else's own. Too, given that sexual identity—which is currently being deconstructed faster and better than almost any other identity category—is potentially invisible, it is worth reminding yourself with an occasional pinch that the philosophical significance of a dude in heels and pasties may be a deeply personal, painful, or energizing question for the professor, frat boy, or dull Pat scribbling notes beside you. I think always of the scene in Nella Larsen's *Passing*: "Nig," John Bellew calls his wife, whose biracial heritage is unknown to him (1986, 170). For many of the students and professors in the classroom you occupy, issues pertaining to identity may be fraught with danger, anxiety, barely concealable glee, or a long history of unsuccessful battles with the current legal system.

One practical way to begin grappling with the tension between poststructuralist and identity-centered texts in the classroom is to contextualize queer texts twice: once within the Western philosophical canon, and once within the lesbian, gay, and bisexual canon (canons that may, in some cases, overlap). It is not enough to teach Butler in relation to Lacan and Derrida. To fully understand her arguments in *Gender Trouble*, her work should also be compared to that of second wave lesbian-feminist writers such as Audre Lorde, Adrienne Rich, or Barbara Smith. (How is it possible, for example, to appreciate genuinely Butler's discussion of the heterosexual matrix (1990) without first reading Rich's essay "Compulsory Heterosexuality and Lesbian Existence" [1986]?). To ignore the lesbian and gay history that precedes contemporary queer poststructuralist theory and to emphasize exclusively its relation to "high theory," is to teach the texts in a vacuum and to do students a vast disservice.

Although the split I experience between my identity as a lesbian and my ostensible nonidentity as a poststructuralist theorist may be highly specific to my particular discipline and academic institution, it is nonetheless related to more widely experienced schisms between theory and practice, and between academic life and the "real world," distinctions some poststructuralist theorists attempt to collapse. Although interrogating such distinctions may usefully remind us that theory and practice, the academy and the real world, can and do interact and overlap, to collapse the terms entirely is to run the risk of assuming that one may be substituted for another without loss. All too often, current trends in (primarily poststructuralist) theory enable academics to neglect local and national political struggles, while reassuring themselves that the highly specialized essays they write will serve, by means of a fantastically complex trickle-down effect, to alter the minds of the voting public. Although I certainly agree that teaching and writing theory can be highly politicized acts, they are not the same as direct political action and do not necessarily have the same effects.

Although academic institutions are sites for political struggle and change, the sorts of struggles and changes they generate are often highly predictable, even choreographed. What seems vital is that local and national political struggles be brought within the walls of the academy; similarly, infusing theory into community politics is a way to begin bridging the gap between a given academic institution and its geographical and ideological context. When direct political action and theory begin to blur, the result is "permeable theory": words and ideas that circulate among academic and nonacademic communities alike, and that remain flexible enough to serve both discursive and activist responses to political struggle. Second wave in impulse (part of that feminism's ongoing critique of patriarchal power structures) yet capable of acknowledging the pleasures and utilizing the conventions of those same structures, this strategy seems characteristic of third wave feminist political work.

One example of the usefulness of such permeable theory occurred in October 1994 when local and state politicians threatened to cut Indiana University's budget by $500,000 if the university used public funding to open an office intended to provide information about lesbian, gay, and bisexual (LGB) issues. When Indiana University president Myles Brand agreed to drop public funding for the office, local and national LGB groups and supporters organized rapidly to protest his decision. The furor that erupted among IU students, faculty, and staff, Bloomington residents, and politicians alike forced all concerned to remember that a university is not an island but a group of buildings scattered across a unit of land that remains subject to city, state, and national governance. When a coalition of LGB groups staged public demonstrations, the site they chose for their protests was highly symbolic. Bloomington's main street, Kirkwood Avenue, runs perpendicular to the campus's best-known entryway: a brick walk framed by elaborate arched gateways. In holding the demonstrations at the joint of this symbolic T, the protesters highlighted the LGB community's role as mediator between city and campus. Rather than aiming its protests strictly at university officials, the coalition forced townspeople and the IU community alike to witness the larger-scale T intersection that had inspired the anger: the intersection of government and academic policy, a joint oiled by economic gift giving and, on this occasion, blackmail.

Moreover, while this direct-action group brought university policies out of the campus closet and into the city, a number of professors and teaching assistants brought the demonstrations from the streets to the classroom, bridging activism and theory by using the flyers, petitions, and even graffiti generated by both sides of the controversy as that week's texts. One of my colleagues photocopied both the LGB coalition's list of grievances and the university officials' statements, asked her students to analyze them in class, and then assigned a written essay in the form of a letter to Myles Brand describing their responses to the controversy—a letter students were invited to drop off at the president's office.

Such moments are valuable because they enable students to see ways in which the analytical tools they've been given might be put to practical use. Poststructuralism, and theory more generally, may then be seen for what it is: an extremely useful analytical tool—not a religion, not a moral code, not an identity masquerading as nonidentity, but a tool that serves as a means to an end. By bridging the gap between theory and practice, by bringing politics into a politicized classroom, permeable theory may enable students and faculty alike to confront more self-consciously their own strategies for "being" in the academy.

Notes

Although I do not wish to implicate her in any of these ideas, I am indebted to Eva Cherniavsky of Indiana University for her advice and encouragement during the writing of this essay.

1. I use the term *poststructuralist* here rather loosely, to refer to a branch of philosophy and/or theory characterized by an antiessentialist bent and by the beliefs that subjectivity is shaped by language, that subjectivity is always-already split or fragmented, and that the self is constructed by ideological structures that actively interpellate it. Many of the theorists I categorize as poststructuralist, such as Louis Althusser, Jacques Derrida, Michel Foucault, and Jacques Lacan, might well reject the label poststructuralist. Importantly, in this essay I include queer theory within the category of poststructuralist theory. Although not all queer theorists are poststructuralists, much of the writing that has emerged out of the queer theory movement has indeed relied on poststructuralist tenets, particularly regarding views on identity politics.

2. See my "Que(e)rying Lesbian Identity" (1995). In this essay I argue that the identity category "lesbian" is continually represented, within lesbian texts themselves, as fluid and changeable. The poststructuralist deconstruction of identity is therefore nothing new; rather, interrogating the borders and boundaries of lesbian identity is an inherent facet of that identity.

Works Cited

Butler, Judith. 1990. *Gender Trouble: Feminism and the Subversion of Identity*. New York: Routledge.

———. 1991. "Imitation and Gender Insubordination." In *Inside/Out: Lesbian Theories, Gay Theories*, edited by Diana Fuss. New York: Routledge.

Frye, Marilyn. 1983. *The Politics of Reality: Essays in Feminist Theory*. Trumansburg, N.Y.: Crossing Press.

Fuss, Diana. 1989. *Essentially Speaking: Feminism, Nature, and Difference*. New York: Routledge.

Guess, Carol. 1995. "Que(e)rying Lesbian Identity." *Journal of the Midwest Modern Language Association* 28, no. 1: 19–37.

Larsen, Nella. 1986. *Quicksand and Passing*. New Brunswick, N.J.: Rutgers University Press.

Rich, Adrienne. 1986. "Compulsory Heterosexuality and Lesbian Existence." In *Blood, Bread, and Poetry: Selected Prose, 1979–1985*. New York: Norton.

Zita, Jacquelyn. 1992. "Male Lesbians and the Postmodernist Body." *Hypatia* 7, no. 4: 106–27.

CHAPTER NINE

Feminism and a Discontent

Lidia Yukman

But do we have a female model?
Do we have an image of ourselves?
I don't think we do.
— Marilyn French

to the reader

Not for nothing have I undertaken a specifically creative project. Although it is true enough that the subject matter of this work concerns teaching and difference, I am also drawing attention to the form of the narrative fragment by submitting it to critical discourse. Part of my premise is that feminist critical language, in many cases, breaks down at the very point at which autocritique might occur. In my mind, critical language itself must be deconstructed, not with itself but with other forms. Which is to say that I am choosing to bring fiction in where I perceive critical language to have a blind spot: at the point of teaching and difference.

This piece is not meant to function as an argument in which a problem is exposed, analyzed, and addressed with a solution; rather, it is meant to construct an opening, a fissure, through which feminist autocritique may find a form. It is my position that fiction creates openings through which new forms of self-awareness might yet arise. The stories we tell ourselves point to bodies and voices that criticism cannot describe fully. As a feminist scholar and a fiction writer, I am daily confronted with different forms colliding and merging. For me, fiction (art) is the place of "hope." It seems fair to ask, then, what fiction can afford us that critical language can't, or in the case of this piece, what happens when one puts fiction up against critical language. My answer is that different forms allow for different expressions. For example, a satirical voice—a voice that speaks through tone or point of view—says something different than a critical voice can. This piece asks, then, what can we hear from a prostitute, a suicide, a junkie, an angry woman, a minority voice, even our own voices, when we listen differently than we do to critical feminist theory?

The effort to keep ourselves interrupted so as not to reproduce a hegemonic theory or practice is always in danger of collapsing. One must fight to keep conscious of the variety of women's stories, in addition to maintaining an awareness of current issues of multiculturalism and liberalism. Like all of us, I will continue to try to struggle with these issues without being careless. I would offer a warning about the dangers of neglecting narrative simply because it is a very different form of expression than the analytical, theoretical essay. Stories may repeat themselves, but that does not make them remain static.

The writing here is, from my point of view, an attempt to hold open and to perform a perspective that is not comfortable, not fully accounted for, and not over-and-done-with by a long shot. It's the "moving on" that this work tries to interrupt, not to block it but rather to bring more with it this time: the woman in a bar, the woman with the fork in her purse, the woman craving a drug, the woman who is paid to perform sex, the woman whose mind holds other logics.

Finally, this writing is part of the text of a performance work; this seems to me an important context for the narrative. The arguments are implicit; the words at the surface are meant only to trigger memories, images, common experiences, viewpoints left for dead. The performance includes a multimedia effort with several other women. However, I think the narratives hold their own in respect to the issues I have addressed. One would hope that narrative itself still has something to show us that we don't already know, because we are yet compelled to tell stories . . .

1. my sister's mother

My sister's mother is not my mother. The gap is eight years, from 1955 to 1963. In 1963, Kennedy was shot. Gap. Let me show you two pictures: in the first picture neither my sister nor my mother is facing the camera. My mother is seated and leaning against the bark of a pine tree. Her legs look uncomfortable—one is actually four inches shorter than the other. Her sitting is never graceful, and in this picture one leg is straight out from her body, the other curled under her like a doe's. Her face is turned slightly, but not completely, toward my sister. My sister is almost seven. Only a slice of her face is visible—her cheek, almost a smile. You can't see her eyes, but you can tell from the angle of the back of her head that she is looking at my mother. My mother's hair is wrapped and wrapped into a bun at the back of her head. My sister's hair is cut short, like a boy's. Really, my sister is almost not in the picture. Her body is bleeding out of the edge of the square.

Even though you can't see it, my father's hands work the camera. My father's hands focus the image of the two little women who won't look at the camera. My father's hands click the shutter. The two women are crashingly silent in the small house of their photo lives. The picture is a question of survival. I am not born yet.

The second picture is of me. There is no mother; she is taking the picture. I am standing alone in the front yard with a gold, a silver, and a bronze medal hanging on crimson, blue, and white ribbons from my smally, mighty neck. My face is scrunched up from the sun. My hair is bleached blond, my skin is bronze, my muscles lie about my gender. My father is at work. My sister is at college. My mother and I have just had a screaming argument. I love screaming arguments with my mother, because she comes out, full fury, more alive than the whole world. We have just had this fight during which she popped me with the palm of her hand on the butt as hard as she could. We both stand there for a long second. I am twelve. I have been a competitive swimmer for seven years already. The muscles in my buttocks are hard as rocks. My mother looks down at her hand; she has broken a blood vessel. You are not a little girl anymore, she says. She wants a picture. She tells me to go and get my medals won the day before. She snaps the shot. She never pops me again. We start to know each other.

When I am fifteen, she takes a whole bottle of sleeping pills and I find her. It's almost like a kiss. When I am sixteen, a gift: she tells me all about how she was kicked out of her high school graduation ceremony for leaving a dance too early. She was supposed to be one of the organizers. She was supposed to help keep everything running smoothly. She was not supposed to dance the night away, she was not supposed to leave her panties on a bush outside the gym, she was not supposed to marry a man whose hands could not be restrained, she was not supposed to let her silence cripple one daughter into depression, the other into anger.

In my sister's picture, little pine needles on the ground are the only comfort the two women can press the weight of their lives down on.

In my picture, I am victorious as rage, courageous as blind fury, I am pure anger let loose in the shape of a little girl. I am my mother's other daughter.

2. from private to social to symbolic

Let's suppose that once she gets there, she just isn't very good at it—being a man, I mean. Blooming consciousnesses being the naive little creatures that they are, what if she makes a lousy man? What if, during intense competition, she walks off the field to write a poem? What if, during important examinations, she laughs too loud, I mean a gut buster, really loud, and even cries once, much to everyone's embarrassment? What if she started out as a cheerleader or a sororal and she can't kick that shopping thing? Can she still be in women's studies? What if she paints her fingernails red and wears a push-up bra? Can she still grab intelligence, or, even more difficult, feminine power? What if she just quits writing theses one day? Can she stay in school, can she get a job, can she publish? What if she sleeps with her teacher? Can she still be dominant? I mean, if she's no good at being a victim, and she makes a lousy man, then what the hell is she?

3. memory: schoolhouse chair, college podium

I can see her sitting out there, arms crossed like wood; face, that dull expressionless void-mask developed over years; body slouched, uncommitted, inviolate. There is a faint, stern bend at her brow. There is mistrust in the molecules of air around her. There is only a crack near the cornea through which anything might be allowed to pass.

I can see her because she is me, the me that stood poised on the edge of anger, before I knew that ideas could save a person's life. How many women beat and swell toward rupture beneath the skin of one angry woman? How many of us sat inside her unbelieving silence, teeth clenched, toes curled, heart broken into the face of artificial attention?

In some deep pool of past, I remember: the other side of anger is the crest of imagination, a second world, the possibility of sight. Anger: not the answer, not the enemy. The border. A possibility.

4. mothering, teaching

You can't keep them all in, you know; some drift out of sight now and again. But you try. You try not to lose one gesture, one expression, one head tilt or fist clench or foot tap. You try to stay with each body in your small vision. But you have only two eyes and one mouth against all those others.

Meanwhile, you spill out words and words at them. You watch as some of the words land gently and perfectly into the waiting sponges, those who are hungry and ready. This puffs you up somewhat, gives you courage to go on.

Other words float around the heads of some; strange bubbles. You try to ease them in near the threshold where the give-and-take of an idea kisses the mind. Some nod, or blink recognition. This also makes you feel confident. You wave your hands around more in victory.

But some of the words slice and gash at the air around one. You try not to notice, but soon it becomes impossible to ignore, every word out of your mouth is an attack, a ripping open of the air around her. It is true enough that the wall surrounding her mind is not your fault. Somewhere someone made her feel less than. Unable to. Not anything enough. Little. You watch as your words crash in and around her, and you are of course horrified, you never meant to, you take it back. You take a step toward her and it is a knife. You back off. You shift your vocabulary up, down. Clenched jaw muscle. You wish you could give her a paintbrush or a musical instrument as more and more words pile on top of her. You inhabit violently different rooms, even in your common language. There is nothing to do but go on.

5. a room of one's own

A woman in a room today is a dangerous thing, Virginia. Right now there is a woman in a room in the back near the door who is only pretending to listen, who has a razor blade and a fork in her bag. Her impenetrable eyes are set on anyone watching, but her heart is on the razor and the fork inside. The razor blade is for her, so that in some moment when there is quiet and the voices burrowing in the channels of her brain have shut up for just five seconds—that's all she needs—she can draw the perfect line on the milk-white wrist, she can slice the thin skin and watch a small mouth open beautifully into blood and veins, she can watch the blue life vessels give way to sweet red inside. The fork is for an attacker, anyone who gets too close or goes too far. The fork comes from the kitchen, from the warm, docile safety where things are cooked and spiced and cradled between oven mitts. The fork is from the kitchen, where dead things metamorphose into culinary delights. She stands there in the back, waiting. For all we know, tonight's the night.

And there is a woman whose face is weathered from years, and she tries to catch your attention just outside the door of the room, because she wants in, she wants a drink, she wants you to buy her a drink; but maybe even more than that, she tries to catch your attention because she has an amazing story to tell and it takes a really long time. Everybody knows this, so they all avoid her eyes. You avoid her eyes too so that she won't talk to you, so that she won't tell you this really long story. But if by chance she does catch your attention, she will shake your hand and introduce herself, and she will begin to tell you the most fantastic tales of riding in a boat on the Nile, of riding in a gondola in Venice, of sailing the seven seas. I mean, this woman has a story about boats from all over the world; it's like she has linked all her experiences to boats out of loneliness, big ones and luxurious ones and fantasies to match—there are boats in every other sentence, and there are lots of sentences. Just about the time you think that is all she is going to talk about, she starts telling you about how she wrote letters to Hermann Hesse and *he wrote back*, so she wrote this really long book about his life, and there were of course many boats in his life, and pretty soon you realize that it's not the boats she needs to tell you about, but her life—*that*'s what no one wants to listen to or hear about, because it's too damn long.

And there is a woman in a room who works a few blocks from here, at a large institution where they have a sort of secret language. I mean, it is as if you need a secret decoder ring just to get in the door. There is a woman from there here, and she is sitting in this room, and she is thinking, I'm so goddamned glad to be in a room where I can use dumb words if I want to. She has fantasies about going on the road with an all-girl honky-tonk band, because she always wanted to put a twang in her voice and play the tambourine on her hip. It's like she's been on a bus, a really ritzy, double-decker bus with a bar and lounge music and scary, pointy-headed guys with postmodern white shirts and black pants, and she couldn't get off, and now she is off and she just wants to stay here in this room and think regular thoughts and use regular words, even though she knows it is true that language is not transparent and that the epistemological ramifications of spending too much time alone in a room are *heavy*.

And there is a woman in a room with way too much makeup, whose face is so familiar in the mirror that she cannot recognize it.

And there are two women sitting next to each other in a room, and one of them has her hand on her belly because she watched the future miscarry last night, and the other has her hand on her belly because she is trying to decide whether or not she can afford to take a leave of absence when the baby is born.

And there is a woman standing with other women who wants a woman across the room; her arm is almost touching the arm next to hers and there is heat-shiver there, and on her other side she can smell another woman's hair like intoxication moving down her throat, making her mind dizzy and her body untamed. All the men in the room seem like children to her, and she keeps wanting to scoop them all up in her arms and say, come now, off to bed, little ones, so that she can turn out the lights and get on with it. And she is paralyzed between the women and the children, and as she stands there with useless hands and an unyielding mouth, she is slowly forgetting her own name to desire.

And there is a brown-skinned woman watching a war-a-week on tv as the u.s. stitches border after border like a big white quilt around its whiteness. And the tv gets more and more animated and the policies get whiter and whiter, until she looks down at the brown skin of her own arm and thinks, how do they tell the difference between molecules of difference? Is my arm ending or beginning?

And there is a clueless woman in the corner who is wondering what to do with her hands. She puts her hands on the table she takes them off the table she holds a drink she sets the drink down she holds a pencil she drops the pencil she brushes her hair out of her face she tucks a strand behind her ear she plays with her lip she scratches her front tooth she touches the rim of her glass she touches the face of the paper she puts her hands underneath her legs she folds them she sees them as incomprehensible.

And that's the trouble these days, isn't it Virginia, that we just don't know what we might do?

6. the glory of the liberal white teacher woman

I am a white woman and I teach a black man and I know that he is an african american man and I have read many books by afro-american authors and I have learned many lessons concerning afro-american politics and I am horrified by rwanda and somalia flashing starving death baby heads and riots of fire melting down l.a. but he keeps looking right at me and I keep trying to look right back at him and this stupid thought keeps coming into my mind: I don't understand the oversized jeans and I never will.

I am a white woman and I teach a woman from china and she is all silence I mean she is more silent than kristeva ever theorized she is a longer and more deafening silence than I can bear and I keep trying to get her to write *personal narratives* because *personal narrative* is a form closer to her experience than argument and logic and I keep telling myself it is because it will help her I will help her we must all help her but really it would help me because if she wrote *personal narratives* then I could give her A's and not C's and I would feel so much better about myself.

I am a white woman and I teach another white woman and I recognize her I think because she looks so angry like I looked when people were trying to tell me what to think what to do what to write how to punctuate how to capitalize and I think we should have a kind of bond because I *understand* her anger and I know not to behave like a militant feminist or a fascist white teacher because that is what she hates but when I take a step in her direction I reach toward her like a comrade and she is closed she is lethal resistance she is like a gun at my temple another life another nation another world another language: who the hell am I to teach her?

I am a white woman and I teach a woman half chicano and half pueblo and I am spilling over with glee that we are studying a native american novel I am spilling over with all my sensitivity and my research into the myths and symbols of native cultures and my slides of petroglyphs from my trip to new mexico and arizona and my spirituality rap and I keep nodding and winking in her direction and her eyes are black and her hair is black and her stare is blacker than the chalkboard backing me up blacker than the words on the white page blacker than night and suddenly I get a jolt like I have been invaded by lethal molecules: get off of me, get off of me.

I am so *lucky* to have such a diverse class, aren't I the lucky one, the little white liberal teacher teaching varieties of new improved knowledge to her very special students.

My students.

7. essay

Each person standing in as a teacher must choose for herself what, why, how, to whom, and so on. What I—an "I" flexing the muscle of past feminist arms and landing a right hook into the jaw of the future— have chosen matters little to another, except that occasionally shared ideas join, mutate, emerge, and this is lucky. But what each person takes from the training, the texts, the teachers, the colleagues, the discussions, the experiences, the history, is never the same. Woman. Teacher. Student. Possibilities between words. What can we ever tell one another that might help?

In the past, women learned to say, I will no longer submit, I will move forward in a new direction of power. Mothers. Sisters. The present gives us the movement of a different lesson: listen to the noise of our differences. Learn to listen, to watch and adapt, and when you have done that, learn it over again, this time through a different sense or language or gesture. It is the women who are not you, the women who are as yet unfinished sentences or emerging stories, who can teach us what we have left to learn. It is the rage inside our differences, not liberal projects of all-inclusiveness, that may yet write new forms of signification.

The students I learn the most from are the most difficult to reach. I know the reason for this. In the first year I was a college student, I had a nuclear rage in me. One teacher told me I could not write a proper essay. This may have been true; instead of writing, I think I mostly ground the pencil lead into shiny smears on the too-white paper. Accordingly, I received a C, a D, and finally, an F. Another told me that if I didn't know how to analyze a text, I shouldn't be in college. I rarely went to his classes. Then I rarely went to any classes. I flunked out. I was not a terrible student. I was an angry student.

Of course my rage was my own, my problems my own, my little overdramatic narratives all mine. The thing is, students bring with them the effects of their lives: anger, hope, confusion, hate, difficulty, shame, or difference—cultural, linguistic, psychological, sexual. But it would have taken only one person to reach me. And when that one person did reach me, she did so through my anger, in spite of it, perhaps even in it. She told me that the problem was not in me but in the barrier between me and a world I had every right not to trust. Try writing about that, she said. What if it isn't an essay, I said. Essay, she said. Attempt, try.

I have not stopped writing since. I remember her words. I remember my mother's voice. I remember my sister's struggle. We move through stories. Like the differences between women, the differences between words interrupt us, connect us, move us.

CHAPTER 10

Masculinity without Men: Women Reconciling Feminism and Male-Identification

Ana Marie Cox, Freya Johnson, Annalee Newitz, and Jillian Sandell

Introduction

Recent work on the "crisis in masculinity" in popular culture has drawn attention to the fact that masculinity has always had an ambivalent relationship to power and domination. For example, masculinity in a straight, white man and masculinity in a gay, black man are differently valued, reminding us that the relationship between sex, gender, and social power is less fixed than we might often think. Masculinity is, in other words, as much a construction and a performance as femininity is. Therefore, the idea that some women might want to assume certain "masculine" traits or consider themselves as "male-identified" does not suggest that women are becoming "like men," but rather that the relationship between gendered social roles and biological sex is more fluid than we have been taught to believe. Although this fluidity never happens in a vacuum, and the kinds of social and political implications associated with it must be interrogated, neither does such a shift automatically signal a regressive step for feminism.

Feminism has often had an uneasy relationship to masculinity. Second wave feminism, for example, taught us not only that the link between biological sex and socially appropriate gender roles is politically motivated to perpetuate male privilege, but also that many of the qualities that society typically celebrates about masculinity are, at best, of questionable value and, at worst, socially destructive. Part of the early feminist project was, therefore, to revalue typically "feminine" qualities and to make them socially desirable for both women and men.

One of the problems we have when talking about "second wave feminism" is that we are, in many ways, drawing upon a caricature of feminism that comes as much from popular culture as from textbooks. This is the feminism of separatism and "women-identified women," the kind of feminism within which the idea that some women might want to take on certain positive aspects of "masculinity" would be considered unthinkable. It would be nice to believe that women have a transparent relationship with feminism, but, like everybody else, our understanding of feminism is filtered through the media. While we understand that we are operating in the realm of stereotypes, these representations were nevertheless instrumental in forming our ideas of what it would mean to be feminists. Growing up, we internalized these stereotypes, and today we are still negotiating them when we call ourselves feminists. Although the reality of 1970s feminism was more complex than the stereotypes allow, third wave feminism has, in many ways, set itself in opposition to a "straw feminist" of the second wave.

Although more feminists today are analyzing masculinity and male culture, some of these investigations are done defensively, as if studying the male gender role were somehow antithetical to a feminist project. Indeed, the defensive, apologetic tone of their work perpetuates and heightens the sense of conflict between feminism and masculinity. A number of books by feminists celebrate masculinity and work hard to open up the feminist project to men. Yet few of them explore what it would mean to be both feminist and male-identified, and when they do, these explorations are generally within the realm of queer and transgender studies.

Each of the contributors to this article thinks of herself, to a certain extent, as male-identified, and each of us is resolutely feminist. Ana Marie Cox (b. 1972) is a journalist for the E-'zine *Suck.com*. Freya Johnson (b. 1970), Annalee Newitz (b. 1969), and Jillian Sandell (b. 1965) are graduate students in English at the University of California at Berkeley. As academics and writers, we often find that part of our work involves thinking through issues related to gender and sexuality. The discussion that follows grew out of informal conversations we have had about our experiences as women who enjoy participating in what is often considered "male" culture. In various ways we all behave in a "masculine" manner. The four of us decided to collaboratively speak out about what it means to assimilate feminist sensibilities and certain masculine gender attributes into the same personality. One afternoon in October 1994, we got together at Annalee's apartment, had some coffee, and tape-recorded the following conversation. Our collaboration became a form of consciousness-raising for us, because in the process of sharing our experiences, we realized we were not alone. We used some of the tools of second wave feminism—consciousness-raising and working collaboratively—to consider an issue that seems central to third wave feminism: where does masculinity fit into the feminist movement?

What is Male Identification?

JS: Perhaps we can start by saying how we feel about being both male-identified and feminist, and what that means for each of us?

AC: I was telling someone about coming here, and my friend said, "What does that mean?" And I realized I had never had to define it before. And the first thing I said was, "Well, I like boys . . ." And then I realized that that was fairly general. I think it means that for a long time, not as long as I can remember, but for a long time, what I've been most proud of is being able to be one of the guys. And that's changed somewhat, and I've refined it somewhat, but that basic feeling of camaraderie with men is something I find pleasure in.

JS: When I was talking to a friend this morning about this project, I had a similar problem, where she said, "So, you're doing this thing on male-identification," and then before I even had a chance to answer, she actually launched into a story about S-M. I thought that was really interesting that in her mind there was actually a connection being made between the sort of power relations we might associate with S-M and being male-identified. I was trying to explain more of what Ana was saying, about participating in masculine culture, or male culture, and enjoying it, and implicitly rejecting conventional feminine culture, and rejecting a sense of femininity that I found really constricting when I was growing up. For me, then, it's partly a kind of negative identity, in the sense that it's not so much that I want to be male-identified, it's that I don't want to be feminine-identified in the kinds of ways I've learned about it.

FJ: Well, for me the male-identified thing definitely keys into my whole gay-boy identification. It opens up a variety of different doors, different things I can do because I can still access the "girly" parts of feminine identification, only I'm doing it from a campy, gay-boy perspective rather than the traditionally feminine one. So it puts a very different spin on, you know—if I want to wear makeup or if I want to

dress up femme, I'm being like a gay man in drag, rather than identifying with a traditional, feminine culture. At the same time, I can appropriate some "feminine" parts of gay male culture without identifying
with the traditional, 1970s-style, earth-mother-centered feminism. So
for me it provides a smorgasbord of different identities. I can switch
back and forth.

AN: I associate my male-identification with enjoying male culture, particularly a culture of hierarchy and power games. Women I've
known also play power games, but it has always seemed to me that
they're not as overt about it, and that I find disturbing. I've never
known how to play that game. I also associate my male-identification
very strongly with a desire for revenge. I think that plays into the
idea of negative identity, because I've always felt belittled by men. As
much as I've always been able to be one of the boys, I believed that I
was a part of the boys because I was somehow being a girl for them. I
think I've always wanted to be more of a man than men are. My male-
identification was a way of getting revenge on men for not allowing
me to participate in their culture as much as I would like to. So, to be
tougher than men is part of it. I think that it comes back to power.
It's an identity based on taking power—and particularly power over
men. [Laughs] So my male-identification is actually about having
power over men as opposed to being one with them. It's about being
their leader.

AC: So, you're using the master's tools to destroy the master's
house. Do you mean that you like to beat them at their own games?

AN: Yeah, beating them at their own game. And I think that's
one of the scary things about male identity. What we don't like about
masculine identity generally as feminists, I think, is the fact that it's
hierarchical and about oppressing other people, and yet I worry that
we have taken that identity on as a way of controlling men, and controlling other women too.

JS: And it also seems like we share a sense that we don't want to
be feminine, that we are rejecting the feminine, at least in the debilitating way in which we've thought about it.

Failing to Be Women

AC: I was thinking about what Freya said about being a gay man when
you "do" femininity—it's a drag identity. One of the reasons why I

became male-identified is because I sort of failed at being a woman. [Everyone laughs and agrees] It's not that I'm rejecting femininity so much, but that I was bad at it, and then I rejected it. It's a bit of sour grapes, you know? [More laughter from everyone]

AN: Last night when I went out dancing at this club with my partner, I was looking around, and a lot of the women were very beautiful, and they were wearing dresses with spaghetti straps and shiny clothes, and I was thinking, "Wow, they look so beautiful." I was wearing big, baggy khakis and a white T-shirt, and I said to myself, "Well, I look good like this. There's just no way I could look good the way they look good." If I wore those clothes, I think I would fail at wearing them.

AC: That's kind of a drag thing—that failed femininity, failed masculinity that's foregrounded in drag. Like right now, I am wearing a skirt, and I've taken in the past year or so to wearing skirts. But I think of it like play. I like the contrast of wearing a skirt and big chunky shoes. I like being one of the guys even though I have a skirt on.

FJ: See, I kind of like to do the feminine thing, like the women Annalee was describing at the club. I venture into that territory sometimes and I do that whole thing and I feel good because I think I can pull it off sometimes. And I like to feel that I'm "undercover"—like, "Ha, I'm inhabiting this particular realm that you guys are all living in, but I'm so completely different from you." It's kind of fun to be able to go in there and speak their language and to produce the same semiotic signals that they are but to be able to subvert it in various ways— which to me is a lot of fun, playing with that.

JS: So it seems like you're saying that it's OK to be feminine as long as you're ultra-self-conscious about it.

AN: Yeah, as if you're really a guy on the inside.

AC: It's not just that we're rejecting femininity, but we're being feminine ironically. "Ironically" is just one of the only ways we can recuperate it.

AN: I've also felt very strongly that femininity rejected me. [Laughter]

JS: Oh yeah.

AN: There was this point at which I could have joined "the girls" and they didn't like me, you know. One of the things that occurred to me is that I've never worn makeup. I never learned to wear makeup. And there was a point I remember when a lot of my girlfriends started wearing makeup and I just couldn't. It was like I just didn't know how to do it. And I never asked anybody to show me how.

FJ: Yeah, for me there was definitely a large part of sour grapes in it. You know, the same thing as with all of us, like when I was a teenager I wasn't good at wearing makeup, I was kind of chunky, and as I got older I studied the feminine gender role and I learned how to play it, but still, every time I enter into it, I become completely aware of the fact that I'm only performing it. I'm being self-conscious about it.

AC: My friend Paul and I were talking about how there's a moment in all the "tomboy movies," like with Katharine Hepburn, where the tomboy gets beautiful, takes off her glasses or lets down her hair, comes down the stairs, and all the guys say, "Uh . . . ," the double-take thing, "That's not Sam." You know how she always has that gender-bending name.

AN: Jo . . .

FJ: Chris . . .

JS: Alex . . . [laughter]

AC: Alex, yeah, I like that. Sometimes I'll try to play that game too, I'll put on something—not really frilly, but something sexy, and wear makeup, and do my hair. I'll do it just to show people that I can be feminine now. Maybe I failed at femininity—once—and that's why I'm a tomboy now, but now I know how, I studied how, I can do it too. It's not that hard—fuck you. [laughter]

FJ: Exactly.

AC: That's how I frame that moment, but I also take a lot of pleasure out of it. I get pleasure out of being able to draw that attention.

What Is "Feminine"?

JS: Well, my experience of femininity was actually quite different, because I wasn't brought up with any feminist consciousness whatsoever, and I didn't become a feminist until I was in my early twenties. As a child I always had short hair. Once I was old enough to decide how I wanted to present myself, I tried really hard to be very feminine. I grew my hair long and would wear lots of makeup. It was only when I started doing women's studies, and began to have a feminist consciousness and being aware of these things, that I just couldn't do it anymore. So for me, I think it really does have something to do with the fact that as soon as I had this feminist awareness of what it meant to be feminine, I couldn't do it anymore—even ironically. I just completely rejected it and basically, for the last ten years, I have continued to reject feminine stereotypes more and more. So it just seems like our relationship to femininity has something to do with self-awareness and irony, but for me, once I was a feminist, I still couldn't do it, even ironically.

AN: Yeah, I think I told you guys last week that there was a while when I did play "femme." For a long time, when I was young, I acted like a boy, and then when I went into graduate school, I started wearing slinky, low-cut dresses. And one of my professors sexually harassed me—repeatedly. He was always leering and telling me how beautiful that I looked. That was the moment at which I had to stop playing feminine. And that was when I pierced my nose and cut my hair and stopped wearing dresses. Essentially, I said to myself, "Oh, this is what's gonna happen if I play the 'femme' role. Men will feel free to do this to me." It wasn't funny anymore—it wasn't a joke anymore at that point. Because this man was slimy—I didn't like him, you know, and it really freaked me out that he felt free to do that. And I do think it was because of the way I dressed. If I were wearing trousers all the time, I don't think he would have harassed me. I really don't.

AC: So we've all had some experience with being feminine, playing with femininity.

AN: What does femininity mean to us?

AC: We all associate it a lot with clothes.

AN: And hair. [Everyone laughs]

AC: We all had long hair. Actually, it's really funny that when I was in junior high I did this modeling thing. Well, I didn't—people put makeup on me and took my picture.

AN: You were a model, admit it!

AC: Right. But I was also really unpopular and didn't have any boyfriends. And then at one point I tried out for cheerleader, and I didn't make it. The next day I went out and cut my hair to what your length is, Annalee [very short].

AN: Ahh . . . you failed to be a cheerleader. [Everyone laughs]

AC: So that's part of what femininity was to me. It was about what I wore and what I looked like. It's interesting because the skirts that I wear now, I describe them to people as "cheerleader skirts"— they're short, flirty things.

AN: [looking at Ana's skirt] It's true. . . . Wow.

FJ: That *is* true!

AC: The skirts I wear are sort of the A-line.

AN: That is a total cheerleader skirt.

AC: A little, kilty thing. . . . I don't know if there's some deep, psychic link here [laughs] or not. So it's clothes, it's makeup, it's how we present ourselves physically. Anything else?

AN: I think it's important to hold on to the fact that being a model for you was where you got your femininity from.

FJ: Being on display.

AC: I think being a cheerleader is being on display. Actually, my dad said that to me—you know, to make me feel better when I failed at cheerleading. He said, "Ana, you don't want to be a cheerleader. They just watch, and they're there to be watched. They watch and they're watched. You wanna be on the field. You wanna play." He was telling me . . .

AN: "Be a boy."

FJ: Well, in contrast to Jillian, my upbringing was different or "alternative." My mom was very much the seventies feminist. And I was raised in what she hoped was a very gender-neutral sort of way, so the moment when I shaved my legs and started putting on makeup— she flipped out and gave me this feminist lecture about "women's gender roles" and blah blah . . .

AN: Wow, lucky!

FJ: But it was sort of a rebellion, you know, "I'm gonna put on makeup!" And it was a rebellion against my mother. So for a while I did the feminine thing, only really ineptly, as a reaction to my mom.

AC: And doing the feminine thing, once again, it's clothes and makeup? Or do we also act differently when we're being feminine? Can we get enough distance from that to say, "We were more submissive then"?

JS: Well, I know for me, wearing feminine clothes made me have a different kind of attitude. Now, wearing jeans, Doc Martens, and a leather jacket gives me the strength of attitude I need to face the world in a slightly different way. And it may be fairly superficial, but I think it does resonate in other ways.

AN: I agree, it's really true, because I basically can't teach if I'm wearing a dress. The only dress I can teach in is the one I have that looks like a flannel work shirt.

FJ: I never wear dresses to teach.

AC: So does that mean you're not feminine?

AN: When I wear dresses or when I play the feminine role, I feel vulnerable, and I feel exposed—I also giggle more, I flirt more. When I dress like a man, I flirt in a different way—I flirt in a powerful way, or something. When I wear a dress, I flirt by acting silly, and I make eye contact with men. For example, last night my partner wanted me to dress up, sort of, for this nightclub that we went to . . .

AC: He wanted you to be feminine?

AN: Yeah, he wanted me to wear a tight shirt. I have, you know, sort of large breasts, and men will stare at my chest when I wear a tight shirt. And it makes me pleased and absolutely want to throw up at the same time. I simultaneously have the urge to vomit and smile. [Everyone laughs] There is this feeling of, "Wow . . . you think I'm attractive!" And you're so grateful, because the failure to be feminine is bound up in feeling ugly, or, well, I felt ugly.

AC: Yeah.

JS: Yeah.

FJ: I did too.

Being Ugly

AC: As my little story about being a model illustrates, feeling ugly had nothing to do with how in any objective sense we appeared.

FJ: I was objectively ugly.

AC: You keep saying so, but I don't think it has much to do with that, really.

AN: I don't either.

FJ: OK, but I went through that period of time when I at least felt ugly and everybody else acted as if I was ugly, so for all intents and purposes I was ugly. [Everyone laughs] If I felt it and other people felt it, then I was. Objectivity doesn't go into this. Well, now at least when I go somewhere and am kind of dressed up and guys are looking at me in that way, I enjoy that and feel pleased yet contemptuous at the same time. I enjoy the fact that I am exerting some sort of power over them, because some of them start babbling like idiots when they try to talk to me and start behaving in a certain way. I can tell that they are behaving differently because of how I look, and it's fun to have the power to change their behavior—because they are the same guys that years ago would have ignored me.

AC: But is that power?

AN: It's power, but—and this is why being feminine makes me want to throw up—it scares the shit out of me when men act like that, because I'm always afraid that they are thinking I'm "meat." I imagine that they are planning how they are going to take advantage of me and kill me or something, you know.

FJ: You see, I enjoy that feeling of danger. Because you are right, there is a definite feeling of danger to that.

AN: It scares me.

JS: It seems that partly that one of the things we notice as women is our bodies as opposed to our minds. It's as if because we're all academics and into being smart and successful, we want to be taken seriously for our minds, and being feminine would somehow just make us all body or something. It draws attention to us as bodies. All the things we're talking about are, after all, external and connected to our appearance.

AN: Men pose a bodily threat to us. So what is that pleasure, then? [To JS:] Did you experience that when you were feminine?

JS: Being feminine?

AN: You know, performing feminine?

JS: Partly, though not that much. Because me trying to be ultra-feminine was also a kind of reaction to people who, when I was growing up, told me I was fat. I think I was determined to prove that I could be attractive, and I tried really, really hard. Of course, I always failed, so I didn't get that thrill of attention that other people are suggesting they did.

Freya's Adventure

FJ: There was this time I was at a bar with this beautiful woman with long, blond hair. It was a straight bar and we started making out right there, and all these straight men were staring at us. They couldn't believe what they were seeing, and I was totally enjoying the fact that they were watching us and seeing this, and this one guy came up to us and he said, "Oh my God, I can't believe this," and he was totally going off, and I'm like, "What's the matter—you're just so turned on you don't know what to do with yourself, or what?" I mean, it's not something I would ever say generally, but I was sort of performing, enjoying the fact that they were watching us. And he said, "Yeah, something like that," and I'm all, "Go rent a video," you know, just completely over the top. "Go rent a video," and then we started making out again and enjoying the fact that they were watching us, you know, just playing with that whole dangerous atmosphere. We were enjoying the fact that they were watching it and totally turned on but sort of aggressive and weird about it too. Because we were in the middle of a straight bar; this wasn't a gay bar. We were just sort of playing with a sense of them watching us, and the danger of it too.

AN: The danger that they might violate you, basically.

FJ: Right.

AN: Because that's the danger. I mean, you're asking, "Are you going to rape me?"

FJ: Yeah, exactly.

AN: When I was being femme, I put myself in those situations a lot—where, had I not been lucky, I could have been raped.

AC: Yeah.

JS: Yeah, me too.

AN: I mean, that's scary. And that's something I only did when I was performing "feminine."

FJ: But going back to what we were saying earlier about feminist identity: part of feminism is trying to refute this idea of "Oh, you were asking for it." So, in a sense, we are kind of performing that by "asking for it." And reserving the right to be furious if anything were to happen. But it's still really dangerous.

AN: That's interesting . . .

AC: It's interesting that you weren't enjoying this other woman.

FJ: Well . . .

AC: But the way you told the story—all we know is that she was beautiful. I mean, were you enjoying it? I mean were you enjoying *her*? If you had been somewhere else . . .

FJ: I was enjoying her like a straight man would. I was enjoying watching the scenario.

AC: You were enjoying them watching you.

FJ: Yeah.

AN: You were being the ubiquitous lesbian topos from a porno movie.

FJ: Exactly. [All laugh] That's why I said, "Go rent a porno flick."

JS: No one will know what "topos" means.

AN: The women who are editing this anthology are English department people, so they'll know "topos." [All laugh]

JS: It sounds like you thought of it as a conquest, because you were referring to her as a straight woman. . . . Clearly she wasn't straight, right?

AC: As straight as . . .

FJ: Well, *I'm* straight. [All laugh]

AN: We'll leave that one aside.

JS: I would hesitate to call you straight.

AN: You know the Kinsey scale. . . . You are probably a one or a two on the Kinsey scale.

FJ: Neither of us had been to bed with a woman before, put it that way. And we were both enjoying the fact that men were watching. And we were performing this sexuality. I wouldn't want to call it a lesbian identity, because real lesbians would probably be completely sickened by this behavior.

AN: What is a *real* lesbian? [All laugh]

FJ: That was a real turn-on . . . watching the men watching me. Knowing what I looked like through their eyes, I enjoyed the fact that I was completely playing with them.

AC: It sounds sexy, just to my conventionally socialized sort of sexual aesthetic. That does sound like a sexy scene. But, umm . . .

AN: But it does sound dangerous.

AC: Yes, it does sound dangerous. But that was what I was getting to, the question we were on before Freya's story—the question "Are you going to rape me?" and the idea that that is a question in being feminine. That question is always there.

"Are You Going to Rape Me?"

AC: If you're a woman, the question "Are you going to rape me?" is a part of your existence. When I have arguments about feminism with guys, I say, "That is the one thing you will probably never experience . . . is that question always being there." And feminism is about wanting to erase that question. Is that the same thing as wanting to make it "OK" to be women?

FJ: I think it means you want to push that boundary. You don't want to say, "OK, men are kind of dangerous, so we shouldn't do this kind of thing; we should stay away from them and stay in our own little women's enclave, because it's too scary to go out there." In a way, performing this type of femininity, going out there and creating these

kind of situations where the typical rape scenario is a plausible out-
come, feeds into our power feminism thing. You're pushing it, you're
saying, "Come on, rape me, fucker" . . .

AC: But what if it really happened? You could just have easily
told us that story and it would end with "And they threw us down on
the pool table and raped us." And it would not be such a cute story.
You would not be going, "And that's what I think power feminism is
all about, is come on, man, rape me," because what if they do it?

FJ: But in a way we were safe. We were in a bar, there were a lot
of people; at the time it didn't occur to me that it could happen.

AC: But it does happen.

AN: What Freya was saying reminds me that one of the problems
with power is that it *does* reinforce the status quo. Because you *do* play
into those rape fantasies by acting like a porno movie. And if at some
level you are actually consciously saying, "Come on, fucker, rape
me"—men *are* picking up on it. The way you talked to that guy was
very provocative, and, sure, that doesn't give him the right to rape you.
But when two guys get into a bar fight and the one guy says, "Yeah
come on, fucker, come on," and the other guy hits him, we say he was
asking for it. Here we are, we identify with men, and I'd say it's a similar kind of situation—one might argue plausibly you were asking for it
in the same way that guy was "asking" to be punched. We're talking
about erasing the question "Are you going to rape me?" and I worry
that certain kinds of power feminism run the risk of replacing that
question with "You won't rape me, 'cause I'll rape you first in one way
or another." This is a version of what you guys were doing in the bar.
I don't mean to suggest that your actions were the equivalent of rape,
but they *were* needlessly aggressive and, to a certain extent, humiliat-
ing for the men around you. You were taunting these men with your
unavailability, with your flagrant display of sexuality, and then saying,
"And you can't have us, and we're going to fuck with you about it."
I think we should be suspicious of our impulses in that direction. Do
we want to become another flavor of "the rapist"? some sort of pas-
sive-aggressive rapist? I do *not* want to.

JS: Do you realize that so far we've talked almost entirely about
how our male-identification or rejection of femininity affects our
interactions with men? It seems to be one of the dangers of being male-
identified—that we are so anxious to assimilate into male culture that
we just want to leave women behind. Perhaps not literally, but cer-

tainly the way in which this is manifesting itself in our discussion, it seems like that could be a danger.

Reconciling Feminism and Masculinity

AN: How do we reconcile our feminist identities with our masculine identities?

AC: I think one of my basic justifications for being male-identified is that I feel that transgressiveness is good, subversiveness is good. I know it's kind of lame to say that so absolutely, but I feel that I am crossing gender boundaries, and by crossing lines you can prove to people that identities are not essentialist, gender is not essential, and that, for me, is a feminist goal.

JS: Well, I'm actually still deeply conflicted about being both male-identified and being a feminist, and one of the ways I reconcile it is that it's only a very recent thing for me to actually accept that men can also be feminists. Somehow in my mind this has been a way for me to reconcile being both male-identified and being a feminist, but I still do find it very problematic, because it does seem like a form of assimilation into male culture.

FJ: For me, the main point is highlighting the constructed nature of all kinds of gender roles. I don't feel that any one sort of identification is any more "real" than any other kind of identification; I always feel like I'm "performing" a role. So I like the idea of being able to perform masculinity or traditional femininity in ways that challenge the idea that these roles are connected with the body—that's why I feel that it's a feminist thing. When I'm performing masculinity, I'm obviously questioning what *is* real masculinity, and at the same time, when I'm performing femininity, I'm questioning the fact that it's rooted in some way to my body, performing it the way men, or gay men, would perform femininity.

AN: It seems like what all of us have ended up talking about is how we reconcile our male half and our female half. Our female half is our feminist half, and somehow we're trying to reconcile it with a non-feminist male half. I have to say that if I were to have any "true" identity, it probably *is* a male identity, and that's hard to reconcile with the fact that for a lot of my life I've hated men for being sexists. I don't know how to reconcile my two halves, because I do feel that being male-identified is not feminist somehow. I think one of the things that we tend to forget about feminism is that it's a methodology which is intended to critique forms of domination, and specifically patriarchal domination. Being male-identified, you're identifying with a set of behaviors which have historically been oppressive behaviors, specifically toward us as women, so it is problematic. It's almost as if the male half and female half inside of me are always fighting—and the male half is always winning. Gender is, after all, based on a notion of hierarchy and its enforcement. Masculinity wins because it's on top. I still can't figure out how to stop having that fight.

JS: I agree with most of what you said, and the fact that we *have* spent most of the time talking about how we participate with men in culture almost speaks to the fact that being male-identified *is* a form of assimilation. We all know of people who feel almost a kind of disappointment at walking into a room full of women, and I think that feeling or experience is extremely negative. I definitely *don't* think that's a goal of feminism.

FJ: I'm not too concerned about oppressing men, but if I thought that I was in some way oppressing other women I would feel really guilty about that; but with men, it's like men can take care of themselves. I know that's not really a good stance to have, because part of gender studies and feminist instruction is to understand that men are vulnerable and men can be hurt too, but for some reason I don't feel the need to concern myself too much about that, though I do worry about hurting other women.

AC: I think we're all conflicted in one way or another. We started out this section with, how do we reconcile our feminist identification with our male-identification? And in a way the question is also, how do we reconcile our male-identified wants with our physical bodies? One could say our male-identification oppresses us, or that we're participating in a culture that is in some ways oppressive to the kind of person who has a female body.

AN: I really like that formulation. So many times I have felt like a stranger inhabiting my body, like I'm an alien who's been transported into this body. And let me tell you, it's deeply puzzling and just weird, because we end up objectifying ourselves. As "men," we have to look at our bodies as objects. We have to be somehow separate from our bodies. I wonder if that's what all women feel. Female-identified women must feel that way too, because having a female body is to be an object.

JS: Although I must say that when I *did* participate in women's culture in a more significant way, that was the time when I felt most comfortable with my body, and it has had a kind of spillover effect on my life now. One of the things that feminism taught me to do was to *not* hate my body, in the way in that being "feminine" had taught me to hate it.

AC: Ideally, feminism should give us a way not to feel conflicted, that our identity and our body don't clash.

What Made Us Feminists?

FJ: Well, I was an anomaly, because I was raised "feminist" by my mom, and I kind of rejected her values for a while. Then I took a women's studies class—the history of women in Western civilization, one of those survey courses—and while reading all the stuff and listening to the professor, it suddenly hit me, "Gee, Mom was *right!*" So for me, my moment of feminist identification was reconciling myself to what my mom had taught me all along, and that's when I became a "feminist." From there I've been rearticulating and nuancing the feminist construction, but that initial moment was, "Gosh, Mom was right."

AN: Well, I don't know if there's an exact moment when I became a feminist, but I would have to say that it was probably when I came to grad school. It's funny, because it was really men who taught me to be a feminist. I have this very distinct memory of the moment at which things clicked for me and I realized the way that women are represented is a problem. I was watching a David Lynch movie with a former boyfriend and a gay male friend of mine, and both of them said, "Oh my God, the representations of women in this movie are completely sexist." And I said, "What? What do you mean? I don't understand." And they said, "Look—all the women are either angels or prostitutes."

AC: What was it, *Blue Velvet*?

AN: No, actually it was a performance art video and it was really abstract. It was a lot like *Blue Velvet*, in that it had certain women who were floating, and other women who were put inside of machines and penetrated by objects—stuff like that. And I said to my friends, "Oh, I suppose you're right." At that moment I realized, "This is what it means to be a female body in my culture." The two of them were saying, "I don't understand how you don't understand this."

AC: So was it within the same moment that you identified as feminist and became a "man" and cut your hair?

AN: It was pretty much at the same time, and it was also around the same time that I identified as queer as well.

AC: My story is somewhat similar, in that my overt identification as masculine-identified became stronger at the moment that I claimed feminism; for me, part of claiming to be a feminist was claiming a male-identification. In high school I was a loud-mouthed bitch, and I realized that feminism allowed you to claim "bitch" as a good thing, or that it at least allowed me to say, "Well, you're calling me a bitch because you don't agree or because you're threatened by me." Calling myself a feminist allowed me to claim a lot of "negative" things as not necessarily bad. Like, calling me a dyke is fine, because I know why you're doing it. Feminism allowed me to see the power structure. The same moment I asserted a male identity, I also asserted a feminist identity, and I didn't see them as being in conflict.

FJ: There's one thing that we haven't quite touched on. In terms of sexuality, a major part of my male-identification—which I think is part of both straight and gay male-identification—is the separation of sex and sexuality from emotions. That's a huge part of my life, because women—both traditionally female-identified women and feminists—talk a lot about how women feel differently than men about sex, conflate sex and emotion, and are inherently nurturing, et cetera. So for me, a major reason for adopting male-identification is in order to reject that model of how women deal with sex. And that's primarily what comes to mind when I think of myself as a male.

AN: Or a stereotypical male.

FJ: OK, the stereotypical man. [Lots of murmurs and laughter]

JS: Well, I have a very concrete moment when I became a feminist. I was an undergrad and I was doing women's studies. The fact that I had enrolled to be a major in women's studies suggests that I was already thinking about "becoming" a feminist, but I hadn't quite realized it at the time. I had a class on the ways in which gender is socially constructed, and it was like the veils were lifted from my eyes; suddenly a lot of things about my life started to make sense. It really affected me in a serious way, although it was also a kind of relief, because things suddenly *did* make sense. Within a year or so, my life was very different. But I didn't associate being a feminist with being male-identified, I actually associated it with being very female-identified, and it was only later that I would say I became male-identified.

Possible Solutions

AC: I think the most interesting thing that I've picked up is that we did talk a lot about how we're men. We can't seem to stop performing maleness, even though we're in a situation where it's established we should all feel comfortable, we should all have that said. And it took us a direct question to get to feminism—you could hear the gearshift turning when we took that turn in the conversation. It's interesting that some of us associated our feminist coming-out with our coming-out as men. And I wonder, is there any lesson to be learned from that? If we felt comfortable as women, at some point, is there a way to be comfortable with it again? Or is the answer to give up on women? I don't think that's the answer.

AN: I don't either. . . . I think if there is any answer, it is something like everybody becoming a hybrid gender. As much as it's really hard for all of us to accept this, it also does involve treating men as our equals, or treating men as we would treat ourselves. Like I said, I've spent a lot of my life hating men and trying to do them one better by being more manly than them—having a bigger dick than them, even though it's not visible—so I know it's hard to imagine doing this. What I want to do is try to figure out what the connection is between male-identification and coming out as a feminist, because I think the fact that we did that may mean we learned the wrong lesson from feminism, a lesson which says, "We can dominate too." Or, "We can abuse men, or treat men the way men have unfairly treated women." To be strong women—feminists—we had to imagine ourselves as men. Maybe this means that there's something lacking in feminism. Feminism needs to send a different message, a message about the fact that men and women are not separate, these identities are not separate. There needs to be some way that masculine and feminist identities aren't in conflict, that these identities are happy with one another, that they're not raping and killing each other.

FJ: Having joyful sex!

AN: Or that they're just friends, you know? They don't have to have sex.

FJ: Yeah, right. [Giggles]

AN: And I would hope that there could be some sort of new brand of feminism that would include men without any questions or discomfort.

AC: It would improve feminism.

AN: And it would make us less angry at men and make men less afraid of us as feminists. Think of all the times that you've scared men shitless by being who you are. We don't want to scare men, we just want to teach them that women are human too.

AC: "We come in peace . . ."

AN: Yeah, we come in peace. It's as if in feminism today we're trying to get revenge, as if we're saying, "Well, you scared us for thousands of years; now look at us, we're gonna scare you." Why? I mean, sexism taught us how bad that was—why do we want to do that?

FJ: Well, there are a lot of things that come to mind. For one thing, my feminist-identification and my male-identification came at very separate times. My feminist-identification was the first step—and that was embracing the feminism of my mother. She taught me that men and women are different, that women have been oppressed, and about a monolithic patriarchy—all these things which were received ideas—and I think it was important for me to do that at the time. I see my male-identification as rearticulating and reforming my mother's style of feminism into *my* new style of feminism. My mom was saying, "So men are this way, women are that way, women have these traits, and it's better to be a woman." I'm saying, "Well, wait, Mom, I can inhabit these traditional male roles that you've discussed, and I can inhabit these traditional female, nonfeminist types of manifestations that you've discussed, and at the same time not be either oppressed or the oppressor." At least in my mind, it may be awfully utopian, but I'm sort of charting new territory. Another thing that you guys talked about . . . is this whole idea of the rape scenario, or rape sex versus what Annalee calls tantric sex, which sounds really dull.

AC: What about just good sex?

FJ: But for me the idea of a rape fantasy or a rape scenario is very different from an actual rape. The idea of playing with rape scenarios does not make it antithetical to feminism or empowerment or "good sex." I guess the episode we were talking about earlier with me in the bar was playing into that kind of rape fantasy, rather than the actual scenario, but as you guys pointed out, that's very dangerous when other people don't see that distinction . . .

AN: When you're not in a safe space.

JS: But I would say that even in a safe space it might be problematic to reenact these kind of power roles. I mean, I find these kinds of scenarios as seductive as everyone else, but I still think it's problematic. Even when we reenact power relations in a safe space—in a playful way, or in a way that transgresses boundaries in this ultra-self-conscious way—I'm not sure that it actually makes that much difference. And, in fact, it can sometimes end up being another form of assimilation, or a way in which we just become increasingly part of masculine or male culture that continues to oppress women. That doesn't seem to necessarily be the answer. I don't think I have an alternative, I just think that we need to be wary of thinking that being playful with our identities is actually going to make that much of a difference.

AN: We do all have rape fantasies, and I agree with Jillian that there's a way in which participating in those fantasies reinforces the status quo and does run the risk of not only being assimilationist but also revaluing violence as positive. It's as if you were saying, "Violence and violation are OK in this scenario. But we don't want them in these other scenarios." Finally, that's a double standard. And how do you teach that without being hypocritical? It's like when men said, "Well, it's OK for men to do this, but it's not OK for women to do this—even though we're all human beings." I mean, it's a similar double standard: "It's OK for Jillian to be raped in an S-M club, but it's not OK for Biff in a bar to rape her." How do we explain that to Biff? How does Biff know if you're consenting? That's the whole thing. How do we teach Biff this stuff? "Well, Biff, it's OK to rape somebody here, but not OK there." Poor, confused Biff.

AC: But there is a difference—it's not rape.

FJ: It's the *idea* of rape. . . . Real rape is very different.

JS: But is it so different? It's still about reenacting these power relations. We're still completely invested in a relationship where someone overpowers us and we are being overpowered. Or, for a change, we might be the overpowerer. Being ironic and self-conscious about power relations is one thing, but does it actually make any difference?

AN: That's it. Ana is now leaving. OK, we're turning the tape off.

Conclusion

As women who came of age in the 1980s and 1990s, we frequently encounter a certain "generation gap" between the kinds of analyses and ideas that dominate contemporary feminism, and our personal experiences as feminists living in the 1990s. Although the recent proliferation of studies on masculinity in the mass media demonstrates that feminists are certainly beginning to study men and male culture, the place of men and masculinity within feminism remains an uncertain one. We are not suggesting an uncritical celebration of masculinity in toto, but we do feel that there must be a place for men and positive, nonoppressive "masculinities" in a feminist politics for the 1990s. As women who identify with certain aspects of masculinity and who often find men to be a source of comfort and solidarity, we feel that a gender politics for the future needs to have a better understanding of the complex relationship between men, masculinity, and patriarchy.

Part of being a "third wave feminist" means grappling with the contradictions of sympathizing with second wave feminism while trying to divorce ourselves from its legacy of separatism. Although it's tempting to call what we are doing a form of feminist praxis, it is more accurately a kind of performance or coping mechanism that helps us reconcile our internalized sense that "masculinity equals power," with our desire for social potency as women. Identifying with men allows us to feel strong, but it also, unfortunately, can reinforce the idea that being female is a form of weakness.

For some of us, male-identification means dressing and acting in a way that might be called "butch"; for others it means enjoying and participating in male-oriented culture, such as violent films or the indie rock scene. Some of us participate in, and identify with, the queer community, whereas others enjoy "straight" culture too. Moreover, we frequently find that our place as academics within conventional departments demands a certain competitiveness—typically associated with men—in order to participate adequately within our chosen fields. While we support feminist-oriented education, entertainment, and events, there are times when we feel more comfortable within "mainstream" (i.e., male-dominated) culture. Sometimes our male-identification manifests itself within the interpersonal realm; at other times, we adopt it as a way of coping with the public—and frequently hostile—world.

However, we all share an awareness and a self-consciousness about gender roles and their relationship to social power and domination in all aspects of contemporary life. What some of us enjoy about violent action films, for example, is the implicit critique of conventional masculinity we can find in such narratives. Similarly, what some of us like about "performing" femininity in a fraternity bar is the sense of irony and subversion such an experience allows. Our relationship to gender—both our masculinity and our femininity—is, therefore, inflected by our understanding that such identities are socially constructed and, by implication, subject to change. We associate our male-identification, therefore, with a sense of possibility—the possibility that every time the automatic connection between men, masculinity, and power is called into question, one might find potential for the power structures of patriarchy and male privilege to be challenged.

But we should end on a cautionary note. It is ultimately dangerous to assert that becoming male-identified women or ironically performing our gender(s) can create a truly just and equal society. We need to reiterate that our gender bending is often simply a coping strategy for dealing with rapidly changing social roles and expectations. Like any coping strategy, our male-identification has allowed us to negotiate and to participate in environments or situations that are largely hostile toward women, particularly "feminine" ones. That is, our "masculinity" has mostly helped us to escape a certain degree of victimization. It has not made us entirely comfortable with who we are.

We should remember, however, that the masculine role offers us positive experiences and opportunities beyond merely coping with a sexist world. For example, we value "masculine" qualities such as leadership, assertiveness, independence, intellect, and feeling welcome within the public sphere. Of course, not all men perfectly embody these qualities, just as all women are not "feminine." Moreover, gender is not the only problem men and women are likely to encounter in society. Patriarchy is, after all, only *one* way human beings create relationships of domination and exploitation. Whereas second wave feminism taught us to dissociate femininity from disempowerment, perhaps third wave feminism can promote the idea of masculinity without oppression. A third wave feminist politics is more properly a politics of gender, which involves critiquing and reevaluating both male and female social roles so that both genders may live in peace with one another. Perhaps the most radical move feminism could make would be to emphasize the commonalities between men and women, rather than the differences.

THIRD WAVE ACTIVISM AND YOUTH MUSIC CULTURE

Copyright 1994 by Barry Baldridge

Miss Lady Hand Grenade, *courtesy of Jen Smith*

Courtesy of Free to Fight!, *Candy-Ass Records (1996)*

THIRD WAVE ACTIVISM AND YOUTH MUSIC CULTURE

Activism in the third wave takes diverse and compelling forms, but one—music production (and consumption)—is particularly important, because of the ways it has spawned so many forms of youth culture. There are good reasons for this. Immediately accessible, emotionally compelling, and most often produced by "youth" themselves, music has long existed as a site of complicated rebellions against, complicities with, and revisions of various forms of the cultural status quo. The late 1980s and early 1990s saw a major insurgence of politically motivated revisionary forms, discussed here under the rubrics "Riot Grrrl" and "gangsta rap/hip-hop."

Music is a potent motivator and can be used effectively as a political tool in the contemporary context because of the communities and frameworks of meaning it seems to offer in a social and cultural context in which lives can often seem devoid of meaning. As Andrew Ross states,

> The level of attention and meaning invested in music by youth is still unmatched by almost any other organized activity in society, including religion. As a daily companion, social bible, commercial guide and spiritual source, youth music is still *the* place of faith, hope, and refuge. In the forty-odd years since "youth culture" was created as a consumer category, music remains the medium for the most creative and powerful stories about those things that often seem to count the most in our daily lives.[1]

Music provides a mode of self-assertion in a world that can feel hostile and indifferent. It's very personal, and it provides an immediate context for bonding. For me, music does "count the most in [my] daily [life]," in those moments when I'm feeling like there's something I need to connect with, something I've simply got to say, such as, "I can kick the shit out of the world, so get out of my way," or, "Yeah, the world's fucking me over, and I want everyone to know." People have their own preferences, and for me there's nothing like the screams of Courtney or Kat or PJ or Ani to make me feel like my sense of reality is valid, that I have a place, that there are people out there who feel like I do.

As Melissa Klein and Jen Smith discuss in their respective essays, "Duality and Redefinition: Young Feminism and the Alternative Music Community" and "Doin' It for the Ladies—Youth Feminism: Cultural Productions/Cultural Activism," a recent movement in music directly informed by social critique was one known as "Riot Grrrl." Riot Grrrl was a young, protofeminist movement that got its start in the punk scene in Olympia, Washington, in 1991 and has since been proclaimed dead by music-scene sound-biters "in the know." Extremely influential in introducing a younger generation of women to feminism and in re-opening the question of women's marginalization within the music and other industries, such as fashion, Riot Grrrl drew aesthetic criticism for its do-it-yourself approach to music, as well as for its antimedia stance and for practices such as holding women-only shows or women-only mosh pits to draw attention to the problem of sexual abuse. Riot Grrrl is seen by many third wave feminists, however, as one of feminism's most active sites, one that spawned a new, specifically third wave feminist culture that goes far beyond the music scene. Like many forms of activism in the third wave, Riot Grrrl relies on the idea of contradiction as a definition. Kim France, writing on the Riot Grrrl movement for *Rolling Stone* in 1993, states, "riot grrrls' unifying principle is that being female is inherently confusing and contradictory and women have to find a way to be sexy, angry and powerful at the same time."[2]

Like Riot Grrrls, women in rap ostensibly made the most noise in the late 1980s and early 1990s. As part of the Native Tongues movement, male and female rappers who endorsed feminist politics in their song lyrics, such as Queen Latifah and Monie Love, set feminist politics to hip-hop grooves. Yet the commercial success of male-dominated gangsta rap has overshadowed their accomplishments. For critic Ronin Ro, gangsta rap is a "national tragedy," because it has ruined the efforts of positive, socially conscious emcees who have tried to alter racist beliefs.[3] But new developments in hip-hop suggest that Ro's elegy has come too soon.

Renewed interest in the Native Tongues movement suggests that gangsta rap is losing its grip on the public imagination and that new, progressively feminist artists are on the rise. Recent features in music magazines such as *Urb* and *Request* document the reemergence of the Native Tongues movement. The current success of the Fugees, A Tribe Called Quest, and Nas (all artists who draw upon gangsta rap but avoid its pitfalls) indicates that masculinist bravado isn't all rap has to offer. From bisexual Me'Shell NdegéOcello's soulful jams to the co-ed Fugees' mix of rock and rap, the current face of hip-hop blurs the lines between muscial genres. Moreover, as Jeff Niesel's "Hip-Hop Matters: Rewriting the Sexual Politics of Rap Music" shows, feminism in rap cuts across many boundaries.

Notes

1. Andrew Ross, introduction to *Microphone Fiends: Youth Music and Youth Culture* (New York: Routledge, 1994), 3.

2. Kim France, "Grrrls at War," *Rolling Stone*, 8–22 July 1993, 23.

3. See Ronin Ro, *Gangsta: Merchandising the Rhymes of Violence* (New York: St. Martin's Press, 1996), 10.

CHAPTER ELEVEN

Duality and Redefinition: Young Feminism and the Alternative Music Community

Melissa Klein

I am twenty-five years old. On my left upper arm I have a six-inch long tattoo of a voluptuous cowgirl. One of her hands rests jauntily on her jutting hip. The other is firing a gun. An earlier feminist might frown upon my cowgirl's fringed hot pants and halter top as promoting sexual exploitation, and might see her pistol as perpetuating male patterns of violence. Yet I see this image as distinctly feminist. Having a tattoo signifies a subculture that subverts traditional notions of feminine beauty. That this tattoo is a pinup girl with a gun represents the appropriation and redefinition of sexuality, power, and violence—ideas characteristic of third wave punk feminism.

I was born in 1971 and am part of a generation of young women who grew up during or after the feminist "second wave" and who, as a result, have mixed feelings about traditional feminism. Many young women hestitate to take on the mantle of feminism, either because they fear being branded as fanatical "feminazis" or because they see feminism not as a growing and changing movement but as a dialogue of the past that conjures up images of militantly bell-bottomed "women's libbers." The issues pertinent to older women do not necessarily resonate in our lives. We do not, for instance, experience the double burden of the proverbial "superwoman"—attempting to be both model mother and ambitious professional—because we often have neither "real" jobs nor children.

A new social context means that within the alternative music community and elsewhere, girls have created a new form of feminism. Much in the same way that race relations in this country have moved from the ideal of the "color-blind society" toward the promotion of diversity and multiculturalism, feminism has moved away from a struggle for equality toward an engagement with difference, an assertion that girls can have the best of both worlds (that they, for example, can be both violently angry and vampily glamorous). This feminism owes much to the struggles of the second wave, yet it differs in many ways, especially in the way it is defined by contradiction.

Third wave feminism is certainly not confined to punk culture. For many women in my age range, because *sexism* is a word in our vocabulary, we have the means to recognize it in our lives, even if this recognition does not occur immediately and even if we have had to find new ways to analyze sexism and to take action. Though we grew up in the so-called aftermath of feminism and have taken some of its gains for granted, we experienced the backlash in areas such as reproductive rights as a rude jolt into action. Activism in the arena of AIDS drew renewed attention to gay and lesbian rights. The resurgence of interest in these and other issues began to shape a new feminism, a new kind of activism emphasizing our generation's cynical and disenfranchised temperament, born of distaste for the reactionary politics and rat-race economics of the 1980s. Our politics reflects a postmodern focus on contradiction and duality, on the reclamation of terms. S-M, pornography, the words *cunt* and *queer* and *pussy* and *girl*—are all things to be reexamined or reclaimed. In terms of gender, our rebellion is to make it camp. The underground music community has served as a particularly fertile breeding ground for redefining a feminism to fit our lives.

For many of us, our paradoxical identity with traditional feminism began in childhood. Thanks to the gains of second wave feminists, we grew up in a comparatively less gender-segregated environment and with expanded expectations of ourselves. My parents made sure the idea that girls are equal to boys was strongly ingrained in me. My mother marched at pro-choice rallies and tried to teach the neighborhood boys how to sew. She subscribed to *Ms.*, and each month I would look over the "No Comment" section (which I liked because it had pictures) and read the stories for kids. My father taught me to read when I was four, ordered science projects by mail for me and my two younger sisters, and played softball and soccer with us in our overgrown backyard. I even had an early introduction to the subject of gay pride when, at my day camp, I kissed another girl on the cheek and a boy said, "Eeeewww! You're a lesbian!" That afternoon when my mom picked me up in our old Ford Falcon, I asked her to explain the word *lesbian*, and she told me it meant a woman who loved other women. Reasoning that I loved my mother and sisters, and not quite comprehending the difference between loving and being in love, I went back to camp the next day and fiercely told the boy, "So what if I'm a lesbian? I'm proud I'm a lesbian."

The remarks of my less-than-enlightened fellow camper demonstrate that despite substantial gains made by the second wave and the influence of these gains in my life, the world around me was not a totally radical place. Within my family I was encouraged to do whatever I wanted, yet in the outside world I was encouraged toward "female" pursuits. I could throw a ball, and I could do more chin-ups than anyone else in my class, yet I spent more time on gymnastics, ballet, and diving—"female" activities that emphasized aesthetics, individual achievement, and grace, rather than aggression, strength, and teamwork. Like many girls, my self-confidence dwindled in adolescence. As I approached an age when peer support became more important than family support, my alienation grew, because I did not fit into the ideal of the popular girl. Whereas before, my self-confidence had come from my status as an academic achiever, I now suspected that my worth depended on my attractiveness to boys.

In the year I turned thirteen, I would smile whenever a female classmate came to school wearing a T-shirt that said, "A woman's place is in the House . . . and in the Senate." Yet that was the year I tried on high heels for the first time and started taking off my glasses at lunch when the boy I liked was nearby, even though it reduced my vision to such a blur that I could barely make him out. As I reached a crisis of confidence, my grades suffered. An often-praised A student in seventh-grade science class, by ninth grade I was getting D's in biology. Instead of doing my homework, I watched soaps, lounged in bed, or experimented in the mirror with makeup. In tenth grade at my new high school, I decided not to try out for the diving team and weaseled my way out of a semester of swimming, because I didn't want anyone looking at me in a bathing suit.

Around fourteen, I became interested in the punk scene. Here mainstream tastes in music and other things were scorned, and thrift-store clothes and outcast status worn with pride. Though my original style was more "traditionally" punk—I favored raccoon-style black eyeliner, combat boots, and the Sex Pistols—I soon gravitated toward the more politicized style prevalent at the time in Washington, D.C., where the close-knit punk community centered on Dischord, a record label started by Ian MacKaye and Jeff Nelson in 1981. The underground music scene provided an alternative to mainstream culture and politics in many ways. There were women within the punk scene who challenged gender ideals and who served as examples of strength and independence: they rode and fixed their own motorcycles, worked at clubs or booked shows, or documented their scene by taking photographs. Yet the punk scene was predominantly male. At this time in punk music (the mid-1980s), there were very few women in bands. When I saw the first show of Fire Party, a local band made up of all women—Kate Samworth, Natalie Avery, Nicky Thomas, and Amy Pickering—I realized it had never occurred to me that this could even be possible.

In 1988, three women, Leslie Clague, Cynthia Connolly, and Sharon Cheslow, published *Banned in D.C.: Photos and Anecdotes from the D.C. Punk Underground, 1979–85*. The photos and stories in this book document the presence of women early in the D.C. punk scene.[1] It is important to Cheslow, who currently both plays and distributes music, to credit the continuum of women in rock. To this end, she has been working on a project documenting women in early punk bands. In a *Village Voice* article about Cheslow's project, entitled "Punk's Matrilineage," Evelyn McDonnell comments dryly, "If you've labored at your art in relative obscurity for a decade and a half, only to suddenly find your milieu—in this case, 'angry women in rock'—touted as the Big New Thing, well you can either laugh or cry, or reeducate forgetful minds."[2]

As Cheslow's project points out, female-powered bands such as the Raincoats, the Slits, the Runaways, and X-Ray Spex played a pivotal part in the early history of punk as raucous waves of sound reverberated across the Atlantic from the United Kingdom to the big cities of the United States. Yet as punk seeped into the suburbs, it mutated into hard-core, fueled by the young male angst of the surfer-skater scene and characterized by pounding drums, frenzied guitar, and testosterone-laden lyrics. According to Cheslow, "As hard-core became more prevalent around 1981, a lot of the girls who had been involved in the mid to late seventies dropped out because of the increasingly macho and violent tendencies of the boys."[3]

Rock, in this regard, has been a kind of last frontier for women. The rock image—being confrontational, lewd, angst-ridden, wild, and loud—has been a male domain met with a head-shaking but tolerant "boys will be boys" attitude. The "bad boy" has always had a sanctioned niche in the mainstream that the "bad girl" has not. The rebel, the James Dean character, wins the heart of the wholesome pretty girl next door. The rock star (even if supremely ugly) marries the super-model, a scenario that has no parallel with the gender roles reversed. Though many girls in the alternative community held as fierce and well thought-out opinions as boys did, when it came to the all-important subject of music, they felt relegated to sideline roles such as fan or girlfriend.

The boys we associated with led "bohemian" lifestyles, questioned mainstream values, and held politically leftist viewpoints. They were unfailingly pro-choice, played benefit shows, believed in gay rights, and so on. And because they had been raised in a society that had assimilated feminist values, they, like us, held less fixed or negative assumptions about gender than any generation before them. Yet the music around which the scene revolved was generally played by boys. Boys occupied the public sphere. They were the ones onstage, the ones literally making the noise; girls occupied a supplementary place.

In a project for the June 1988 issue of the self-published fanzine *Maximum Rock'n'Roll*, Cynthia Connolly, Sharon Cheslow, Amy Pickering, and Lydia Ely arranged three sessions in which groups of sixteen women and eight men answered questions about the issues of women in the D.C. punk scene. The introduction of their article states, "In our music community, most men and women treat each other first and foremost as human beings." Yet one of the questions posed by the women was this:

> Why has our "alternative" society developed in the same way
> that "mainstream" society has—where females do organizational,
> behind-the-scenes tasks, and men perform? When we developed
> the list of people to invite for this, almost all the men were in
> bands. Most of the women were involved in some ways, but not
> in bands—like working for Dischord, or working on fanzines, or
> doing booking at clubs. Promoting, encouraging, supporting.

I see punk, like the antiwar and civil rights movements before it, as a place where young women learned or solidified radical means of analyzing the world and then applied these powers of analysis to their own lives, only to realize that, as girls, they felt disenfranchised within their own supposedly "alternative" community.

In 1970, women's rights leader Robin Morgan wrote of the experience of women in the student movement, "Thinking we were in-

volved in the struggle to build a new society, it was a slowly dawning
and depressing realization that we were doing the same work and playing the same roles in the Movement as out of it: typing speeches that
men delivered, making coffee but not policy . . ."[4] Despite the similarities in coming to consciousness, the means and methods through
which women in the alternative music community chose to express
themselves differed from those of earlier feminists, because they
stemmed from our experiences as girls in a subculture whose roots lay
in disaffection, destruction, and nihilism rather than in peace and love;
that is, we were punk rather than hippie. The 1960s counterculture
represented a challenge to conformity and an optimism that society
could change. Punk was also a reaction against conformity, but one
tempered by a disillusionment with the 1960s. Punk feminism grew
not out of girls wanting sensitive boys so much as girls wanting to be
tough girls; instead of boys wearing their hair long and getting called
pansies, girls cut their hair and were called dykes.

Yet the seeds of our feminism did grow out of our participation
in structures established by the second wave: taking women's studies
classes in college, volunteering at a battered women's shelter or at the
rape crisis hotline, attending pro-choice events. For me, the foreshad-
owing of my punk feminism was the frustration I felt when I would go
out with my boyfriend, who was in a band, and other boys would
come over, sit down without saying hello to me, and start talking to
him about music and "the revolution," which was mainly one of aesthetics rather than politics. I began to wonder what was so damned
revolutionary about staying up all night and combing your hair a certain way, when I had gotten up at four o'clock on a freezing January
morning to hold hands with other women defending a clinic, and had
listened to a boy whose girlfriend was inside having an abortion as he
confided that he had sold his stereo to pay for the procedure and asked
me how he could help her when it was over. I began to wonder, as
many other girls did before and after, why we did not get or give each
other credit for the contributions we made, and why toughness, anger,
and acts of rebellion were considered a male province.

As we began thinking individually about how we had experienced
oppression on the basis of gender, we also started making connections
with each other. We critiqued both popular culture and the underground culture in which we participated. We thought about school and
the books we had read, about the way that despite the second wave,

we had learned history with no idea how or whether women could be great or brave. We realized that early on in life we had learned a self-conscious sense of the male gaze, a constant awareness of the physical impression we make. Boys cannot appreciate this, unless perhaps they imagine as constant the feeling of walking alone at night through an unfamiliar neighborhood under hostile scrutiny. Upon examination, we saw that we shared with other girls experiences of being made uncomfortable, unsure of ourselves, or even abused because we were female. Girls began to draw parallels between different experiences: shame at being fat and bitterness at caring so much about our looks; secret competitiveness with other girls, coupled with self-dislike for being jealous; the unsettling feeling that we could not communicate with a boy without flirting; the sudden, engulfing shock of remembering being molested by a father or stepfather when we were too small to form words for such a thing. Straight and bi girls talked about having to give anatomy lessons every time we had sex with a boy. Queer and questioning girls talked about isolation and about mothers bursting into tears when they learned their daughters were gay. Girls who wanted to play music talked about not knowing how to play a guitar because they had never gotten one for Christmas like the boys did. Girls who played music complained that they were treated like idiots by condescending male employees when they went to buy guitar strings or drum parts. We began to see the world around us with a new vision, a revelation that was both painful and filled with possibility.

Young women's anger and questioning fomented and smoldered until it became an all-out gathering of momentum toward action. In the summer of 1991, the bands Bratmobile and Bikini Kill, self-proclaimed "angry grrrl" bands, came to D.C. for an extended stay, on loan from Olympia, Washington. Bikini Kill promoted its ideas under the slogans "Revolution Girl Style Now" and "Stop the J-Word Jealousy from Killing Girl Love." While subletting a room in the house where I lived, Allison Wolfe worked with Bratmobile bandmate Molly Neuman to produce Riot Grrrl's earliest manifestation, a pocket-sized fanzine by the same name. An initial experimental all-girl meeting evolved into a weekly forum for girls to discuss political, emotional, and sexual issues. That August also saw the International Pop Underground Convention (IPU), a brainchild of stalwart Olympia indie K ("No lackeys to the corporate ogre allowed"). IPU opened with Girl Day. As the idea of Riot Grrrl spread via band tours, fanzines, high school and college networks, and word of mouth, chapters sprang up around the country. A year later, in July 1992, the weekend-long Riot Grrrl Convention took place in D.C. Women gathered together for workshops on topics including sexuality, rape, unlearning racism, domestic violence, and self-defense, as well as attending two shows featuring female bands and spoken-word performers, and the "All-Girl All-Night Dance Party."

Riot Grrrl meetings owed much to the "personal as political" precedent set by second wave feminists. In *Civics for Democracy*, Katherine Isaac writes about women from the 1960s Student Nonviolent Coordinating Committee and the Students for a Democratic Society, who felt frustrated at the lack of seriousness with which the concerns of women's rights were taken:

> Many of these women began to meet with each other to form a separate movement. They used their organizing skills to set up small "consciousness-raising" discussion groups, which quickly multiplied across the country. As historian Sara Evans describes these groups, "The early meetings were intense and exhilarating. In a style they had learned in the civil rights movement and the new left, women explored the political meaning of their personal experiences. Again and again, individuals were shocked to discover that their lives were not unique but part of a larger pattern. The warm support and understanding of other women empowered them as they reclaimed the lost legacy of sisterhood."[5]

Like earlier movements, Riot Grrrl also relied on the strength of numbers to question male territory, but for purposes specific to punk. In "Revolution Girl Style Now," a 1992 *L.A. Weekly* article later reprinted in *Rock She Wrote*, Emily White writes:

> One of the most engaging metaphors of the Riot Girls is their dramatic invasion of the mosh pit. In Olympia, bands often don't perform on risers, so only the people up front can really see, and, given the violent crush of the pit, those people are almost always boys. The girls got tired of this. But most of them didn't want to dance in the pit—it hurts your boobs. And getting touched by a bunch of sweaty male strangers has all-too-familiar, nightmarish connotations for many girls. Perhaps moshing is just another one of what Barbara Kruger calls those "elaborate rituals" men have invented "in order to touch the skin of another man." But the girls wanted a space to dance in, so they formed groups and made their way to the front, protecting each other the whole way. Any boy who shoved them had a whole angry pack to deal with.[6]

Early Riot Grrrl ideology was much like the "safe-space," women-only feminism that characterized the second wave. Riot Grrrl often used second wave activist techniques but applied them to third wave forms. The "safe space" Riot Grrrl created was more often the mosh pit than the consciousness-raising group, but lyrically the music often functions as a form of CR. And whereas some second wave feminists fought for equal access to the workplace, some third wave feminists fought for equal access to the punk stage.

One of the most obvious ways that girls strove collectively to end the disparities within punk music was to put women onstage. The phenomenon of girls playing music grew explosively and exponentially. Girls taught their friends how to play instruments and encouraged through words or examples. Some chose to play with other girls to demonstrate unity, whereas others avoided the "girl band" stereotype and proved that they could "rock with the guys" by doing exactly that. There was encouragement to overcome intimidation, to just get up and play. Sometimes this resulted in debate about whether just playing, or "going for it," was the most important thing, or whether it undermined the status of women in rock to perform ill-played sets. I remember wincing at certain overly cutesy, discordant performances. Yet there is something about the mere image of a woman playing guitar that is thrilling, that gives me the same impression as the painting of Rosie the Riveter on my kitchen wall—a strong woman with a power tool waiting to be bent to her will.

While reworking feminism, these girls were simultaneously reworking punk, getting back to its roots, to a time when raw honesty of expression counted for more than perfect playing. Interviewed by Andrea Juno in *Angry Women in Rock*, Lois Maffeo, who had an early-1980s all-girl radio show and has been performing music herself since the mid-1980s, discounted the idea of musical "virtuosity":

> Men think that if you can do a really flawless guitar solo, you're a great musician! To me that's bogus. My own career is based on the eradication of the guitar solo. I think that is just complete wanking, and I don't want anything to do with it! People talk about hooks and bridges within songs and I'm like, "Call 'em whatever you want, I can only write a song as it comes out, and my songs don't have to have a structure that's already well-defined in male-dominated music." . . . It's not virtuosity, it's mimicry in a lot of these people who are supposedly great musicians.[7]

Maffeo was an early supporter of punk feminism's do-it-yourself ethic, which functioned, as male punk had functioned in relation to the rock establishment before it, to challenge conventional notions of authenticity, greatness, and aesthetic value.

It is important to remember that not all music created by young women was the same, despite press coverage that made it sound that way. Nor did all feminists in the alternative scene identify themselves as Riot Grrrls, though journalistic overgeneralization sometimes made it seem so. Valerie Agnew of 7 Year Bitch complains that on her band's first European tour, they were labeled "Riot Grrrls from Seattle," although "Riot Grrrl was always peripheral to us. . . . It was the new bratty young women's way of feminism—which I don't relate to."[8]

Rather than constituting a homogeneous mass, the different bands girls played in were characterized by the contradictions that distinguished other aspects of their lives. They reflected the full spectrum of personas among which young women felt pulled. The music and lyrics combined toughness and tenderness, vengefulness and vulnerability. A political message was often conveyed through graphic personal stories. The songs ranged from fierce exaltation in female anger, to anguish about the pain of relationships, to celebration of noncompetitive love between girls. Stage presence often reflected duality as well, for example, contrasting a physical emphasis on overt sexuality with lyrics about sexual abuse. Vocals swung back and forth between harsh, wrenching screams, sweet, soulful siren intonations, and childish singsong.

As women began to form and perform in more bands, they not only changed the face of punk but changed its fabric. They reclaimed punk as the legacy of the outsider, and previously marginalized issues became more prominent. Early influences on the new punk feminism were the self-published queer-girl fanzines *Sister Nobody*, by Laura Sister Nobody, and *Chainsaw*, by Donna Dresch, who was later to start a record label of the same name and play in the all-dyke band Team Dresch. In the introduction of *Chainsaw* number 2, Dresch writes:

> Right now, maybe CHAINSAW is about Frustration. Frustration in music. Frustration in living, in being a girl, in being a homo, in being a misfit of any sort. In being a dork, you know, the last kid to get picked for the stupid kickball team in grade school. Which is where this whole punk rock thing came from in the first place.

NOT from the Sex Pistols or L.A. But from the GEEKS who decided or realized (or something) to "turn the tables" so to speak, and take control of their (our) lives and form a Real underground. Which is ALSO where the whole heart of CHAINSAW comes from.

Feeling in multiple ways like outsiders as feminism became more prevalent among younger women, these musicians demonstrated the punk ethic of bypassing the co-option of the mainstream through self-sufficiency, by photocopying fanzines and distributing them by hand or by mail. These 'zines became a means of feverish expression and collaboration. They employed a format traditionally used to review records and conduct band interviews, not only to spotlight female musicians but also to share insights, ideas, and information (such as how to induce a late period through herbal teas), to rant and reflect, and to tell personal stories—some humorous, some horrifying, some uplifting. Like other means of expression, fanzines embodied an attempt to process a wide variety of past and present images of femininity. Illustrations ran the gamut from photographs hyping girls currently involved in music, to cartoon sex kittens, to torrid lesbian pulp-fiction covers, to hilariously wholesome advertisements from old *Life* magazines. Fanzines helped girls form a network with each other, not only between towns such as Olympia, D.C., and San Francisco, but also among other places, smaller places, suburbs. Hard-core enabled young suburban boys to vent their anger at the world; Riot Grrrl allowed young suburban girls to vent their anger at the world of suburban boys.

Like the women's bands, not all angry-girl fanzines will go down in history as brilliant masterpieces. Often they were crudely constructed and consisted entirely of free-form rants, fragmented diatribes, and uncensored accusation. I have picked up fanzines that I have found literally impossible to read. Yet because young women are so often made to feel invisible, it is vital for them to elevate their everyday lives outside the everyday. I liken this to Frida Kahlo painting herself over and over. It is the pounding of the fist on the table, claiming, "I exist, I exist." Maybe creating a fanzine is cathartic to one young girl alone in her bedroom. Maybe it helps another young girl, reading it alone in her bedroom, come out or speak out or just feel less alone. And if these things are true, then that fanzine has fulfilled its fundamental task of fostering creativity and communication.

For me, fanzines were and are important because I did not have a desire to play music—I express myself through writing. Moreover, Riot Grrrl itself felt less vitally necessary to me, because I had already taken women's studies courses and had already processed many of these issues. It was not a revelation to me that Barbie's blond tresses, wasp waist, and permanently high-heel-molded feet provided a less-than-wonderful role model. I undertood the anger, because I felt it myself, particularly around issues such as street harassment. This anger and figuring out how to confront it were important in defining a feminism particular to young women. We tend to live in neighborhoods that are not homogeneous, and harassment often involves undertones of racial or socioeconomic friction. The lifestyles we lead and the fact that we can't always afford cars means that we are outside often and sometimes late at night, and because we are young we are considered prime sexual targets by men. They lounge on street corners and outside stores to hiss insolent comments at us. They drive by in cars and holler or honk their horns, startling us out of daydreams or conversations. We feel as if we are entering a war zone every time we walk down a crowded sidewalk wearing shorts.

Constant sexual appraisal is exasperating and degrading. Yet we want to be able to feel good about our bodies, and we do not want to give up our freedom to walk anywhere or to wear what we like. We refuse to return to the days of masculine protection, asking boys to walk us home or to fight anyone who insults our honor. We are not damsels in distress who stand idly by, hysterical, high-pitched screams issuing from our mouths while the knight in shining armor slays the dragon. We want to be our own warriors.

Street harassment is something all girls have in common, and the discovery and discussion of this served as a catalyst for widespread feminist activism. Talking about it together made us view our experiences not as degradation by men but as a source of communal action among women. Girls who began bands sang raw, outraged anthems about the subject; girls who wrote fanzines banged out their aggression on battered Smith-Coronas. We pondered the mind-boggling possibility that our harassers considered their bruising words to be compliments. We found that sometimes if we stopped to engage one of them and told him he was hurting us, he would feel ashamed and apologize profusely.

Many girls discussed guerrilla tactics, and even if we never carried them out, we felt better for thinking about them. I remember laughing gleefully when a girl told me that a mutual friend had confronted a man who would not stop bothering her, by taking a used maxipad out of her bag and throwing it at him. My then-roommate Nikki Chapman and I contemplated a secret plan of assault with squirt guns filled with pee. Wanting to claim my looks as my own and to challenge the double standard of judgment, I learned to respond to someone yelling, "Hey baby, looking good!" by spitting back something like, "Yeah—that makes one of us."

Fanzines and punk shows created forums for young women to speak out as survivors of sexual abuse and to share success stories and painful secrets. As in any movement, it was and is important to rise from pure anger to action. The do-it-yourself ethic in towns such as Olympia and Washington, D.C., has long dictated that the answer to a problem lies not just in pointing fingers but also in creating solutions. No place for your band to play? Play in your friend's basement, in a church, in a community center. No record labels will put out your band's music? Start your own label (Dischord and K Records, started by Calvin Johnson, being the primary examples in D.C. and Olympia, respectively). Thus, women looked not only at the problem of sexual assault, but also at innovative solutions. From this was born the idea of *Free to Fight! An Interactive Self-Defense Project*, a twenty-eight-song CD and thick booklet released on Portland-based label Candy-Ass, owned by Jody Blyle of Team Dresch. The CD intersperses self-defense instructions, anecdotes, and songs, including rap by African American and Latina women.[9]

As with some aspects of second wave feminism, issues of violence against women form a basis for biracial, cross-cultural coalition. But, perhaps because our scene has punk rather than hippie roots, because we grew up in a more violent society, and because we feel frustrated at the seeming lack of progress in preventing rape, we are more likely than some second wavers to see violence as a legitimate form of equalizing gender dynamics, of reclaiming power. Harassment of young women occurs not only on the street but also at work. We often have the types of low-paying jobs in which sexism is an undercurrent. I worked for six months as a cocktail waitress in a nightclub where the waitstaff were all female, every bartender and barback but one was male, and all the doorpeople were large, male, and black. I knew that my being hired and the amount of money I would make in a nightclub depended on my ability to look cute and to chat in a friendly, flirtatious manner with drunken men. To accomplish this, I had to endure guys trying to put tips down my shirt and asking if they could lick Jello shooters off my breasts. My favorite holiday present that year was a button that my little sister Alison gave me, which said, "That's not in my job description."

Because young women often feel exploited in the workplace, we see sex-trade work in less black-and-white terms than older feminists do. We reason that because our bodies are appropriated through looks or comments anyway, we might be better off at least profiting from it. Young women sometimes have a fascination with the idea of being a stripper or a dominatrix, because we see it as having a kind of subversive glamour, and as a means of "exploiting our exploitation." Yet this engenders debate about whether this fascination is healthy, whether it is empowering to utilize blatantly our sexuality, or whether it is simply falling prey to societal demands to objectify ourselves and make our looks the most important thing about us. An interview I conducted with Kathleen Hanna of Bikini Kill, which appeared in the February 1993 issue of *off our backs*, illustrates this debate:

> MELISSA: How do you feel about the whole idea of exploiting your exploitation? Working as a dancer, do you feel that since this attitude already exists of having your body appropriated— that every time you walk down the street, through looks or comments your body is being appropriated by this male audience— that if this male attitude already exists, you might as well make money from it? That you might as well use the system that already exists to your advantage?
>
> KATHLEEN: Yeah, yeah. I mean, exactly. The guy on the bus jacks off under his coat and looks at me and he doesn't give me money, but the guy in the club does give me money. And in a way I don't think my work is any more fascinating than working at Burger King. I think that when I worked in a McDonald's as a pretty female who was 15 years old and pregnant by the way, and working there to get an abortion, I was being exploited because they made me wear a uniform that was two sizes too tight in the middle of summertime in Richmond, Virginia where it was over a hundred degrees. And they made me stand up in the front line and all the girls with acne or who were fat were put in the back cooking. It's totally ridiculous because they were exploiting my little sexual figure to sell burgers. And yet I was being paid $4.50 an hour, $4 an hour, whatever it was at the time. I don't see that huge of a difference between what I'm doing except that I make a lot more an hour. And it's really, really disgusting to me how peo-

ple discriminate against sex trade workers. . . . I might be pretty
and I might be near the ideal and I am exploiting that to my own
benefit. But I'm not exploiting, I'm NOT exploiting anyone else,
you know? . . . And when people discriminate against me because
of that, when people tell me I'm not a feminist because of that,
they can go fuck themselves because that's bullshit. I fucking feed
my friends. I take care of my friends when they're sick. I am one
person in this community who gives girls rides places at night.
People call me and come to my house when they're sexually
abused and talk to me and I can do that because I don't have to
go to work fucking five days a week for The Man and make shit
money. I make enough money in two days a week that I can live
off of that and support other people at certain times.

    MELISSA: Well, I don't know—sometimes I have a problem
just in general with that idea because it sounds like ends justifying
means. . . . It's like the whole idea of, OK, would I do a commercial for a product I don't believe in because it would give me a lot
of money and I could do beneficial things with that, or do I not do
a commercial and then just in my own life, I'm less capable financially but maybe I'm providing more of a . . . positive example?[10]

This debate, although ongoing, marks a difference from the social context of the second wave that is historically specific: the sheer number of
women of all races and classes in the workplace.

    Although reflections about rape, relationships, and reclaiming
our sexuality constituted the burgeoning of our feminism, they also revealed important differences between our definition of it and that of
the second wave. Though old stereotypes reverberate in modern gender dynamics, they do not exist in the same clear-cut form. In a society
that takes premarital sex for granted, the "virgin/whore" dichotomy
that underpins much earlier feminist theory has mutated. Instead of experiencing strict sexual repression, we are taught through advertising
that sexuality determines how we are rated; it is a potent form of
power we must struggle to possess. Yet it is not a power we ask for or
control. In the aftermath of 1970s feminism, we experience both the
loss of chivalrous standards that require "respect for ladies," and the
post-"free-love" backlash against women's prominent sexuality, which
uses our sexuality to thwart us.

    Unlike older, Dworkin-MacKinnon feminists, young punk femi-
nists tended to be very pro-sex, more likely, for example, to celebrate
female-centered pornography than to censor male-centered porn. This
comes partially from a distaste for the censorship in creative circles that

developed during the mid-1980s: the Parents' Music Resource Coalition's record-labeling efforts, the outcry over Robert Mapplethorpe's sexually explicit photographs, and the attempted anti-flag-burning amendment. We were also influenced by the publication of the RE/ Search book *Angry Women* in 1991. An ad for the book asks, "How can you have a revolutionary feminism that encompasses wild sex, humor, beauty, spirituality *plus* radical politics? How can you have a powerful movement for social change that's inclusionary—not exclusionary?" The ad then goes on to tout the book as covering "a wide range of topics: menstruation, masturbation, vibrators, S/M and spanking, racism, failed Utopias, the death of the Sixties and much more."[11] The book contains in-depth interviews with sex activists Susie Bright and Annie Sprinkle, as well as cultural critic bell hooks. The influences of these women can be seen in the pro-sex attitudes and analyses of racism in later angry-girl music and writing.

Conflicting ideas about the meaning of sex and sexiness are often reflected in the way punk feminists look. Punk fashion has always reflected irony. Because clothes come from thrift stores, they reflect whatever era of clothing people are discarding at any given time. Wardrobes consist of the past, bought for pennies and reworked, reinvented. In this way, the idea of identity is turned on its head. This might mean wearing a gas station attendant's jacket with someone else's name on it. It might mean wearing army gear although you are antimilitary. It might mean mocking capitalism by wearing a T-shirt advertising a ridiculous product you would never buy. For women, punk fashion irony has often been reflected through gender parody.

During the heyday of hard-core and the early politicization of punk in D.C., girls felt compelled to dress and act like guys—black jeans and no makeup were de rigueur. But ultimately, as girls came into their own, the solution became not to demand equity but to celebrate difference, whether this meant strutting their butchness or being a vampy femme or combining both. Punk female fashion trends have paired 1950s dresses with combat boots, shaved hair with lipstick, studded belts with platform heels. We dye our hair crazy colors or proudly expose chubby tummies in a mockery of the masculine ideal of beauty. At the same time, we fiercely guard our right to be sexy and feminine. We might get harassed less if we dressed and acted exactly like boys, but we would see this as giving up. We are interested in creating not models of androgyny so much as models of contradiction.

We want not to get rid of the trappings of traditional femininity or sexuality so much as to pair them with demonstrations of strength or
power. We are much less likely to burn our bras communally than to
run down the street together clad in nothing but our bras, yelling,
"Fuck you!"

Another paradox of punk feminism is that it exists within what
has traditionally been youth culture, yet no one stays young forever. So
what do we do now? How do we grow up? And how do we negotiate
the media representations of our efforts? Laura Sister Nobody self-
published a fanzine that contained a prophetic warning about the fick-
leness of media attention to the Riot Grrrl movement:

> Us, we are women who know that something is happening—
> something that seems like a secret right now, but wont stay like
> a secret for much longer. . . . why does usa today, abc, nbc, cbs
> and every other corporate media fuck want to get a hold of bikini
> kill and riot grrrl? because theyre not fools—they know some-
> things happening too—but theyre terrified of it and they want to
> take it and twist it and package it and spit it out to the masses as
> the next latest thing in order to kill it. we have to understand that
> they will try sneakily and unrelentingly to suck the life out of our
> fight and we have to be ready.

Early Riot Grrrl publications pointed out that the name was not copy-
righted and encouraged other women to start their own groups. It was
never a movement with membership rolls and dues; thus, the media
pronouncements of its rise and fall are mostly hype. I am less interested
in the EKG status of Riot Grrrl than in the idea that women's work is
definitely thriving, though, for what it is worth, Riot Grrrl does currently exist on-line and as a fanzine-distribution press.

For me, looking at the past, present, and future of women in the
alternative music community, I see a continuum of struggle, spiraling
upward. This struggle does not depend on the name it takes. Punk has
assimilated the demands of girl revolutionaries—there are women tour
managers, engineers, and label owners, as well as a plethora of women
musicians. But perhaps more important to me is not only that women
make up a much more equal balance of those playing music, but also
that as women occupy a more respected space, support grows for their
work outside the traditional punk music arena. Initially we had to fight
just to breathe, to keep ourselves alive. Now that we can stop and take
a breath, we can go more in-depth, we are freer to branch off into our

specific interests, to leave our own lasting landmarks combining creativity and social change. My friend Dara Greenwald, discussing the idea of starting an alternative school for at-risk girls using music as a focus, says, "We need to start creating our own institutions."[12] I am inspired as I see women mobilizing to hold on to creativity and the do-it-yourself ethic while stepping beyond the traditional guitar-bass-drums punk rock arena. A sampling of recent self-published fanzines illustrates this diversity. In issue 3 of *I'm So Fucking Beautiful*, Olympian Nomy Lamm's confrontation of fat oppression includes a comic of herself in a tight T-shirt, proclaiming, "No more mumus!" In *Bamboo Girl* number 4, from New York, Sabrina Sandata tackles bands, breast biopsies, and Tagalog tidbits from a take-no-prisoners queer Filipina perspective. In *Femme Flicke* number 5, editor Tina Spangler, from Cambridge, Massachusetts, interviews queer-core filmmaker G. B. Jones and lists resources throughout the country for girls to get their own films seen. In *Doris* number 5, from Berkeley, Cindy writes sad and beautiful personal stories wrapped in red duct tape. In my own recent San Francisco *Inkling* number 2, I document the often forgotten history of women outlaws in the Old West and humorous trips to places of historical interest to women.

I would like to see this branching out continue in other areas. For example, I have had to step outside the punk scene into social service work to confront race, aging, and poverty issues, because the punk scene remains predominantly young, white, and middle class. I would like to see us use punk feminist tactics to deal with these issues in an innovative way. I would like to see a feminism that does not grow lazy because of certain gains. I would like us to question the ways that major-label–MTV co-option of "alternative" music has impacted our scene even if we personally have steered away from it—for example, by asking ourselves how the recent punk trend toward superskinniness, supershort skirts, plucked eyebrows, and platform heels is influenced by a mainstream, media-friendly aesthetic.

I am confident that we have the structures to continue questioning, collaborating, and creating, whether this takes the form of *Free to Fight*, Cha-Cha Cabaret, or Sharon Cheslow's Women in Punk project, and whether we call it making music, movies, comics, fanzines, or social change. The dueling images of femininity and feminism found in music and writing produced by young women may initially seem confused or confusing. Yet these fanzines, songs, and other forms of expression represent a mode of activism that is challenging rather than didactic and that leaves room for different and changing roles—for boys as well as for girls. I regard the willingness to experiment, to accept duality, and to have more questions than answers, as positive attributes—attributes that have given birth to a new brand of activism, a striving for social change unique to the young women of my community and my generation.

Notes

This essay is dedicated to Sharon Cheslow for her great encouragement, Jen Smith for her genius and friendship, and to my mother, Kim Florence Klein, for constant inspiration.

1. Leslie Clague, Cynthia Connolly, and Sharon Cheslow, *Banned in D.C.: Photos and Anecdotes from the D.C. Punk Underground, 1979–85* (Washington, D.C.: Sun Dog Propaganda, 1988).

2. Evelyn McDonnell, "Punk's Matrilineage," *Village Voice*, May 21, 1996, 57.

3. This and subsequent quotations from Sharon Cheslow are taken from a personal interview by the author in San Francisco in July 1996.

4. Robin Morgan, ed., *Sisterhood Is Powerful: An Anthology of Writings from the Women's Liberation Movement* (New York: Vintage, 1970), xxiii.

5. Katherine Isaac, *Civics for Democracy* (Washington, D.C.: Essential, 1992), 106, quoting Sara M. Evans, *Born for Liberty: A History of Women in America* (New York: Free Press, 1989), 282.

6. Emily White, "Revolution Girl Style Now," *L.A. Weekly*, July 10–16, 1992; reprinted in *Rock She Wrote*, ed. Evelyn McDonnell and Ann Powers (New York: Dell, 1995), 398–99.

7. Lois Maffeo, interview by Andrea Juno, *Angry Women in Rock* (New York: Juno Books, 1996), 132–33.

8. Valerie Agnew, interview by Andrea Juno, in ibid., 107.

9. *Free to Fight! An Interactive Self-Defense Project* (Candy-Ass Records, 1996). See Jen Smith's "Doin' It for the Ladies—Youth Feminism: Cultural Productions/ Cultural Activism" (this volume) for a fuller description of this project.

10. Kathleen Hanna, "Revolution Girl Style Now!" interview by Melissa Klein, *off our backs*, February 1993, 11.

11. Andrea Juno and V. Vale, eds., *Angry Women* (San Francisco: RE/Search Publications, 1991). The advertisement quotation is from a promotional postcard for the book.

12. Dara Greenwald, conversation with author, San Francisco, July 1996.

CHAPTER TWELVE

Doin' It for the Ladies—Youth Feminism: Cultural Productions/Cultural Activism

Jen Smith

> *The fear of exposure, the fear that one's deepest emotions and innermost thoughts will be dismissed as mere nonsense, felt by so many young girls keeping diaries, holding and hiding speech, seems to me now one of the barriers that women have always needed and still need to destroy so that we are no longer pushed into secrecy or silence.*
> —bell hooks, Introduction to *Talking Back*

> *She writes it down quickly before it fades away. The ink is black permanent Sharpie. She chose her pen well.*
> —Nikki McClure, *My Super Secret* fanzine

> *We meet in underground passages, a handshake will pass my message to you. Then we will move on, separately, as if nothing has happened. But my story has become a part of you now. It is a story about us and how we will create our own meaning.*
> —*In Sequential Order* fanzine

I am a punk feminist interested in telling a story. This is a story about the creation of an alternate meaning system. It is a story about identity, about networking, about community. It is also a story about cultural resistance from a particular cultural location. But maybe it is a story about conquest and domination, the human body as a landscape defined by political boundaries. Maybe it is a story about fragmentation, about synthesis, about physiological dysfunction. Maybe it is a story disguised as a pamphlet about toxic shock syndrome. Maybe this story is called, "What every girl should know." Maybe it is a story about motherhood. Maybe it is a story about urban violence. Maybe it is a story thick with signs and signifiers. Maybe this is a story about alternative technologies historically relevant for the stories they tell and the connections, both existentially real and theoretically abstract, that they present. Maybe it is a story that destroys diaries by making them public. Maybe it is a story about all of these things.

In June 1996, I attended the SPRGRL (pronounced "supergirl") Conspiracy Convention in Portland, Oregon. While running around downtown Portland searching for makeup, false eyelashes, and my very first curling iron, I strategized what the night's performance would be. Because I was a friendly acquaintance of one of the organizers, Geneva Gano, I had been asked to serve as mistress of ceremonies as a character I had been developing, Miss Lady Hand Grenade. Donning garish (and oh so *glamorous*, darling) makeup and flashy clothing I had made, Miss Lady stood in sharp contrast to the fashion sensibility of the ladies in attendance. The butch-girl look was heavily represented. One friend encouraged, "What's butch without femme?" But would these women understand the nature of my message? Would some be offended? Did it matter? I remained determined to stay atop my silver-glittered platform heels despite how my feet might bark and moan. This femme fatale was doing it for the ladies, and whatever the night might hold, it must include total dedication.

The SPRGRL Conspiracy was a three-day event held at Portland State University, a gathering of mostly young, punk feminist women. There were bands, performances, movies, fanzines, and workshops that focused on women's issues of voice, power, and identity. Exploring oppressions and privileges as well as possibilities, issues addressed included white skin privilege and racism, classism, sizeism, self-esteem, depression, domestic violence, and women's self-defense, as well as how to make a video, how to fix bikes, and how to buy used guitars without getting ripped off. The organizers hoped to promote issues of accessibility and inclusion. In the fanzine directory for the event, the *SPRGRL Conspiracy Guide*, Gano writes:

> Something that I have been considering a lot when trying to organize this convention has been race and class. My role as one of the organizers has included calling and writing to artists and performers I admire and respect in the hopes that they would participate in the convention. Taking a glance at the schedule, it would probably be no surprise to anyone to learn that I am a white, middle-class lesbian girl. So are many (probably the majority) of the participants. My peer group is also a source of inspiration to

me. Though I find it exciting and encouraging to see so many
girls out there doing things who are a lot like me, it also makes
me really aware of my own social circles, the limitations I, as
one of the organizers of a project of this magnitude, live and act.
While I have been trying to make this convention as accessible
and diverse as possible, I know that it falls considerably short of
my hopes. What that means to me, personally, is that despite my
firm commitment to working against racism and classism, I still
have so much more to do. . . . I think that the performers, artists,
workshop leaders and organizers of this convention each have a
commitment, at some level, to make art, inspiration, and education accessible for everyone. (2)

Having clearly located themselves on a larger political spectrum and
having named their ambitions and shortcomings, the organizers could
begin to get down to the scheduled events. This space was going to
host a variety of experiences, from a very emotional multimedia theater performance piece confronting domestic violence, called "Open Sea-
son," to a dyke kissing booth.

The whole event was a hub of women-powered activity. Many
girls were engaged in creative endeavors during the convention. Amber
Dawn from Vancouver, British Columbia, had brought a quilt project
to which she hoped girls would contribute. Lois Maffeo (Olympia,
Washington) and Sarah Dougher (Portland) showed a video in which
women they interviewed shared their ideas about courage. A walk by
Kinko's a few blocks away revealed girls busily copying their fanzines.
On a trip to the bathroom, one had to pass through a bunch of girls
laughing uproariously as they spontaneously rehearsed choreographed
dance moves that they performed to bands later that day. I was really
inspired by the buzz of activity. Here were girls encouraging each
other, directly and indirectly, to put their ideas into the world.

This influence was especially important to me because I had been
loosely involved with the early days of the Riot Grrrl "movement."
Certain issues had made me reluctant to think that Riot Grrrl was *the*
definitive liberatory possibility for the girls and women in my young
punk feminist scene. During the summer of 1992, I went to the very
first Grrrl convention. I was excited that this sort of grassroots organizing and outreach was taking place in my community, but I was already the ancient age—from the movement's perspective—of twenty-
two. I recognized the vital importance of this opportunity for young
women (women in their teens or those lacking access to or interest in a

college campus). Also aware of my own history, I saw how much I had needed this kind of information when I was a teenager.

At this first convention, I recognized notable landmarks, things that would have helped so much if I had had them earlier. At an outdoor show connected to the convention, women confronted a man who was heckling the performers and audience members with lewd comments. Several women escorted this man out of the park and lectured him about respect for women. At shows, all women bands asked that girls come to the front of the stage. They would proceed to make a cacophonous sound to lyrics that urged resistance to male power. In front of the stage, women's sweaty, gyrating bodies confirmed our growing sense of power and possibility. It was fun, and, if only for a moment, it felt like liberation. Our ability to transform a space collectively as performers, as audience members, as women, was a critical example of self-creation and the possibility of feminist community.

Yet, despite my compassion and enthusiasm, I still felt weary. The urgency of some of the women was alienating to me. There seemed to be an overwhelming specter of patriarchy. Implicit to the sense of power we were cultivating was a constant rejection of white male authority. Though I would concur that a vigorous examination of these issues will always be necessary to subvert old definitions of power, it seemed to me that a lot of energy was spent in anger and rejection. *Koo Koo*, a fanzine at the convention self-published by singer-songwriter Lois Maffeo aptly asserted:

> I think it is time to stop worrying about the problems of being a woman playing rock and roll and start working on the solutions. I'm tired of seeing young women's inspiration go down the drain because it is put under scrutiny by someone who doesn't really care. Put your anger to work for you by channeling it into energy for your band or magazine or life. The end product of your work will be an example for others to start.

In a 1994 interview by Gail O'Hara in the self-published fanzine *Chickfactor*, artist Stella Marrs speculated that "maybe riot grrrls are the James Deans of the 90's or late 80's. There was this image of this group of girls that was never able to express anger in the culture. That's really powerful and threatening as an image in the culture—riot woman or whatever. But there is some sort of image past that." From my perspective, the SPRGRL conspiracy is concrete evidence of the "image past" Riot Grrrl, and marks a transition in youth feminist culture. It is a turn toward an attitude of independence rather than simple repudiation, and is firmly entrenched in the power and inspiration of a feminist community. Probably due to the anger and reactionary struggle of these earlier incarnations of Riot Grrrl or young punk feminist activists, women are currently more free to explore not only the terrors and frustrations but also the possibilities of their lives. At SPRGRL I noticed a lot less discussion of white male authority and more discussion focused on our responsibilities and aspirations.

Nowhere was this more apparent than in the discussion group "Workshop on Women Owned Businesses; or, How to Quit Work, Get a Real Life, and Work Harder Than You Ever Have." Led by a twenty-six-year-old local independent magazine and fanzine store owner, Chloe Eudaly, a panel of women talked about their experiences running their small businesses, as well as various other projects. Less concerned with the mechanics of running a business, each woman gave a personal narrative of the process of having an idea and turning it into something public. After a while, one of the participants asked, "What if you don't have any talent? I don't have any hobbies or interests. I'm not particularly good at anything, but I don't want to work for somebody else." Her voice was edged with vulnerability and despair. The women in the room rushed to reassure her. Jody Blyele, of Candy-Ass records, counseled, "Just think of something you want to exist in the world and doesn't. Then try to make that idea happen." It turned out that most women on the panel felt that they were not particularly adept at what they did, just dedicated. Most went on to say that their projects had begun with very little money. I watched as the women in the room, ranging in age from fourteen to thirty-seven, shared success stories, ambitions, and strategies, shaping meaning. Their lives demonstrated feminist agency, and their work was an example and an inspiration to others.

Beyond Riot Grrrl: New Punk Feminist Cultural Productions
The Big Miss Moviola project: Miranda July

Miranda July is a young filmmaker and performance artist in Portland, Oregon. She is also involved in the punk feminist music scene. In the early 1990s, she was frustrated that there were few ways for women who make low- or no-budget movies to network with each other. Information about recording and distributing one's music or songwriting abounds in our community. Interest in homemade cassette recordings, low-budget records, and independent record labels, as well as formal and informal distribution networks, has made it possible to publicize one's music to an audience broader than one's immediate community.[1] A culture of photocopied, self-published fanzines, passed through the mail and sold at specialty shops, has allowed the same publicity for one's writing. July started the Big Miss Moviola project in an attempt to create this same accessibility and networking for women filmmakers. July explains:

> One big reason why there is no cinematic equivalent of the independent music scene (i.e. an "indie" section of the local video store) is that movies are so expensive to make. All the equipment related to movies is pretty pricey and unless you are in college ($), there are very few cheap places to rent or borrow equipment. One of the goals of this project is to connect-up women who could share each other's resources (scams, equipment, brilliant ideas, grant writing techniques, time etc.).[2]

July's plan was simple: to create a video chain letter. July asked women of any age and background to send her a self-made movie, five dollars, and a personal statement. July asked that, in this statement, any pertinent information about the video or about the filmmaker's interests be specified: "If you are a Jewish lesbian and you only want to work with other Jewish lesbians then write that. Or if you want to be non-specific or brief that is also okay." Sequencing the movie with other women-made movies (about eight total) on a videotape, July would then send that tape, plus a fanzine guide of the personal statements, back to the participant. These directories would include the women's addresses. The five dollars would cover July's cost of producing both the video and the guide (she bought used videotapes from thrift stores and other sources), plus shipping (book-rate postage was $1.24). She also put together a pamphlet with her ideas about the necessity of this project, its goals, and instructions for how to participate.

Initially, July distributed these pamphlets by hand at punk shows, the occasional bus stop—wherever she was. She had some help spreading the word, as friends in touring bands told women in other cities about the Big Miss Moviola project. Soliciting work in this manner was a slow process. One year later, she had received enough movies to make the first video, *Big Miss Moviola Chain Letter #1*. It comprised the first nine movies that were sent to her: "None of these women read about Big Miss Moviola in a magazine. They either got a flyer from me at some event or they heard about it through word of mouth. Friends of friends. This means that these movies are all reflective of my crowd or scene (even though I only know two of the ladies)."

Eventually, July decided that if she was going to fulfill her goal of wider representation of women's movies and voices, she ought to take a more aggressive approach toward publicizing her project. Having no professional training in media outreach, she sent her pamphlet to a variety of women's and art magazines. The first magazine to respond was *Sassy*, a major teen girls' magazine. July was skeptical that the *Sassy* editors were interested in her endeavors, largely because she physically "fit" into the images of women (thin, white, with bleached white hair) in the magazine. However, she decided that it was still an important opportunity to tell women who might otherwise never hear about the Big Miss Moviola project. July was fearful this representation was beyond her scale of control. She did not want Big Miss Moviola to become a video pen pal service for *Sassy* magazine. What resulted, however, was an interview and photo shoot that became the first of a regular feature called "She's Way Sassy."[3] This motivated July to approach other magazines and to pursue screenings at colleges, which she did with some success. She has also had showings at independent film festivals.

During intermission at Big Miss Moviola screenings, July sets up a camera in a bathroom or closet and asks audience members to spend two minutes with the camera, completing the sentence, "Nobody ever told me . . ." At the end of her screening, she shows the audience the tape they have made. She says that this has been an interesting exercise in getting audience members to recognize themselves as participants in the spectacle they have been observing. Women identify themselves and each other, unconsciously becoming empowered to think of themselves as artists, stars, interesting people.

July says that "legitimate" women filmmakers have responded with fervor to her project, due to the film industry's general lack of interest in women's ideas and movies. Through her work with Big Miss Moviola and the Missing Movie Report, Miranda July is building an infrastructure to make women's movies more accessible. Further, she is deliberately creating a network of women. She has located a need in the community, a need in her own imagination, and is pursuing its realization.

Girlhero: Megan Kelso

Girlhero is a comic book series by Seattle artist Megan Kelso. Even when she was first drawing comics as a college student in the early 1990s, her work received a lot of attention and support. In January 1993, she applied for a grant from a group called Xeric. Established by Peter Laird, one of the original Teenage Mutant Ninja Turtles creators, the grant would fund production costs for one three-thousand-copy print run. In her proposal she had *Girlhero* number 1 almost fully drawn and included research about how to print and market her new comic. According to Kelso,

> I said I wanted to do a comic from a very specifically feminist perspective. I was going to work really hard to find a way to sell these comics to women and girls who don't normally read comics—because girls just don't shop at comic stores generally. A big part of my proposal was talking about how I was going to try and get my comic in other places than comic book stores.[4]

Kelso speculates that it was this clear set of goals that got her the grant, which enabled her first issue to have a color cover and a print run of three thousand. By selling these copies, she was able to make a second issue.

These developments provided a crash course in the comic business, and Kelso quickly found out how to get her comic into the world. She is involved with two major comic distributors, a few magazine distributors, and an underground comic-fanzine network. Getting a distributor to agree to take on the responsibility of selling something new is a struggle, but connection to a variety of distributors has allowed Kelso to meet her goal of getting her comic to women who would not normally see it: "I got a letter from a girl who bought my comic at Barnes and Noble in Boston. I also got a letter from this old woman whose husband bought my comic at a newsstand somewhere in Pittsburgh." These letters lead Kelso to believe that the comic's feminist message has been fairly widely disseminated.

In issues 1 through 6, the "Bottlecap" story was a regular feature. Exhibiting pressing third wave concerns, the comic is set in a gloomy industrial setting. The narrative focuses on a group of women friends who work on the assembly line at a local corporation. Due to poor wages, subjugation, drugs that "keep them healthy," and assault by the male foremen, the women initiate a campaign to organize the women at the plant. During this process, two of the three women turn themselves into "superheroes." One character modifies her arm by installing a rivet gun, and the other has a computer placed directly into her brain. (The third woman was "born" with superhuman powers.) In a brutal turn of events, the women are sought out by corporation executives, who want them killed. According to Kelso,

> I wanted to do a kind of science fiction story. I wanted the women to be super heroes. I wanted them to be feminist. I wanted there to be a group of them. I wanted them to work together. I wanted them to have to deal with issues of violence. I wanted them to not necessarily agree. I wanted them to be coming from different points of view as far as how violence should be used or contained or if it should be used at all.

"Bottlecap" is one example of the third wave feminist struggle with issues of violence and community, feminist organization and coalition.

Yet from fellow male comic artists, Kelso has received a lot of criticism about her decision to use superheroes: "A lot of the alternative comic scene is about people rejecting the use of super heroes and trying to get away from that image. And it's true, I don't know if there is any other medium that is so driven by a particular genre." But Kelso was fascinated about what the superhero image says about our culture:

> Superhero comics are usually about a single person coming in and saving the day and rescuing people. They are just the ultimate male fantasy. So I thought how would a super hero be female and how would a super hero be feminist? And I kept thinking, there would be more than one of them and they would work together. They would help people but in the process help those people help themselves. I got the idea that they would make themselves into super heroes. They would create that.

Despite the surreal setting of the story, the characters in "Bottlecap" have an important message for women. Their ability to recreate themselves into superheroes exemplifies the possibility of transformation. By networking within their own community, they are able to find the skills to create their own vision of themselves, their own solutions, their own meaning.

Free to Fight! An Interactive Self-Defense Project:
Anna Lo Bianco, Staci Cotler, and Jody Blyele

Several women in the Portland, Oregon, women's rock scene are self-defense instructors. Through their friendship, Anna Lo Bianco, Staci

Cotler, and Jody Blyele decided to make a self-defense record (also available on CD) and workbook. The project, *Free to Fight!*, incorporates self-defense instruction, success stories, rock, rap, folk, writings, and the voices of many women from their community, and it is produced and distributed through Blyele's record label, Candy-Ass.[5] The organizers distributed *Free to Fight!* to record stores and had some success with it in women's bookstores. Proceeds went toward funding *Free to Fight!* tours and free women's self-defense classes in Portland. By including a large and diverse community of women, the organizers also relied on word-of-mouth networking.

Realizing that the *Free to Fight!* recording could never substitute for an actual self-defense class, the organizers wanted to give women exposure to the possibility and prevalence of self-defense in their lives. The introduction to the workbook includes this passage:

> Some one told our parents not to teach us to hit and not to talk about it loudly. Self defense is the equalizer. When a girl defends herself verbally she may feel she is putting herself in a physically threatening position. But when she knows how to fight, she can feel more able to say whatever she wants. When you have the physical, you have the back up for the verbal and the non-verbal attitude, how you feel inside. When you feel how strong you are physically, your will to protect yourself can surge. This is why we know how to fight. This is why we made this.
>
> This is not a consumer item "You've Bought Self Defense." We already have self defense in our lives. We do with what we've got to survive. Whatever it is we are creating: comix, zines . . . You are keeping yourself alive. You are defending your soul. Like rock. Playing rock is the power to create and those creations are a force field against all the other shit in the world. The stage and this record are our soap boxes for public talk, to call the shit shit and we direct that dialogue. Unlike most straight white boy bands, we do not have the luxury to not allow that conversation to exist.

This interactive recording and workbook is one way of perpetuating that crucial conversation, a conversation that can save lives.

The *Free to Fight!* recording and workbook include success stories. These stories allow the listener-reader to recognize that each self-defense approach described increased the teller's safety: the teller either averted or survived an attack. Here is one story:

> So I was on this bus and there was this guy who was sitting kitty corner in back of me. I saw that he had his dick hanging out of his pants. There was a girl sitting next to him but she was asleep

and I didn't know what to do. So I kinda slyly caught his eye and then I stood up and yelled really loudly "EXCUSE ME SIR! BUT COULD YOU PLEASE PUT YOUR DICK BACK IN YOUR PANTS!" And he did. I was afraid that he was gonna attack me right after we got to the bus station. But instead, he just disappeared and I never saw him again.

Free to Fight! also offers a very broad definition of abuse. On the recording, different women's voices say the following:

> I was raped.
> My boyfriend always tells me I am stupid and fat.
> My co-worker lisps and prances around to imitate queers.
> My history teacher only calls on the boys.
> My boyfriend's parents didn't want me to go out with him
>   because I wasn't white.
> I was molested by my grandfather when I was ten years old.
> Violence is violence.

This plurality of voices tries to sketch out the enormous range of womens' experiences with violence. Elsewhere, the workbook specifically addresses issues of violence between lesbian women. Ironically functioning as a motivation for feminist coalition, violence is an everyday threat for women of all colors, class backgrounds, ages, and sexualities.

Examples of defense strategies are included in both the recording and the workbook. Nonphysical strategies include confident body language, boundary setting, trusting intuition, safety planning, and verbal techniques. Physical strategies locate an attacker's primary targets— the weakest and most sensitive points of the male body. A sing-along of these points is included for easier memorizing. Seeking to spread its applicability in a grassroots way, *Free to Fight!* also offers advice on how to start self-defense classes in any town.

The next step for the organizers was to host shows that incorporated self-defense demonstrations. They took these shows on tours throughout the United States. In 1995, Blyele's band, Team Dresch, an all-lesbian rock band, took self-defense instructor Alice Stagg on tour with them. At each show, Blyele and Stagg would introduce themselves and explain their project:

> I'd say I [Jody] was in a rock band and Alice was a martial artist
> and self-defense instructor and that we were from Portland.
> We said we were going to do some role playing and self-defense
> scenes and that all the girls should come forward. Everybody

should feel free to yell along and participate as if they were seeing this on the street or whatever. Then we would say that all the attackers were men unless we said otherwise.

It was totally different on different nights. Some nights we'd be really serious and some nights it would be really funny. We would adjust our skits depending on who was in the audience. If it was a queer show, we'd do mostly queer skits. We'd do lesbian battering stuff whereas if it were a more straight forward punk show, we'd do more teen dating issues—date rape, battering.[6]

Making use of humor, role-playing, and theater, *Free to Fight!* is an important introduction for girls and women to the spectrum of abuse and the challenge of self-defense. By making this project fun and using a medium that young women already recognize, the organizers present self-defense as a possibility in the listener-viewer's life. By enabling women to name their environment, *Free to Fight!* and women's self-defense provide one avenue toward empowerment.

Cultural Productions as Community Activism

Riot Grrrl has evolved into broadly based activist communities. At the SPRGRL conference and in my own community, I have met a variety of women engaged in this kind of work. Some make music. Some write. Some run their own record labels. Some keep track of all of these efforts, producing directories for other women. Some make movies. Some do performance art. Some organize events. Some own spaces where these activities can exist. Some make visual art. Some are teachers. Some volunteer at shelters. Some teach self-defense. Some are moms. Some are gay. Some are old. Some are young. Some are environmentalists. Some are doctors. Some always hated school. Some are strippers. Some are fat. Some are women of color. Some are from working-class or poor backgrounds. Some have been abused. Some are a combination of these things. All have known the threat of violence in their lives, all are resisting. All are trying to do their work. All want to contribute their voices to a larger community of women. All are feminists.

Meeting these women and others like them, and exploring our experiences, hopes, and fears, has been and continues to be a vital part of what I see as feminist agency. Don't misinterpret my meaning: this community is not always supportive, I don't always get along fabulously with every woman, and I think some women are malicious and misguided. But by naming our experiences in workshops and in our writing, music, movies, and performances—that is, in our art—we begin to connect (to each other and to our own ideas) in new and insightful ways. It is these connections that directly challenge mainstream frameworks of power and dominance. Employing a do-it-yourself ethic, we use alternate production and distribution methods. We make our ideas a reality and then give public life to our endeavors by participating in independent networking systems. By using different and immediate ways of showing and sharing our art, we are often intimately involved with our creative and commodification processes. The ways we exercise our ideas, our art, and our livelihoods are the ways in which we engage in activism. These processes construct both a physical and a psychic space for articulating our realities. By connecting with one another in these different spaces, we both create and participate in the making of our identities and our community.[7]

Notes

1. Simple Machines, a woman-owned record label in Arlington, Virginia, put together a comprehensive guide called "An Introductory Mechanic's Guide to Putting out Records, Cassettes, and CDs" (1992). It explains the process of mastering a record, listing everything from companies throughout the United States to the cost of making one thousand records or CDs.

2. This and subsequent quotations from Miranda July are taken from her fanzine, *Big Miss Moviola* (1995).

3. "She's Way Sassy," *Sassy*, April 1996.

4. This and subsequent quotations from Megan Kelso are taken from her conversation with the author, 10 December 1994.

5. This and all subsequent quotations, unless otherwise noted, are taken from the recording-workbook package *Free to Fight! An Interactive Self-Defense Project* (Candy-Ass Records, 1996).

6. Jody Blyele, conversation with author, 15 December 1994.

7. Addresses for the artists and organizations featured in this article include Simple Machines, P.O. Box 10290, Arlington, Virginia 22210–1290; The Big Miss Moviola Project, c/o Miranda July, P.O. Box 14284, SE Portland, Oregon 97214; *Girlhero*, c/o Megan Kelso, 4505 University Way NE, Box 536, Seattle, Washington 98105; and *Free to Fight!* c/o Candy-Ass Records, P.O. Box 42382, Portland, Oregon 97242. The author herself performs with the Cha-Cha Cabaret, P.O. Box 7293, Olympia, Washington 98507.

CHAPTER THIRTEEN

Hip-Hop Matters: Rewriting the Sexual Politics of Rap Music

Jeff Niesel

Check it out. Warning: If you want an album, an hour's worth of music, that's all senseless violence and ignorance, all done in the name's sake of realness, you have received the wrong album. If you consider that to be dope, so be it. But this is not it.
　　　　　　　　—Ras Kass, promotional for *Soul on Ice*

I was watching this comedian one day who was talkin' about rappers, and he said that all they do is grip the mic, and walk around holding their dicks. Our whole thing is, we want to show that there's much more to hip hop than what people think.
　　　　　　　　—Wyclef Jean (of the Fugees), press release for *The Score*

By the time I graduated from high school in 1986, the popularity of alternative and indie rock had started to soar—and not because record labels were pushing their artists down consumers' throats as though they were the latest soft drinks. As I started writing about popular music for my college newspaper, I noticed an increase in the number of artists who cultivated their fan bases through grassroots channels and played music unlike anything heard on mainstream radio. Female singers with feminist perspectives (Suzanne Vega and Siouxsie Sioux), male singers with ambiguous sexual preferences (Michael Stipe and Morrissey), and co-ed rock bands (Sonic Youth and Game Theory) all stood out as real alternatives to David Lee Roth's sexist swagger or REO Speedwagon's heterosexist clichés about romantic love. This music spoke to and came out of a whole generation of younger men who, like myself, were lost when it came to bragging about sexual conquests or competing to see who could bench-press the most weight during physical education classes. I found that my tendency to cry when rebuked by coaches for my lack of masculine prowess, and the empathetic role I played as my female friends' confidant excluded me from the province of traditional maledom. I felt no more affinity for the braggadocio of Roth than I did for the testosterone-driven male athletes who participated in high school sports. Because of my own ambiguous feelings about heterosexuality, my heroes were the ones who blurred lines between the genders—not those who enforced the idea of sexual difference.

When I started reading feminist theory in college, I found a theoretical framework for what I had experienced. My education, family, and religious upbringing had all contributed to the construction of a masculinity based upon competition, exclusion, and the denial of emotions. But in the contemporary scene there were alternatives. To me, Michael Stipe sounded as vulnerable as Suzanne Vega, and I identified equally with each of them. As I have continued to write about music for magazines and daily newspapers, identification across lines of gender and race has become increasingly important in my life, especially as some of the most compelling musicians I have interviewed and reviewed have been female and/or black. As complicated as their differences are, their exclusion from the public sphere and the various ways they articulate that disenfranchisement have helped create and validate the nontraditional models of gender I have lived.

When I first started listening to rap music in the early 1990s, however, I found that the gender paradigms presented there had more in common with David Lee Roth and the masculine posturing of male athletes than with the alternative music that wasn't pumped with the same male bravado. I liked the way artists such as Public Enemy and NWA used urban slang to criticize racism and economic inequality, but their macho attitudes were often alienating and presented views of women with which I could not identify. When I discovered the Jungle Brothers, Queen Latifah, and De La Soul shortly afterward, I realized that there was an alternative to gangsta rap. These artists served much the same purpose as alternative rock had done in the mid-1980s—by blurring the boundaries between male and female and between black and white, they suggested that for political activism to be truly successful, coalitions must be built across the lines that divide people according to race, gender, and class. For "alternative" rappers, rap music had the most potential of any music to inspire social change, and, unlike gangsta rappers who separated racism and poverty from sexism, alternative rappers explicitly included women, demonstrating that for their work to be considered effectively political, race activists need to include rather than exclude feminists.

My introduction to rap music started with NWA's 1989 album *Straight Outta Compton*—not the first gangsta rap album, but the first one to have, as Ronin Ro puts it, "a far-reaching influence on American youth" (2). With *Compton*, which has sold more than two million copies since its release, NWA realized every parent's worst nightmare—armed and dangerous black males had (figuratively) invaded their kids' bedrooms. Not even Satan-worshiping heavy-metal rockers could shake the walls of suburban homes with as much force. NWA had the powerful effect of putting fear in the hearts of parents, politicians, and even black leaders, and, with the incendiary track "Fuck tha Police," it also continued rap's tradition of mixing social commentary and music. But NWA did not just direct its rage and frustration toward symbols of authority. In tracks such as "A Bitch iz a Bitch" (with lines such as "the title bitch doesn't apply to all women / but all women have a little in them / bitch, eat shit and die") and "Quiet on the Set" (with lines such as "this so-called women's lib / I'll retire it. / That's why I'm a walking threat"), NWA included women and feminists on its list of social threats. Like NWA, other G-funk, gangsta, and pimp rappers (such as Snoop Doggy Dogg, Ice-T, and Short Dog) have attacked women with sexist lyrics, videos, and album covers at the same time that they decry social and economic injustices based on race.

Gangsta rappers have caused rap's proponents to struggle for ways to explain why, in gangsta rap, sexism accompanies the powerful demand for social change. The best explanations link rap's apparent misogyny to social conditions and the overarching sexism of white patriarchal society. For Tricia Rose, the economic impoverishment of most black males conflicts with cultural norms about masculinity and economic power, causing male rappers to make up for their social emasculation by bragging about their sexual prowess and denigrating women.[1] For bell hooks, the story is even more complicated: "the sexist, misogynist, patriarchal ways of thinking and behaving that are glorified in gangsta rap are a reflection of the prevailing values in our society, values created and sustained by white supremacist capitalist patriarchy" (1994, 116). Hooks argues that the film *The Piano* depicts women in a manner as sexist as any gangsta rap song, but it isn't attacked because it doesn't threaten bourgeois values, as rap music does.

For hooks, gangsta rap reproduces white patriarchal values without the upper-class rhetoric: "they [rappers] give voice to the brutal, raw anger and rage against women that is taboo for 'civilized' adult men to speak" (122).

Other examples within popular music confirm hooks's argument that the misogyny of black male rappers is unfairly criticized. Neil Young, Johnny Cash, Tom Petty, and Henry Rollins have all written about strong-willed male characters who resist the temptation of seductive women (a gangsta rap trope), but they are rarely attacked for their sexism. In just one example, Johnny Cash's 1994 song "Delia's Gone" (from *American Recordings*) celebrates the shooting of an uppity woman in a manner as celebratory and gratuitous as that of any rap lyric, but the boasting only confirmed Cash's status as a rebel hero rather than a misogynist public enemy.

Although denunciations of rap are usually inflected with racist rhetoric, justifications for gangsta rap's sexism ultimately come up short.[2] NWA interprets women to be just as much a threat to black male pride as are police and lawmakers. It may be unfair to criticize rappers with more scrutiny than musicians in other genres, but there's virtually no way of viewing the depictions of women in material by gangsta rappers such as Snoop Doggy Dogg, Ice-T, and Too Short as anything other than degrading. It is important, however, to ensure that rap music on the whole is not equated with misogyny, an assumption that supports the stereotype that black males are unrestrained sexual animals. Because rap has such a powerful effect on youth, its representations of gender and race have great significance.

A variety of responses to gangsta rap within the hip-hop community suggest that, as *New York Times* pop music critic Jon Pareles writes, "gangsta rap has been an artistic dead end" (1996). A new generation of black male rappers currently offers radical interpretations of gender while still representing the language and attitudes of urban street culture. Although it may at first appear otherwise, much of rap music plays a significant role in advocating feminist principles. The Native Tongues movement of the late 1980s brought male and female rappers together to show that life in the hood is not glamorous for either sex and is nothing to be celebrated with bravado. None of the Native Tongues rappers advocate censorship of gangsta rap, but they present an alternative to it that suggests that truly subversive politics can't be sexist. Rapper Michael Franti (of the Disposable Heroes of

Hiphoprisy and of Spearhead) writes about ghetto life and advocates treating women fairly in relationships. In addition, self-reflexive songs about black masculinity, such as Chino XL's "Kreep," Ras Kass's "The Evil That Men Do," and Nas's "I Gave You Power," along with the reconfiguration of black male sexuality on the AIDS awareness album *America Is Dying Slowly,* demonstrate that rap music, although often ambiguous and contradictory in its treatment of gender and race, offers a critique of the social constructions of identity as complex as the work of any social scientist or literary theorist.

Stephen Rodrick argues that "alternative" hip-hop (the examples he cites include Arrested Development, Basehead, and the Disposable Heroes of Hiphoprisy) doesn't attract black audiences like "gangsta rap" does. Rodrick says that "alternative rap has drawn little more than barely concealed yawns from other rappers and urban audiences," and concludes that it is simply "a way to make rap safe for white liberals" (1995, 115–16). But making rap music that appeals to mass audiences isn't simply about selling out. Because much of the mass media associates rap music with violence, alternative rap, as the recent "Smokin' Grooves Tour" illustrates, provides an important counternarrative that isn't just about making rap "safe for white liberals." Sponsored by the House of Blues, the thirty-four-city "Smokin' Grooves Tour" (which took place in the summer of 1996) was an effort to dislodge notions that live rap concerts breed the violent behavior of fans. Because of these assumptions about rap music and violence, the tour wasn't simply about attracting white audiences. Several highly publicized incidents have contributed to fears of violence at rap concerts (forty people were injured at a 1986 Run D.M.C. concert in Long Beach, and a fan was stabbed at a 1988 rap show at Long Island's Nassau Coliseum), causing promoters to balk at booking rap bands, even though "hundreds of rap concerts have taken place peacefully in clubs around the country since the genre began catching the pop imagination in the mid-'80s" (Coker 1996b). Most rap concerts include metal detectors at the venue entrances—not even punk and metal concertgoers, who have just as much potential to become violent, are subject to the same degree of scrutiny.

Featuring Cypress Hill, A Tribe Called Quest, the Fugees, Nas, Ziggy Marley, and Busta Rhymes, the "Smokin' Grooves Tour" showcased rappers (with the exception of Marley, a reggae singer) who don't fit the mold of gangsta rap yet still speak about the troubled economic and social conditions of African Americans in the United States. Although many of the bands have been labeled alternative (Cypress Hill and A Tribe Called Quest even played on Lollapalooza tours), their crossover success hasn't prevented them from staying true to a street ethos. As the Fugees' Prazakrel Michel says, "There's nothing alternative about us. If we were truly 'alternative,' brothers in the hood wouldn't be gettin' with our music. You got the Mobb Deep fans loving it, and the Red Hot Chili Peppers fans loving it. . . . That's mass appeal" (qtd. in Coker 1996b).

The tour has the potential to make touring safe for other rappers as well. Refuting Rodrick's claim that gangsta rappers aren't interested in alternative rap, Ice-T, one of gangsta rap's best-known practitioners, says, "There was a time in hip-hop where it was really wild and it hurt us. That's why I pray to God that this [Smokin' Grooves] is a peaceful tour, because it means there will be more tours if things go well" (qtd. in Coker 1996b). The surging popularity of alternative rap groups such as the Fugees and Busta Rhymes suggests a renewed interest in the Native Tongues movement, which started as a way to counter representations of aggressively sexist black males in gangsta rap with ones that didn't depend upon the denigration of women.

Without creating a rift with gangsta rap, the Native Tongues movement of the late 1980s articulated new ways of representing black masculinity. In addition to female rappers Queen Latifah and Monie Love, male rap groups such as A Tribe Called Quest, De La Soul, and the Jungle Brothers avoided using gangsta rap's epithets, such as "nigger," "bitch," and "ho," when they began recording in the late 1980s. Instead of competing with each other, they played on each others' albums to show support and to inspire unity. By calling themselves "Native Tongues," the rappers represented an attempt to speak a language that, for them, predated the street slang of gangsta rap. Tricia Rose cites De La Soul and A Tribe Called Quest as two examples of artists whose lyrics "not only chastise men for abusing women but also call for male responsibility in childrearing and support the centrality of black women in black cultural life" (1994, 150). Although the Native Tongues movement is no longer unified, A Tribe Called Quest has continued to be progressive and musically innovative, and its most recent album, *Beats, Rhymes, and Life*, was the top-selling album in the country during its first week of release.

One of the most critically lauded and commercially successful acts associated with the Native Tongues movement (so far, two of its albums have sold more than one million copies), A Tribe Called Quest has always made a point of including women's issues in its lyrics. Since forming in Queens, New York, in 1988, the band has released four albums: *People's Instinctive Travels and the Paths of Rhythm* (1990), *The Low End Theory* (1991), *Midnight Marauders* (1993), and *Beats, Rhymes, and Life* (1996). In songs such as "The Infamous Date Rape" (on *The Low End Theory*) and "Description of a Fool" (on *People's Instinctive Travels*), the group criticizes black males for mistreating women. In "Separate/Together" (on *Beats*), Tribe maintains that black men and women need to work together to effect any real social change.

Like the coalition politics advocated by women-of-color feminists such as Bernice Johnson Reagon of Sweet Honey in the Rock, Tribe suggests that inclusion, not exclusion, is the key to successfully changing social hierarchies.[3] By mixing vocals on top of each other in "Separate/Together," the group provides an aural representation of different voices working toward the same end while simultaneously maintaining their distinct characteristics. By including Faith Evans as a guest vocalist on "Stressed Out" (on *Beats*), Tribe shows that women experience poverty and racism with as much anguish as do African American males—a reality most gangsta rappers refuse to acknowledge. When Evans sings the refrain ("I really know how it feels to be stressed out when you're face to face with adversity / . . . we're gonna make this thing work out eventually"), she doesn't just empathize with the plight of African American males. Rather, Evans suggests that she has also experienced the pain and misery of everyday life, and that racism and poverty are not lived only by black males who, according to gangsta rap's separatist paradigms, strike back with vengeance.

For Tribe, unity and collective action can only be achieved if men and women work together—a striking contrast to Public Enemy's "brothers gonna work it out" ideology. Tribe hasn't reduced its critique of social reality to platitudes, either. Even though its lyrics often refer to abstract notions of achieving peace and harmony, Tribe still uses images of violence—in "Crew" (on *Beats*), the gunshots and sounds of a party being broken up by the police are just two examples. Unlike gangsta rappers, however, Tribe doesn't rap about how black males need to be invincible in the face of death, and it doesn't exclude women from its project of social renewal, both of which are key concepts to developing nonsexist versions of masculinity and inclusive, third wave feminist politics.

Although not part of the Native Tongues movement, the Disposable Heroes of Hiphoprisy and Spearhead, two acts fronted by rapper Michael Franti, take hip-hop in a similar direction. Franti writes about AIDS awareness, poverty, and ethnic and gender stereotypes in the mass media. Franti, who was born to a black father and a white mother but was given up for adoption to white parents, presents himself without the usual bravado that accompanies "gangsta rap." His approach to his multiracial upbringing is paradigmatically third wave. Because of his multiracial heritage, he embodies the inclusive racial politics that is a part of third wave coalition building suggested by thinkers such as hooks, Cornel West, Hazel Carby, and many others, and that is embodied in the interracial, transgendered, multisexual organization the Third Wave.[4] As Franti says in the autobiographical Disposable Heroes song "Socio-Genetic Experiment" on *Hypocrisy Is the Greatest Luxury* (1992), "You see I'm African, Native American / Irish, and German / I was adopted / by parents who loved me. / They were the same color / as the kids who called me nigger." Franti recognizes that he is the product of many cultures, as is the case with third wave feminists who recognize the imperative to include men and women of different ethnicities.

For Franti, gangsta rap contributes to images of black masculinity that are damaging, because they continue a legacy of racist depictions of blacks in popular culture. In the Disposable Heroes song "Famous and Dandy (Like Amos 'n' Andy)" (on *Hypocrisy*), Franti criticizes gangsta rappers for perpetuating stereotypes about black males that are not unlike the racist stereotypes presented in *Amos 'n' Andy*, the racist 1950s television comedy: "We learn not to feel, for protection / And we learn to flaunt when we get an erection." What distinguishes Franti's perspective is that by using the pronoun *we*, he includes himself as one of the perpetrators of gender stereotypes. Franti doesn't pretend to exist outside the socially constructed norms of masculinity. In Disposable Heroes' "Music and Politics" (also on *Hypocrisy*), he doesn't brag about his sexual prowess but instead admits "that sometimes I use sex to avoid communication / it's the best escape when we're down on our luck." Rather than bragging, Franti makes frank comments about his sexuality that demonstrate a different version of black male sexuality than the one gangsta rap puts forth.

Because Franti recognizes his own weaknesses, he presents a view of masculinity that exemplifies third wave revisionist beliefs that masculinity is not a solid, self-reliant structure.

Black male rappers often identify with the skills of male basketball players, but Franti refuses to idolize them, even though he himself played basketball at the University of San Francisco for two years. In Spearhead's "Dream Team" on *Home* (1994), he writes about the symbolic value of the Olympic Dream Team that featured NBA players for the first time: "So could ten Africans represent America? / Bullshit / It didn't mean a thing / cause in the same year / we saw Rodney King." For Franti, who constructs his own dream team out of male and female African American intellectuals and political activists, it's important that sports do not become the only option for African American males. In the Spearhead song "Of Course You Can" (also on *Home*), Franti says that African American males should aspire to attend school and to educate themselves, even though the federal government doesn't want them to. Franti doesn't write off gangsta rappers, either. In fact, he stands up for Ice-T. Like bell hooks, Franti exposes the contradictory nature of the way critics attacked Ice-T but left alone antiauthority songs by white males: "They're fuckin' with Ice-T but they don't even care if / Eric Clapton's singing 'I Shot the Sheriff.'" As Tricia Rose writes about Disposable Heroes' "Music and Politics," "rapper Michael Franti acknowledges how crucial personal sexual awareness and transformation are to cultural and political revolution" (1994, 175). For Franti, transformation starts on a personal level but eventually includes building alliances between different cultures and different sexes—a telling example of third wave feminism's most pressing projects.

Michael Franti and A Tribe Called Quest present views that correspond to feminist politics with few inconsistencies. In their music they openly address issues such as rape and sexuality, and criticize gangsta rappers who try to perpetuate stereotypes of promiscuous and gold-digging women. For Franti and Tribe, political activism and feminism are inseparable. Nas, Ras Kass, and Chino XL, however, present contradictory images of women, some of which are feminist and some of which are not. In many ways, though, they represent a new direction in rap music—their hybrids of gangsta and alternative rap contain the potential to rewrite stereotypes about black masculinity.

Nas (Nasir Ben Olu Dara Jones), a twenty-two-year-old rapper who grew up in the housing projects of Queensbridge in Long Island

City, New York, comes across as hardened and streetwise on *It Was Written*, his second album (1996). As a teen, Nas dealt drugs after he dropped out of school in ninth grade. When his best friend died when Nas was eighteen, Nas turned to rap music. Nas explains in a *Los Angeles Times* interview:

> I hate to sound corny, but there's a problem between a lot of
> teachers and black boys. They don't understand our attitudes
> at an early age. They treat us like violent animals and throw us
> in special classes where we can't develop ourselves as people.
> But even if you get through that, you have to deal with society.
> As a young black man, sometimes you think the whole world is
> against you, and ignorant people—some teachers especially—
> will feed that to you (qtd. in Coker 1996c).

For gangsta rappers such as Tupac Shakur, taking on the world becomes a mark of male self-sufficiency and bravery. Nas offers a different perspective. *Written*, which topped the national sales charts in the first week of its release, opens with the sounds of men preparing for a lynching, and, in a voice-over, Nas says, "Damn this place. Damn these chains." The track both conjures up the history of African American enslavement in the United States and suggests a new reality, which is what *Written* envisions despite its materialistic lyrics.

On *Written*, Nas employs sounds and images associated with gangsta rap. For many music critics, Nas doesn't represent anything different from the glamorization of gangsta lifestyles in Snoop Doggy Dogg and Dr. Dre. In the first track, "The Message," Nas brags about killing a man who threatened to step on his turf. But in other songs, Nas writes about interracial harmony and equality between the sexes. In "I Gave You Power," Nas imagines himself as a gun, but he doesn't equate black masculinity with the power of a pistol. He initially makes the analogy in sexual terms: "Always I'm in some shit, my abdomen is the clip / the barrel is my dick uncircumcised / pull my skin back and cock me I bust off . . ." Although it may seem otherwise, "Power" isn't simply about the phallic power of a gun; the slow piano melody and drumbeat reflect the song's ponderous mood. At the end of the track, the gun refuses to fire because it is "sick of the blood, sick of the thugs, sick of the wrath of the next man's grudge." Nas portrays the identification of violence with black male sexuality, with his metaphor of the gun only to show how it is counterproductive and contributes to black-on-black crime. Nas doesn't just criticize current conditions, either. He looks forward to a time when life for African American men and women will improve. For Nas, men and women have equal roles in trying to create economic equality and racial harmony.

In the successful first single from *It Was Written*, "If I Ruled the World (Imagine That)," an update of the Kurtis Blow song by the same name, Nas imagines a world in which blacks participate in consumer culture to the same degree as whites. The fact that the Fugees' Lauryn Hill sings the refrain with Nas suggests that ending racism requires men and women acting together. For Nas, the project of creating a better material world in order to change values and beliefs involves women as much as it does men. With references to Armani clothes and Mercedes-Benz automobiles, "If I Ruled the World" may come off as materialistic, but it's empowering for African Americans participating on a level equal with whites in consumer culture. As Nas sings, "don't nobody want a nigga having shit." "If I Ruled the World" is not about male power but about imagining a world in which African American men and women can be raised in peaceful, multiethnic neighborhoods where black males are not the target of police harassment (the image at the beginning of the song). Ras Kass and Chino XL present similar perspectives, but their views are much more contradictory.

Because they spend so much time disrespecting other artists, Ras Kass and Chino XL could be dismissed as fast-talkers with little concern for addressing social issues. Still, Ras Kass (John Austin), who named his album *Soul on Ice* (1996) after Eldridge Cleaver's book, scrutinizes his masculinity and is critical of black men who don't respect women. As he says in an interview in the *Source*, "See [Cleaver's book] motivated me to look at myself: like, I wanna be a good brother" (T-Love 1996). In "Evil That Men Do," Ras Kass, who grew up in poor neighborhoods in Watts and in Carson, California, adopts the persona of a "nappy headed nigga" whose father leaves him at age twelve. It's unclear if the song is autobiographical, but the boy's only role models in the song are an alcoholic uncle and grandfather who constantly hit each other. While growing up on the street, the narrator of "Evil" "mastered the art of hatred" and survived by stealing. As he matures, he "fucks sluts," getting one woman pregnant. At age eighteen, he kills someone while driving drunk and ends up in jail. Although the song could be read as an endorsement of the gangsta lifestyle, Ras Kass makes clear (and the song's title is an initial indication) that he doesn't condone the man's behavior. At one point the man tries to make himself white, covering himself with baby powder. For Ras Kass, this man's loss of self-respect stems from the conditions into which he was born. The final refrain, "Every nigga on my street can't stop / and he won't stop / and he don't stop," is repeated several times, showing that African American men need to break out of the cycle of denying responsibility in order to create social change.

On his debut album, *Here to Save You All* (1996), Chino XL, dubbed the "King of Ill Lines and Punchlines," lists the celebrities, magazines, and other rappers he disdains. What prevents Chino XL, who is part black and part Puerto Rican, from becoming another gangsta rapper out to hype his skills and boost his ego is the fact that he includes himself in his list of fools. The song "Kreep" is the best example of the self-reflexive nature of Chino's songwriting. As Cheo Coker says in a review of the song, Chino "spends his misogynist verses blaming his woman for all the problems in his life, and in the hook he loathes himself for being such a confused, sexist jerk" (1996a). The song's refrain ("I'm a creep, I'm a loser, I wish I was special") mixes Beck's "Loser" with Radiohead's "Creep," but Chino doesn't employ Beck's sarcasm to distance himself from the self-indictment. In "Kreep," he says he "becomes jealous at the drop of a dime" but blames the woman for being a "tease" and for poisoning him. Chino XL brags about the women who flock to him but admits he is disappointed that his plans to grow old with his lover haven't materialized, revealing a sensitive, emotional side to his persona. At the start of the song "Vampire of the Ghetto," a woman confronts him: "I just think it's hella exploitive to take these metaphors and butcher icons from the urban community. What are you some sort of vampire? Where did this come from?" Her voice provides psychologist-like criticism of Chino's style, making listeners question his antagonistic approach.

The Red Hot Organization compilation *America Is Dying Slowly* (1996) represents yet another way in which the hip-hop community has responded to gangsta rappers who brag about their promiscuity and shrug off the threat of AIDS as though they are too tough to be concerned with it. In his lyrics, NWA rapper Eazy E often boasted about his sexual conquests and bragged that he didn't worry about wearing condoms when having sex. His tragically ironic death in March 1995, of complications due to AIDS, stirred the hip-hop community to the point that rappers were finally interested in contributing to a compilation by the Red Hot Organization, which has earned more than $6 million for AIDS relief since 1989 by hosting rock concerts and releasing benefit albums. As Red Hot executive producer John Carlin says in a press release, "Until recently, AIDS awareness among the hip-hop community was lacking. There was a general feeling that the disease was out there, but that it didn't hit close to home. But with Eazy E's death people started to take notice and realized that if it could happen to him it could happen to them." Carlin also cites figures indicating that "HIV infection is rising five times higher in communities of color than in any other group in the U.S. And AIDS is the number one killer of young black men."

It's especially significant, then, that most of the rappers on *America* are male, and that they advocate that protection against AIDS is a male responsibility: "use a condom when your third leg stands," rapper Pete Rock advises in "The Yearn." *America* is also significant because it features both alternative (De La Soul) and hard-core rappers (Wu Tang Clan) working together to restructure black male sexuality. Granted, rappers Sadat X, Fat Joe, and Diamond D. write about AIDS in a reactionary manner, placing the blame on promiscuous, disease-carrying women in "Nasty Hoes." But most of the contributors recognize that AIDS doesn't afflict just gay men, and in the process, they present images of responsible black males in control of their sexuality. The album's politics of inclusion (blacks, whites, males, females, straights, and gays are all mentioned) clearly situates this movement in hip-hop within a coalition-based third wave politics.

For some critics, gangsta rap represents an irreversible wrong turn for hip-hop, a view I've tried to contest with examples of new rappers who rewrite gangsta rap's sexual politics at the same time that they invoke many of its beats and rhymes. At a time when the economic and social structure of the United States has been particularly debilitating for black males, who "make up less than 7 percent of the U.S. population, yet comprise almost half of the prison and jail population" (Donziger 1996, 102), rap music can provide an important way to counter the representations of violent black males in political campaigns and in the mass media. Lawmakers and police have targeted African American males to the extent that "one of out every three African-American men between the ages of 20 and 29 in the entire country—including suburban and rural areas—was under some form of criminal justice supervision in 1994" (102). It's no wonder, then, that African American male rappers such as Ice Cube, Ice-T, and

Chuck D have used their words and music to fight racism and to depict scenarios in which black males retaliate with violence when they are treated unfairly.

But the way these rappers place women on their list of enemies doesn't make much sense. Women don't represent the same threat as police, Hollywood filmmakers, and government legislators do. Like African American men, women of all ethnicities (some much more than others) suffer from low pay, discrimination, and acts of violence, making the alliances between African American men and women in the work of many new rap artists all the more compelling. As part of the third wave feminist project of rewriting traditional masculinity and forging alliances between different races, sexes, and classes, hip-hop puts theory into practice as the voices of male and female rappers of mixed racial heritages combine to invoke a furious call for political activism.

Notes

1. Rose says, "Some of this hostility toward women is related to the dominant cultural formula that equates male economic stability and one's capacity to be a family breadwinner with masculinity, thus making black men's increasingly permanent position at the bottom of or completely outside the job market a sign of emasculation, dependence or femininity" (1994, 171).

2. In "African American Women between Hopscotch and Hip-Hop: 'Must Be the Music (That's Turnin' Me On),'" Kyra D. Gaunt defends "gangsta rap," linking her attraction to rap to her attraction to schoolyard games because of the "sing-song, declamatory nature of the vocal line, the emphasis on rhythmic punctuation and style, the use of the musical break (or interruption of sound but not musical line), the emphasis on narration and linguistic play" (1995, 278). Gaunt's analysis, however, leaves intact stereotypes about black male rappers as the instigators of violence and misogyny. Gaunt isolates the blurring of boundaries as something that happens, for the most part, in the lyrics of female rappers:

> The mediation between access and discovery signs found in rap music for African American women is illustrated through obscured boundaries between masculine signs ("hardness," the street, theft, sex, penetration, etc.) and feminine signs (softness, romance, commitment, children, the female body, etc.) in the lyrics of female rappers, the dress of both performers and fans, and the masculine and feminine musical constructions that are now a part of the rap aesthetic. (288)

The mediation between masculine and feminine signs is not solely featured in the work of female rappers. Male rappers, too, combine masculine and feminine aesthetics.

3. Bernice Johnson Reagon's "Coalition Politics: Turning the Century" is one of the most influential pieces from Barbara Smith's landmark collection *Home Girls: A Black Feminist Anthology*.

4. See especially hooks's *Outlaw Culture* (Routledge, 1994) and Rebecca Walker's New York organization the Third Wave, whose mission statement is widely available on the Internet (and a portion of which is quoted in the Introduction of this volume).

Works Cited

Cash, Johnny. 1994. *American Recordings*. American Recordings.

Chino XL. 1996. *Here to Save You All*. American Recordings.

Coker, Cheo Hodari. 1996a. "Here's to the Good Life—and the Jerks." *Los Angeles Times*, 21 July, 56.

———. 1996b. "Security Problems Have Thwarted Big Rap Tours, but 'Smokin' Grooves' Could Change All That." *Los Angeles Times*, 22 July, F1.

———. 1996c. "It's a Beautiful Feeling: Nas' Journey Has Taken Him from a Queens Project to the Top of the Charts." *Los Angeles Times Calendar*, 11 August, 62.

Disposable Heroes of Hiphoprisy. 1992. *Hypocrisy Is the Greatest Luxury*. 4th & B'Way Records.

Donziger, Steven R., ed. 1996. *The Real War on Crime*. New York: HarperCollins.

Gaunt, Kyra D. 1995. "African American Women between Hopscotch and Hip-Hop: 'Must Be the Music (That's Turnin' Me On).'" In *Feminism, Multiculturalism, and the Media*, edited by Angharad N. Valdivia. Thousand Oaks, Calif.: Sage.

Hooks, bell. 1994. *Outlaw Culture: Resisting Representations*. New York: Routledge.

Nas. 1996. *It Was Written*. Columbia Records.

NWA 1989. *Straight Outta Compton*. Priority Records.

Pareles, Jon. 1996. "Can Rap Move beyond Gangstas?" *New York Times*, 28 July.

Ras Kass. 1996. *Soul on Ice*. Priority Records.

Reagon, Bernice Johnson. 1983. "Coalition Politics: Turning the Century." In *Home Girls: A Black Feminist Anthology*, edited by Barbara Smith. Latham, N.Y.: Kitchen Table: Women of Color Press.

Red Hot Organization. 1996. *America is Dying Slowly*. Elektra Records.

Ro, Ronin. 1996. *Gangsta: Merchandising the Rhymes of Violence*. New York: St. Martin's Press.

Rodrick, Stephen. 1995. "Hip-Hop Flop: The Failure of Liberal Rap." In *Rap on Rap: Straight-up Talk on Hip-Hop Culture*, edited by Adam Sexton. New York: Delta.

Rose, Tricia. 1994. *Black Noise: Rap Music and Black Culture in Contemporary America*. Hanover, N.H.: Wesleyan University Press.

Spearhead. 1994. *Home*. Capitol Records.

T-Love. 1996. "Ras Kass: On Earth as It Is in Heaven." *Source*, August, 25.

A Tribe Called Quest. 1990. *People's Instinctive Travels and the Paths of Rhythm*. Zomba Recording.

———. 1991. *The Low End Theory*. Zomba Recording.

———. 1993. *Midnight Marauders*. Zomba Recording.

———. 1996. *Beats, Rhymes, and Life*. Zomba Recording.

Contributors

Barry Baldridge, the contributor of several photographs in this volume, was born in Tucson, Arizona, in 1966 and he's still there and not even complaining about it. He received a B.F.A. in photography from the University of Arizona in 1991. His work has been seen in two solo exhibitions and numerous group and juried exhibitions. For four years he lived in a fixed-up garage that contained a darkroom. Now he lives in a house next door to the gallery where he works. He is currently president of a Tucson visual artists organization called the Group for Photographic Intentions. His work has consistently explored topics such as gender identity and media influenced (read invaded) sexuality.

Ana Marie Cox was born in 1972. She is the executive editor of *Suck.com*, a daily experiment in buzz-saw journalism on the Web, popularly described as "smart media for smart-asses." Her foray into graduate study in American history at the University of California at Berkeley devolved into an obsession with popular culture; she considers herself lucky.

Jennifer Drake was born in 1965 and remembers wearing white go-go boots, a beaded choker, and a suede fringed vest (not all at the same time—at least she doesn't think so). She's moved around a lot and has landed most recently in Terre Haute, Indiana, where she is an assistant professor of English and women's studies at Indiana State University. She teaches courses on U.S. women writers, multicultural U.S. literatures, and creative writing, and has a long-standing commitment to teaching in community-based settings and affirmative action programs.

Currently, she is revising her book "Art Activism America: Cultural Hybridity and Representation" for publication.

Ophira Edut was born in 1972. A recent graduate of the University of Michigan, she cofounded *HUES* magazine at age nineteen. Based on her achievements in self-publishing, Ophira was awarded a full scholarship to New York University's 1994 summer publishing institute. There she worked closely with veteran magazine consultant Jack Nessel, a founding force of the *New Yorker* and *Psychology Today*. In addition to publishing *HUES*, Ophira writes direct-mail copy for Gauthier & Gilden in New York. She has designed packages for *People*, the *Atlantic Monthly*, *Glamour*, and the *American Journal of Nursing*. Ophira's articles and political cartoons have appeared in *Ms.*, *Glamour*, *Sassy*, the *Detroit News*, and *New Moon: The Magazine for Girls and Their Dreams*. She now serves *HUES* as both the designer and the editor-in-chief.

Tali Edut was born in 1972. She is a graduate of the University of Michigan with a degree in photography and computer graphics. Born into an Israeli family in Oak Park, Michigan, Tali has a firsthand interest in cultural issues. At nineteen, she cofounded *HUES* (Hear Us Emerging Sisters) magazine, which focuses on diversity among women. In 1991, Tali won *Sassy* magazine's second annual Reader-Produced Issue Contest. From this experience Tali gained an understanding of the complete magazine production process, which she then applied to *HUES*. In addition to running the daily business operations of *HUES*, Tali enjoys working as the magazine's creative director. She is currently collaborating with fellow womanist publications *New Moon*, *Teen Voices*, and *Hip Mama* to create a network of shared resources and support.

Carol Guess was born in 1968. Her first novel, *Seeing Dell*, was published in 1996; her second novel, *Island a Strata*, is forthcoming.

Leslie Heywood was born in 1964. She has a B.A. and an M.F.A. in poetry from the University of Arizona, and a Ph.D. in English from the University of California at Irvine. She is the author of three books, *Dedication to Hunger: The Anorexic Aesthetic in Modern Culture* (1996), *Bodymakers: A Cultural Anatomy of Women's Bodybuilding* (forthcoming 1998), and *Built to Win: The Rise of the Athletic Woman as Cultural Icon* (forthcoming), which chronicle, among other things, the cultural and historical contexts of her experiences as a female athlete. She has recently won bench press competitions in New York State, does performance art pieces that explore athletics and female identity, and is an assistant professor at the State University of New York at Binghamton, where she teaches gender and cultural studies and twentieth-century literature.

Freya Johnson was born in 1970. She is a doctoral candidate in the Department of English at the University of California at Berkeley, where she is studying twentieth-century American literature and popular culture. She is currently writing her dissertation, "Mocking Sex: Transgression, Irony, and the 'Negligee of the Emotions,'" which is about dark humor and irony in representations of transgressive sex and violence. She is a frequent contributor to *Bad Subjects*, and she is also inexplicably obsessed with T. S. Eliot.

Melissa Klein was born in 1973. She writes short stories and publishes the fanzine *Inkling*. In 1995 she moved to San Francisco from Washington, D.C., with her cat, Addison, whom she feared would exceed the carry-on baggage weight limit on the plane. Since moving to the West Coast, she has taught creative writing to high school students studying English as a second language, has worked at a women's resource center, and has waged a losing battle against the corruption of her speech by the word *rad*. She has also been described by one inside source as "Melissa Klein, superfine—likes ice cream, got a big behind."

Dyann Logwood was born in 1973. Born in Ypsilanti, Michigan, Dyann is currently working on her third degree from the University of Michigan. As a first-year student, Dyann was responsible for cofounding *HUES* magazine. In 1994, Dyann cofacilitated a summer journalism program for youths at risk. A gifted orator, she has spoken on issues of race and gender at numerous conferences, including the 1996 National Women's Studies Association conference in Saratoga Springs, New York. Her inspirational speeches and writings have appeared in the *Ypsilanti Press* and the *Ann Arbor News*. She is a member of Black Women in Publishing and Blacks in Advertising, Radio, and Television.

Dyann is responsible for connecting *HUES* to a network of women's studies departments and classes.

Annalee Newitz was born in 1969. She is a freelance cultural critic and a Ph.D. candidate in the English department at the University of California at Berkeley. Her articles on pop culture have appeared in newspapers, journals, and books. She is coeditor, along with Matt Wray, of *White Trash: Race and Class in America* (1996), and is codirector of the E-'zine *Bad Subjects*, which publishes articles devoted to political education for everyday life. She is also completing a book, *When We Pretend That We're Dead: Monsters, Pyschopaths, and the Economy in American Pop Culture*.

Jeff Niesel was born in 1968. He has an undergraduate degree in comparative literature from the University of California at Irvine, and is ABD in cultural studies at the University of California at San Diego. Because he has his doubts about the academy and likes to hang out at seedy bars, he writes about popular music for the *Orange County Register* and the *San Diego Union-Tribune*, a job that brings perks in the form of free concert tickets, interviews with obnoxious stars, and roomfuls of free bad CDs.

Jennifer Reed was born in 1963. She completed her Ph.D. in comparative culture at the University of California at Irvine. She currently teaches versions of cultural studies, women's studies, ethnic studies, and American studies all over southern California and is looking for a permanent gig.

Jillian Sandell was born in 1965. She is a graduate student in the Department of English at the University of California at Berkeley studying contemporary U.S. literature and popular culture. Her articles have appeared in the journals *Bad Subjects*, *Bright Lights Film Journal*, *Film Quarterly*, and *Socialist Review*, as well as in the anthologies *"Bad Girls"/"Good Girls": Women, Sex, and Power in the Nineties* (1996) and *White Trash: Race and Class in America* (1997).

Leigh Shoemaker was born in 1972. When she was eight years old, she wanted her parents to vote for Ronald Reagan; she no longer retains any Republican leanings. She received a master's degree in philosophy from the University of Kentucky in 1995, along with a graduate certificate in women's studies. Due to an insidious addiction to school, she is currently pursuing a master's degree in information sciences from the University of Tennessee at Knoxville. Every now and then, in the privacy of her own room, she likes to put on the only Rollins Band CD she has left and punch the walls.

Michelle Sidler was born in 1968. She is an ABD doctoral student at Purdue University specializing in rhetoric and composition, and is researching the influence of cultural studies, computers, and feminism on composition studies. She is cowriting a textbook titled *Networks of Writing: Online Culture in the Information Age*, a rhetoric reader for the networked composition classroom.

Deborah L. Siegel was born in Chicago in 1969. An Aquarius, she has lived by water all her life; it comes to her as no surprise that she is now studying a wave. A doctoral candidate in English and American literature at the University of Wisconsin at Madison, she has published a nationally distributed report on sexual harassment, a cultural history of Nancy Drew, and a third wave reading of Gloria Steinem. She entered graduate school after working at the National Council for Research on Women, where for her the intergenerational dialogue began. She now serves as adviser for Grrrl Club, a Madison-area group for girls in high school.

Jen Smith was born in 1970. Mistress of meow, queen of cabaret, diva with guitar, she is an artist living in Olympia, Washington. Very interested in the stories women tell, she works to create situations that allow for the telling. These efforts culminate in the variety show Cha Cha Cabaret, where she hopes to continue to showcase (and experience) the dynamic variety and possibility of radical girl culture.

Carolyn Sorisio was born in 1966. She is an assistant professor of English at the University of Akron. Her scholarship focuses on race and gender in nineteenth-century American literature, and she is currently researching a book that investigates the relationship between scientific theories of race and gender and the body politics of "radical" American writers.

Lidia Yukman was born in 1963. She is the editor of *two girls review*, a nationally distributed magazine of arts, literature, and cultural critique which "crashes culture with bodies and words," and "believes in the labor of art." Lidia teaches fiction at Pacific University. She has published criticism, poetry, and fiction. A collection of her short stories, *Her Other Mouths*, is forthcoming, and a cinematic novel is in the works.

Index